D1152958

AMERICAN SCHOOLS

A Critical Study of Our School System

BY HENRY C. MORRISON

Cres- Vita
cat Sci- Exco-
entia latur

THE UNIVERSITY OF CHICAGO PRESS

CHICAGO · ILLINOIS

THE UNIVERSITY OF CHICAGO PRESS · CHICAGO

Agent: THE CAMBRIDGE UNIVERSITY PRESS · LONDON

COPYRIGHT 1943 BY THE UNIVERSITY OF CHICAGO. ALL RIGHTS RE-
SERVED. PUBLISHED MARCH 1943. SECOND IMPRESSION APRIL 1944.
COMPOSED AND PRINTED BY THE UNIVERSITY OF CHICAGO PRESS
CHICAGO, ILLINOIS, U.S.A.

PREFACE

AS ONE reads the intimate history of the educational system of the United States, he can hardly fail to be impressed by the fact that there has never been any generally accepted underlying body of principles in the minds of leaders by which it could be guided. The result has been what anybody of intelligence might expect. At the best, it has been empiricist, and at the worst it has descended into the intellectual anarchy of a long series of fads administered by "experts" drawn from the pseudo-sciences.

We find running through the years a long succession of enterprises based upon what founders "would have." I suppose that Benjamin Franklin in his academy at Philadelphia was in a way the great precursor of that whole way of looking at the problem. We find it in the early notions of the eminently practical Leland Stanford, as he gave of his riches to found he scarcely knew what, certainly not what in due season appeared in his great foundation. We find it in the absurdities of numerous scattered colleges founded and administered by men who were convinced that they, and they alone, had—it must have been by revelation—the recipe for "what education ought to be."

Again we find examples of a better type of reformer and reorganizer whose stock-in-trade consisted of convictions copied from England and Germany, with little critical knowledge of the validity of English and German conceptions as applied to the new society launched in the United States and with indifference to the native schools which had rudely grown up here in adaptation to the requirements of that society as those requirements were to be apprehended by the eye of common sense.

Finally is the bane of a speculative philosophy of education, so called, as the source of all principles, ranging from those which govern in the classroom to those which enter into the management of the revenues. One cannot go very far with that sort of a program before he comes to realize that the chief result is the setting-up of a

iii

family of creeds to which converts give adhesion in very much the same spirit as that found among religious sects or political partisans.

For about twenty years past, I have been attempting to bring some sort of intellectual order into our activities in Public Instruction, utilizing as well as I could the methods which are common to all the sciences and especially to the social sciences. In so doing, I have thought to cover the disciplines which seem to be fundamental to our whole valid conception of the American public school and its operations.

Three volumes have preceded the present publication. The four are, in logical order although not in order of appearance, *Basic Principles in Education, The Curriculum of the Common School, The Practice of Teaching in the Secondary School,* and *American Schools: A Critical Study of Our School System.*

HENRY C. MORRISON

CHICAGO, ILLINOIS
November 1942

TABLE OF CONTENTS

PART I. MAJOR EDUCATIONAL INSTITUTIONS

PART II. SCHOOL STRUCTURE

v

PART III. SCHOOL SYSTEM

PART I
MAJOR EDUCATIONAL INSTITUTIONS

INTRODUCTION

THE title of this work is *American Schools: A Critical Study of Our School System*. Very well, why not proceed at once to the subject? That is the way most things have been done in our country in the "do-it-now" spirit. It is especially the way, as we shall abundantly see, in which our whole existing system of schools has been developing ever since the time of Horace Mann. It all has to be done over again in much the same guesswork fashion, perhaps after years of futility.

It is simple enough to proceed at once with our great subject and perhaps arrive at satisfying conclusions, in a similar unbalanced and ignorant manner, unless we first of all come to see that nobody can possibly understand the school structure and school system except he see both in their inevitable normal and logical relationship to the whole effort in systematic public enlightenment and, indeed, to the whole process of the conservation and transmission of Civilization itself.

Hence, in this Part I we shall endeavor to get into the background of our apprehension of things social:

First, an awareness of the School as a major institution, without reference to the particular schools with which we are familiar and which we perchance once attended. This will in large part be a re-calling of what has already been covered in other works.

Second, some notion of what the University is as a social institution, again without reference to alma mater or to our favorite football coach and his fortunes.

Third, an understanding of the immense importance of technological schools in the national economy, all the way from city and county technical schools to conservatories of music and teachers' colleges.

The second and third issues we shall study only in so far as seems to be necessary to a full understanding of the place and functions and

3

nature of the Common School, but concretely with a view to becoming intelligent about what belongs to each of the three principal institutions in our educational economy. There is much more than that to the University and Technical School, but we shall leave the more particular study of these to another and further work.

CHAPTER I

THE SCHOOL

IN THE pursuit of most of the concerns which make up the modern world we are referred to scientific foundations, from which we are supposed to start. In the various branches of engineering, in medicine, in law, and in the crafts, we are in the habit of recognizing that there are *principles* to which obedience must be given if we expect to arrive at useful and intelligible results. Schools we take for granted, much as we do the eating of three meals a day. We have all been at school somewhere and, after graduation, have not thought much more about it until the perplexities of having children of our own in school have appeared. Going to school—and to college, too, if possible—is the thing. Besides, they make you go to school anyway. It is, I suppose, quite safe to say that not one person in a thousand—and very few school people, indeed—has any notion that schools have a logical place in the universe and that they cannot depart very widely from that place if they are to accomplish anything in particular.

Well, is not that insouciance the natural attitude of everybody with respect to all that does not fall within the scope of his own business? It is indeed, but note that schools differ from most institutions in that they are in the end directed by popular vote. That fact makes us look upon validity in the conduct of schools as being anything the public directly or indirectly decrees, and yet validity eventuating in practical results is as objective here as it is in any other human enterprise, in the cure of disease, for example.

Now, when we use the familiar word *school*, we probably have in mind some particular school or else the generic term, "school," covering schools of all sorts. In the present chapter, as our point of departure, we are concerned only with the abstract noun "School" as the name for a universal institution, part of the order of wholesome life in any possible society. The concept is as much a part of the logic of one of the three primary forms of existence as are the mechanical things we use and the health we enjoy parts of the logic

5

of the two other forms. The mechanism and the health have reason behind them; and so has the School. We cannot do as we please with any of them without suffering some kind of consequences. It follows that the establishment and conduct of schools, if not guided by sound principles, is a meaningless undertaking, scarcely more than the setting-up of a traditional nursery on a colossal scale.

In endeavoring to get at and understand these principles, we have to study and deal principally with four fundamental intellectual disciplines: (1) The Theory of Education itself; (2) the Curriculum, or the valid content of Education; (3) School Structure and School System, or the way an individual school and a system of schools must be put together in order to make the attainment of educational ends possible; and (4) the Principles of Pedagogy, or the nature of learning products and the valid methods of attaining them.

I. THE SCHOOL AS UNIVERSAL INSTITUTION

The human infant is peculiar among animals in that he has to learn all that he will ever be or be able to do. So far as we can make out, the child differs from the chick or cub or kit or pup in that he brings into the world with him no inherited adjustments, commonly called instincts; or, if he does, the human instincts are so evanescent as to be negligible. Passions as driving forces, certainly; but not ready-made adjustments. Moreover, utterly beyond any other creature, the human adult under Civilization is dependent on his kind, so that he can in no sense achieve his destiny outside of what we call "Society." Since the child is devoid of instincts and has to learn, infancy is the point at which Society appears in the universe and becomes a comprehensive logic parallel with Nature, but not at all the same thing. Living under social conditions means that ways of living together at once begin to evolve, and, in general, we call them *folkways, mores, customs, institutions.*[1] Nobody ever invented Society any more than anybody ever invented Nature. Both of them had to be. Nor were any of the institutions ever invented. They arose out of the necessities of living together, and they are still social necessities in civilized existence.

[1] See chap. ii of *The Curriculum of the Common School*, the preceding volume in this series (Chicago: University of Chicago Press, 1940).

All this signifies upbringing of children in the family and, beyond that, instruction in the school. But there is no upbringing and no instruction except as ways of living together are transmitted. From the earliest times the School as an institution has existed because boys and girls had to be provided with something that would guide their minds when they had passed beyond parental and scholastic tutelage and guide their acts when they were beyond the reach of the police. That something, moreover, must be what is right in itself rather than what is decreed by authority or inculcated by propaganda. In short, what is transmitted must be the elements of Civilization in the arts and sciences and moral attitudes which constitute civilized existence.

II. THE COMMON SCHOOL

The question at once arises: To whom does the School apply? In the logic of things, does it apply only to a selected group in the population composed of those individuals who are presumably best qualified to profit from instruction, or does it apply to all?

The answer must be that of necessity it applies to all, not only in this nation but in all nations. Otherwise, there is no adjustment of folkways, customs, and mores to the primary universal condition of happy living which is civilized society as a going concern. Let us see.

In the sanitary protection of a local community, it boots nothing to segregate and protect the few and let contagious disease run rampant elsewhere. In spite of all precautions, infection invades the protected precincts. There is no security for some unless all be secured.

Ignorance and primitivism are more fundamental menaces to humanity than disease. The mores which in the end govern everything, even in absolutisms, arise out of the persons of all—in slave times even out of the persons of slaves—and there is always and everywhere a tendency for the immature generation to regress to the lowest cultural level to be found in the surrounding population, unless the youth are prevented from so doing by competent upbringing and instruction.

I suppose that there has seldom been a better illustration of the principle than has been our experience with young people, and middle-aged infantiles, during the period which followed the War of 1914–

18. Moral, aesthetic, and intellectual laxity and nihilism in general ran rampant for nearly a full generation. The youth of the period, and their aged congeners, proclaimed enlightenment, advanced ideas, a new era. To them, anything which existed before they were born was out of date. Costumes became those of the underworld, and cosmetics those of the primitives of Central Africa and the Polynesian islands. Books which were written to cash in on the situation justified the youth and helped them to discharge their lack of confidence in themselves.

And yet very few people whose memories ran as far back as William McKinley failed to observe that these youthful illuminati did nothing else than was commonly done in low-grade sections of towns and cities in other times; and language became singularly like what one used to hear in the smoking-car of a lumber-jack train or in a back-country livery stable where one waited for a rig. The literature and art of the period reflected the age-old nastiness of the small boy who has not recently been spanked for it.

In short it was a typical case of cultural regression on an international scale brought about by an undisciplined generation. The same thing, or a similar thing, has probably happened all the way back to the Stone Age. It is noteworthy that it was constantly happening in Rome after the Mediterranean conquests had brought about a great expansion of slave labor.

⌐ We acknowledge the principle in the only constitutional basis for our tax-supported schools. Jefferson once stated it in the formula: "Only an educated people can be free." Ever since the nineteenth-century political revolutions eventuated in universal suffrage, statesmen have proclaimed the principle: "We must educate our rulers," and that means everybody who will eventually have a vote. To a discouraging extent, we have been obliged to learn the lesson that if we leave a lower class uneducated, presently the whole body-politic becomes incompetent and corrupt. We all know that universal schooling is one of our corner-stone institutions.⌐ Nor did our founding statesmen, and others in the Middle Period, ever countenance the notion that our schools should engage in the inculcation of the virtues of our form of government. They held rather that an enlightened people would prize our Republic and that, if it turned out to be otherwise, they could safely be trusted to alter it.

It follows that School as universal institution is Common School. It exists not primarily for the behoof of individuals but for the transmission of Civilization and, in that sense, for the benefit of the Community. The individual benefits in proportion as he himself becomes civilized and in proportion as the community in which he lives becomes more civilized and more capable of defending him in his rights, of saving him from the attacks of criminals, and of protecting him from the consequences of economic collapse. A community becomes more civilized in proportion as it contains more civilized persons.

Hence it is that the School has as its subject the Common Man—not common man in the demagogic sense but all of us in our nonspecialized, personal character, the citizen as distinguished from the professional man, the craftsman, the businessman, the learned man. All of us, or most of us, are in the end specialized in some sense—in our vocations, in our interests, in our lot in life—but we are all in the first place, and most importantly, Common Man.

III. LOGIC OF THE COMMON SCHOOL

We are thus brought somewhat more precisely to further study of the School as institution.

OPERATES UPON INDIVIDUALS IN PUPILAGE

First of all, a school is a body of children and young people who in the nature of their presumed stage of personal development are pupils and not students. In legal terms they are *in statu pupillari*, and a considerable body of law has grown up to regulate the status. The presumption is that they are in that status, or may be, until the age at which legal majority is reached. They are pupils, for the natural reason that they have presumably not matured out of that condition.

Nevertheless, age in itself has nothing to do with the issue. The individual does not wake up on his twenty-first birthday to find himself personally different from what he was the night before. The law has to deal with what the makers thereof believe to be collectively true. But in truth one is, educationally if not legally, a pupil until he has reached educational maturity as described below. If in fact he has reached that stage prior to the age of twenty-one, he is no longer a pupil, whatever his scholastic status may be. If he has not reached educational maturity by the age of fifty, then he is educationally still a minor, even though he has voted for twenty-nine years and is a Member of Congress.

PERSONAL MATURITY

Such statements as these call for elaboration.

As the individual develops personally by learning things which are essential to his adjustment in the world, he sooner or later tends to reach the stage at which he is competent himself to direct his further learning. Adaptability has become established in him as a social being. He is fit to be trusted as a safe citizen. Education is complete. He has passed out of pupilage.

Let us look at the major elements of personal maturity.

Social or ethical maturity.—The individual has learned the elements of right living with his neighbors and prefers things that way. He can be trusted in his moral career. And not only in what is strictly his moral career: he has further found his self-respect in courtesy and good manners. He has sloughed off the conceit of adolescence which has often made him such a nuisance and has found the fundamentals of Taste. We say that he has grown up.

Volitional maturity.—Perhaps the kernel of adult personality is in the power to make an effort, even when the latter is directed to an uninteresting or even unpleasant end. And it is equally the power of self-restraint. These things have to be learned. The volitionally mature has reached a stage at which a "good time" is incidental and not the whole business of life. There is some measure of real confidence in one's self, and for that reason there is less need of showing off. The volitionally mature can be depended upon to take the trouble to keep his promises, to work at the needful thing without being driven to it, and to show some sense of the value of money. He is not infantile but grown up.

Intellectual maturity.—Firm and wise discipline in the hands of mature persons of basically sound personality, in the homes and the schools, does much to guarantee the maturity which has been described. Indeed, we would fain believe that most American adults have in these senses "arrived," despite the noise which adult infantiles make in the world. Certainly, one knows many noble and useful citizens who are to that extent educated—in some cases conceivably even when they are illiterate.

But intellectual maturity is something rarely achieved, by age twenty-one or any other age. The schools are not adequate to the purpose in either curriculum, structure, system, or the character of the teaching.

What is meant by this phase of personal maturity?

In the first place, the intellectually-mature person can, and commonly does, express himself correctly in well-ordered discourse, both oral and written. He is not obliged to resort to a patois of slang, profanity, or obscenity in order to attract the attention of others and to impress his meaning on them.

Correlatively, he has become able to follow an argument at length and become convinced by it, or else to perceive why he is not convinced.

In the third place, he has learned how to use books for the purpose of study, including books which are not fed out in assignment, and, since he has become able to use books, he can and does feel some confidence in his ability to learn from reputable books in the various fields of human concern. He has lost his feeling that nobody can know anything without taking a course in it, and equally he has lost his feeling that taking a course is a guaranty of knowledge.

In the fourth place, he has learned to think straight, since he has learned the principles to which valid reasoning must conform, and has become able readily to detect the common fallacies.

Finally, he has become able to form his own opinions through the attainment of intellectual maturity in the preceding four aspects and equally to refrain from expressing opinion on matters about which he knows nothing. The intellectually mature has learned to distinguish between what is and what is not matter of opinion, and he discriminates between opinion, on the one hand, and desire or intention, on the other. And he has sloughed off the intellectual impertinence of youth.

The bulk of our graduates, to say nothing of the untutored, form

no opinions of their own. At the most, they accept ready-made opinion from newspapers or books or follow the trend of popular fancy.
In times of acute political stress especially, it is amazing to see how
large a proportion of presumably educated people accept some particular journal or periodical as the authentic scripture.

MATURITY NOT COMPLETENESS NOR PERFECTION

The mature young person is what people in reality have always
judged him to be, when they have given any serious thought to the
matter at all. *He or she has become the kind of person who will know
what to do, or will know how to find out, and who can be trusted to do
right.* The development of such persons is the objective of Instruction.

The educationally mature person has become adjusted to the elements of the fundamental laws which govern in Nature and in Society, as they are known in his time; that is to say, he knows them and
accepts them. He has become adaptable, for he has become able to
learn more as occasion requires, indefinitely. He is not a learned man
and in most cases will never need to become one; but he has acquired
background capacity to become such if his destiny so decrees. He is
qualified to hold opinion on matters of public concern, and public
opinion which arises out of the opinion of such persons is worth
something. He is qualified to vote and hold elective office, and nobody of less capacity is qualified to take part in governing others in
a true republic.

But he is not personally complete; personal growth is not at an
end. Physiological analogies are sometimes useful. When puberty
has been established, the individual is in possession of all his physiological functions, so much so that primitives commonly make that
the customary basis of majority. But physical growth is not at an
end; the boy will have thirty years to go before he is definitely past
his prime.

So it is with personal or educational maturity. The individual
will never be any more truly educated than he is now. He may acquire a profession or a craft or a business technique, and we hope that
he will acquire a sound philosophy, all made possible by his education. He may go on learning until death—and perhaps after death

—but he will be acquiring something else than education and beyond education—wisdom perhaps. He is out of pupilage and will no longer require instruction under discipline either in a University, if that be his destiny, or in the common concerns of life in a community.

The term which applies peculiarly to the instruction of pupils is *discipline*. The word has drifted so far away from its essential meaning that comment is perhaps called for.

The word itself was originally pretty nearly synonymous with "instruction," and instruction was the practice of the schoolmaster or pedagogue. That is all far away and long ago, but the essentials of original meaning still abide as right meaning.

There is signified the use of authority of some sort in maintaining instruction, and we recall that Instruction is the process of bringing about Education.

When military and naval officers prescribe a routine, for themselves and their men to follow, with the purpose of establishing and maintaining certain personal characteristics which are likely to prove needful in battle, we call the process *discipline*. If discipline is conducted by enlightened authority, the outcome in the disciplined is normally self-respect and confidence. If authority is not enlightened, the so-called "discipline" becomes merely a cloak for petty tyranny.

When schoolmasters and teachers prescribe a school routine, the object of which is to create a constraint in the direction of active learning, to overcome the traces of infantile negativism which linger in a great many pupils, and to counteract the inner opposition to learning which observant teachers know so well, the process is *discipline*. If the school authority is of good will and enlightened, the result is that pupils learn to learn as a matter of course and that the generation in them of self-respect and confidence is furthered. I suppose that most veteran teachers have often had occasion to observe, as I have, that firm authority of that sort is a great deal more likely to prove popular with pupils than is consistent time-serving and popularity-hunting. It is usually the teacher who held authority justly and firmly that pupils in afteryears thank for his services. The bully and the mean tyrant are those whom pupils despise and for whom they often cherish a lifelong hatred.

Again, the term is accurately applied to the proper subject-matter of study. Grammar, Mathematics, Science—and, in fact, all the subject-matter of instruction which belongs to the Curriculum at all—are often called *disciplines*, and so they are. They are authoritative. And so they are used as implements of instruction and are not pursued for their own sake as they would be in the University.

INTELLECTUAL DISCIPLINE

When thorough learning as distinguished from slipshod half-learning has been insisted upon, we say that the pupil has been under intellectual discipline, and the outcome is the building-up in him of a trained intelligence or intellect.

But the pupil's mind is not thereby influenced. Perception, a mental process, continues to be what it always has been in that particular individual, but new percepts and appercepts are built up and organized. Memory, power of recall, a mental process, is not altered, but there will be more in the memory system. Imagination is still imagination; but new ideas, logically coherent within themselves, about which imagination can and will play, come into the field of consciousness.

DISCIPLINE IS OF THE SCHOOL

Discipline in the sense in which we have developed the meaning of the term is of the School and not of the post-School.

In adult life we are constrained to do some things and restrained from doing others, but compulsion is of the law in either civil suit or criminal process. Most of us obey the law—about in proportion as we have been under discipline in school and at home—but we detest arbitrary personal authority of any kind. On the other hand, in nonage, personal authority in parent and teacher is of the essence of upbringing and instruction, that is, of discipline.

It is especially true that discipline in any of its aspects is no part of the regime of the true University. Students are supposed to be grown up when they matriculate, although, as matter of fact, very, very few of them in our country are mature in any sense. A school in its nature can exercise the extreme penalty of expulsion only as a sort of sanitary precaution, when a pupil has become such that his presence is an incurable menace to 'the school and to other pupils. To expel for curable delinquency or failure to learn is to repudiate the School's institutional obligations. Not so with the University. Students in a university avail themselves of a privilege; pupils are compelled to attend school. In principle, a university may rightly expel any matriculate on the ground that he has shown himself incapable of University work or on the ground that he will not conduct himself in a manner befitting a scholar.

✓ THE SCHOOL COMPLETE IN ITSELF

The status of a minor is that of infancy in either a natural or an artificial family. The status is recognized in a variety of legal principles, all of them predicated on the known immaturity of the minor and on the presumption that he has not yet attained the personal stature at which responsibility can be attributed to him. The parent has custody and control. The child is bound to obey his parent, and the parent may enforce obedience. The parent is responsible for his child's conduct in the community and may be sued for damages perpetrated by the child. The minor cannot make an enforceable contract or act as a legally responsible agent.

All that is legal status. It is legal because it is socially reasonable and not primarily because a lawmaking body has set up the status. In the main, and in principle, it is good for minority and does not apply to half-a-dozen different levels in status before the age of twenty-one is reached.

Much the same reasoning applies to educational status. The individual does not cease to be in pupilage until he has reached educational maturity, and then he does cease. He cannot have one status as a pupil in elementary school and another as a pupil in high school and still another as an immature matriculate in college. Moreover, the educational process is continuous up to maturity, and then formal education is complete. There can be no such thing as "kindergarten education," "high-school education," and perhaps least of all, "college education." These separate schools, and others, are merely administrative devices which have grown up, presumably for the purpose of furthering the educational process itself, and not as things-in-themselves. We shall have much to do with them in later chapters.

Thus, on every count, whether legal or educational, the School is complete in itself. It is not a collection of schools in series. It does not lead to a university, nor to anything else save the attainment of General Education at educational maturity. The moment a university sets up entrance requirements in subject-matter, at that moment it becomes a school and ceases to be a university. It can retain University status only by resolutely refusing to accept the immature as matriculants.

The School uses culture for the purpose of generating Intelligence, Conscience, Taste, under discipline.

The University engages in the pursuit of culture for its own sake in quest of Philosophy, either general or professional.

The Technological Institute pursues specialized forms of culture in order to make its students proficient in the practice of some art which has an extended underlying logic, either of science or else of aesthetic accumulations.

CHAPTER II

THE UNIVERSITY

THIS work deals with the School, with its rational structure, and with the system in which many schools are knit together in order that the School may accomplish its normal institutional function in the Community. Why should we so early pass to the study of quite a different institution?

The answer is that there is no possibility of arriving at a comprehensive understanding of the School without also understanding the University in its essential social function and in the organization which makes the accomplishment of that function possible. Moreover, in our own country, schools and universities are so tangled up in their administration that the universities are in the main schools, and schools are largely dependent in their administration on the policy of universities. I am sure that many if not most of my readers would almost automatically exclaim at nearly every point I am making, both in Parts II and III of the present work and in the previous work: "What does he suppose the universities would say to that?" Now, anybody who has achieved any sort of grasp of the essential function of the University in Society, and therefore in our national economy, will recognize at once that universities have properly no more to do with the conduct of the schools than has the United States Steel Corporation or the American Federation of Labor. Members of faculties as citizens, like other citizens, no doubt; but not the universities as such.

I. AN INDEFEASIBLE SOCIAL FUNCTION

When societies were in the early stages of evolution, and the definition of Civilization as the art of living together in communities was just beginning to be written in human experience, nearly everywhere there was to be found an ever-interesting functionary called the "shaman," the medicine man of our Indians. He was a very powerful individual in most tribal communities, a sort of brain trust

17

of the Stone Age. He was diviner; he professed communion with the
spirits which were supposed to be indwellers in all things—somewhat
perhaps as the modern scientist professes knowledge of natural laws
—he was a sort of *maire de palace* to the tribal leader. He seems to
have been charlatan and trickster, but it does not follow that he saw
himself in that light. What charlatan ever does? He was physician,
Supreme Court, Bureau of Standards, Congressional Commission—
wherever the unseen world was felt to have something to do with
public affairs. Later on, in more refined times, we find him expanded
into the Delphic Oracle and the Roman College of Augurs, and, still
later, when kings needed to consult about the right and wrong of
things, into the University of Paris.

Now call that University or call it something else; the function is
the important thing. That function is the interpretation of Nature,
the accumulation of wisdom, the conservation and application of the
customs, the cure of disease, and more of the like. The form changes
from age to age, and the content expands beyond all knowledge, but
the substance remains much the same. At bottom in social meaning,
in one way or another, the function is what Oxford and Cambridge,
Leipsic and Paris, Harvard, Columbia, and Chicago—all of them
with more reason than shaman or priest ever had—have said they
were fulfilling ever since they got started. Without that function being well and truly performed, Civilization soon withers and then disappears out of the mores, and society as a going concern disinte-
grates. Plainly, here is something different from the School and
more fundamental in social meaning.

ANCIENT UNIVERSITIES

While it is doubtless true that no universities existed in the ancient world which were in form similar to those foundations with
which we are familiar, it is nonetheless true that the University
function was carried on in Babylon and ancient China, in Greece,
and in sundry centers in the Hellenic and Roman worlds. It appeared as studies in rhetoric, mathematics, ethics, metaphysics, logic, and, especially at Alexandria, as such positive science as there
then was. Grown men from all over the Mediterranean Basin, including some of those destined to be the greatest, resorted to Athens

and Alexandria because they were interested and desired to spend a time in study. What they studied was called Philosophy, and out of that pursuit has descended our little-understood College of Arts and Sciences.

II. THE INCORPORATED UNIVERSITY

But it was left to the early Middle Ages for the time to be ripe for the incorporated institution to arise. It was *Universitas*, the name for a corporation in the Roman law. In the great twelfth century the organized University as we know it was launched. As Professor Haskins has remarked, all our universities and colleges are the heirs and successors of Paris and Bologna.[1]

The essential structure of the true University which in those days emerged held good, with sundry adaptive variations, down to the collapse of universities in the twentieth century under the impact of world-wide materialism and hedonism and of totalitarian absolutisms, their legitimate children.

TERMS

The terms in that structure are still valid, and they are very germane to our main subject.

UNIVERSITY

As soon as usage had become established, the central term, "university," came to be defined as "an incorporated company of masters and students." It had nothing to do with "universe" or "universal." As we have just seen, it was a legal term meaning corporation. It was not a school or body of pupils under discipline.

COLLEGE

The parallel term, "college," meant then, as it still fundamentally means, a body of men set apart to perform some special function in State or Church. There had been the Roman College of Augurs, and the College of Cardinals was not very old. In time we set up our Electoral College. The Scotch call their courts the College of Justice, and the English call their organized practice of Medicine the College of Physicians and the College of Surgeons. So the aca-

---

[1] C. H. Haskins, *The Rise of the Universities* (New York: Henry Holt & Co., 1923).

demic meaning of College was that of a particular company of masters and students working in some particular field, in most instances what we should call a *profession*.

In Paris, and especially in the English universities, College came to mean a body of students and masters living in a residence hall, and then the word was applied to the residence itself with the addition of library and provision for tutorial instruction.

Our State Universities use the word correctly in their Colleges of Law, of Medicine, of Engineering, and so on.

The American use in early days corresponded to the English use, and Harvard College was at first a building under that name. Many a time I have heard citizens refer to the buildings about a campus as the "colleges."

The nuisance in terminology is the present American practice of defining the College as a grade in instruction between High School and Graduate School, part of the graded-school notions about which we shall hear much. Our American colleges since about 1870 have more and more lived up to this conception. In all their "collegiate" ways, they are far more like English secondary schools than like Oxford and Cambridge. "College-bred man" as a step in our peerage is almost the exact equivalent of their "public-school man," and "loyal son of old Siwash" is like "old-school-tie" man.

FACULTIES

The academic meaning of "faculty" is not teaching staff but rather a body of masters or professors devoted to some particular pursuit. The old faculties were everywhere: Philosophy, which has come down as our Science-Arts College and not as the department which deals with Metaphysics, Logic, Ethics, and sometimes Aesthetics; Law; Theology; and Medicine. In the great days of the German universities when American students resorted to them if they wanted to learn much, the four faculties were those just named.

III. DEFINITION OF UNIVERSITY

What, then, is "University"? We have already found a sociological definition, but that does not carry us very far if we desire to discriminate between what is and what is not "University." For that

purpose we shall probably do best if we resort to description by list-
ing attributes. We turn away from the period of origins and come
down to our own times.

Any valuable definition has in it the element of discrimination or
makes discrimination possible. Hence, part of our definition is contained in chapter i. That at least marks off one of the fields from
which the University is excluded.

If we begin in the period following the Civil War, in the administration of Charles W. Eliot at Harvard, in the founding of Johns
Hopkins, and the refounding of Chicago, in the expansion of Columbia—as well as in the history of others, notably Cornell, Michigan,
and Wisconsin—we find diligent study of the problem, active development of universities, and interest in finding a compelling definition. Many, if not most, of our university executives have at one
time or another essayed definition.

Put the tale all together—historical origins, academic and scholastic facts, presumably competent official views—and extract the
substance: you will find something very like the following as a critical description of the true University, marking it off especially from
the School, on the one hand, and from the Technological Institute,
on the other:

1. A University is a company of scholars, some of them professors and some
of them students, devoted to the pursuit of knowledge for its own sake and to the
pursuit of the learned professions.

2. It is a company of educationally mature persons. The student body is not
made up of schoolboys and schoolgirls.

3. It is confined to the pursuit of scholarly and scientific subject-matter. The
latter is not used for disciplinary purposes as is the subject-matter of the School.
The interest is cultural and not instructional.

4. Students are self-dependent in their academic pursuits, under the guidance and co-operation of men who profess advanced knowledge of the subjects
pursued. Teaching is not didactic and study not a matter of assigned tasks.

5. The University is conceived in the spirit of independent search for knowledge and reinterpretation of knowledge. That is the essential presumption of
scientific and scholarly study. The University is not so much devoted to research
as that its study is research.

6. The several faculties of the University are composed of learned men who
are capable of guiding advanced study, of interpreting its results, and of competently lecturing on subject-matter not yet available in published form.

IV. AMERICAN UNIVERSITIES

This section might well be written in the form of the brief sentence of the famous chapter on snakes: There are no American Universities. What goes under the name with us, or else under the name of College, is, *in varying proportion of ingredients*, a combination of graded school, trade school, daily journal of professorial opinion about life, amusement club for adolescents, propagandist forum, public entertainment park, employment agency, matrimonial agency, and University proper. Enough of the *corpus delicti* is in the daily newspapers, in the common knowledge of all who directly or indirectly have to do with the institutions, and in the pages which follow, to justify the indictment. Nor is this section the first publication on the subject.

There is in the aggregate a deal of true University work going on in the higher cultural foundations of the United States, but nowhere in companies of scholars organized for the purpose. There are indubitable Masters in many fields on faculties, and many of the matriculates are truly students, but there is nowhere an incorporated body of such and nothing else. So long as this condition prevails in our national economy, there can be no Common School, and any wisdom which creeps into the conduct of our national affairs will arrive there by accident.

Specifically:

1. *The student body is nowhere a company of educationally mature men, or men and women, and is nowhere in fact professed to be.*

On the contrary, our colleges and universities matriculate boys and girls who admittedly have not yet finished their schooling. A large proportion of them would make no claim whatever that they are in the university or independent college in pursuit of cultural ends. They are admittedly in residence in pursuit of a good time, hopeful of a job, and at any rate expecting a recognized place of superiority in the world. As one young Hypatia whose career seemed to need explanation put it to her dean, "I came here to be gone with and I haven't been went."

2. *Our higher institutions, even the best and most distinguished of them, are by no means confined to the pursuit of scholarly subject-matter.*

The allegation will be self-evident to anybody who can read a college catalogue. When we find courses like home gardening, biography, golf, and clog dancing offered in partial satisfaction of the requirements for a degree, there is no need of proficiency in educational science to enable anybody to form a valid judgment.

In the first place, there are so many school courses offered that it is perfectly evident that most American universities and independent colleges are at least half secondary schools with no pretext whatever for calling themselves universities, on the showing of their course offerings alone.

In the second place, it is clearly in the evidence that a considerable part of their offerings which are not of the schools nevertheless belong to teachers' colleges, technical schools, conservatories of music, art institutes, and similar enterprises.

In the third place, of what remains, much is in the form of courses which are merely elucidation of young professors' views about the world, many of the views being decidedly nihilistic in import.

3. *Study is not self-dependent under guidance and co-operation.*

Be it repeated emphatically that there are now and always have been individual students who are not only capable of self-dependent study but, in fact, pursue it in accordance with their cultural interests, despite college and university limitations. They are, in fact, University students and pure gold for such of the faculties as are University professors.

These are the rare exceptions. The catalogues of all the science-arts colleges contain conclusive internal evidence that the great majority of their students find their way through a labyrinth of courses, under severe restrictions designed to prevent them going astray, and work at their books only under pains and penalties for failing to accumulate "passes" translatable into permission to stay in college, and ultimately exchangeable for a Bachelor's degree—much as Tom Sawyer exchanged his colored tickets for a copy of the Scriptures. Having attained the degree, they are entitled to call themselves college-bred, to attend alumni gatherings, and to have title to priority in football tickets. To them in all honesty that is college education.

Such individuals are not students but only mismanaged pupils.

4. *Nor is the American university conceived in the spirit of research.*

A university may be academic home to able and productive investigators, men of international reputation;

It may maintain a publicity department which exploits every trivial discovery made within its walls;

The word "Research" may be uttered within its precincts with an unction only less fervid than that applied to "alma mater" at alumni meetings—and yet it may still fail to be conceived in the spirit of research. Research is essentially the self-dependent pursuit of knowledge, even without thought of discoveries. When the spirit of research is genuinely present, discoveries of real moment take care of themselves.

5. *Are the faculties composed of learned men?*

Some of them are, and there are learned men on most faculties. If we estimate by the number of substantial contributions to knowledge, in the form of discoveries, in that of extension of old knowledge, or in that of reinterpretation of knowledge, then there are assuredly more professors of the highest standing in our universities today than there have ever been. It is a pity that they have to be wasted on school children.

V. THE UNIVERSITY-IDEA MOVEMENT

Scholars, men of affairs, and university executives seventy years ago recognized the defects in our higher institutions of learning, although the defects of those days were nothing like the unthinkable list which has since appeared. Some of the executives were men of great capacity, discernment, and aggressive activity. Notable in the early days were Charles W. Eliot and Daniel C. Gilman, but they had many contemporaries who were only less vigorous. Somewhat later appeared others, among whom William R. Harper at Chicago and Woodrow Wilson at Princeton were conspicuous.

Eliot at Harvard devoted himself to the building of competent professional colleges and to opening up the Science-Arts College to true University work.

Gilman had the opportunity of launching a new university, and the result was Johns Hopkins in its best period. Later on, Wilson attempted to turn the Science-Arts College at Princeton into an enterprise possessed of University aspirations on the principles, largely, of Oxford as Oxford then was.

Altogether, we made marked progress throughout the University field, and the movement came to be known as that of the "University Idea."

CHICAGO AND THE JUNIOR COLLEGE

But neither Eliot, Gilman, nor Wilson seems to have been aware of the crux of the whole matter, namely, that the so-called "undergraduates" were still school children and that they could not be lifted out of that status by mere presidential and decanal decree, promulgated at an early meeting of the Freshman class. Harper did see the crux.

He turned this way and that in efforts to set in motion forces which would keep school children where they belong and reserve the University for mature men and women. But for his untimely death, he might have succeeded. On this point, it is worth while to pause, for on Harper's action hangs an essential part of the argument of the whole volume.

Where Eliot and Gilman retained the undergraduate college and built a Graduate School on top of it—on the principle that if a little of a bad thing does not work well, defects may be cured by doing a good deal more—Harper would probably have sent away the two lower years altogether if he could. I am sure that his successor, Judson, would have done so. Failing that, Harper entered into an understanding with the authorities of the Joliet High School in Illinois, the terms of which were in substance that the High School should extend its course to include the misplaced two years in college and that the University should admit graduates, otherwise qualified, to its Junior year.[2]

[2] An important documentary account of the transaction can be found in an article in the May (1941) number of the *Junior College Journal* under the authorship of Dr. Lewis W. Smith, who was long the superintendent of the high school and junior college, although not at the time of the agreement. Attention is especially called to the statement of Mr. C. E. Spicer, a teacher in the high school, tending to show that the latter had long been building up in the direction which culminated in the Harper move. Mr. Spicer's contention, in the opinion of the present writer, contains the meat of the meaning of the whole junior-college movement. It suggests, what may be amply con-

The two years, whether added to the High School or kept as Freshman and Sophomore years in the Science-Arts College, came to be dubbed "Junior College"—a fair illustration of the persistence of graded-school ideology. The two additional years were no more "college" than any other years. The only reason for the Chicago-Joliet agreement was in the principle that the first two years of the existing Science-Arts College, elsewhere as well as at Chicago, were and are secondary, Common School, in content, in method, and in meaning.

And then came the end of an era, reaching from the inauguration of Eliot in 1869 to the debacle of war in 1914; and the end came chiefly because of deep-seated and far-reaching changes in the national society itself.

We shall frequently have occasion to note the sudden expansion of high-school enrolment which began at the turn of the century. Along with it went expansion of college enrolment, and, of course, a wave which appeared in the high schools about a given year tended to break over into the universities four years later. The colleges and universities became so far swamped in increasing enrolment that structural defects became fatal. The higher institutions could not keep on being grade schools and amusement resorts and at the same time become Universities. And the end of the first World War brought about the impossible. The universities fairly swarmed with students, the great bulk of whom had never any background which would support real intellectual life at all. The brighter students could learn the jargon of the pseudo-sciences, and that was about all. One might go on and ungraciously name more sinister influences which were demoralizing our higher institutions and, indeed, our whole national life. Be that as it may, an era of progress was at an end.

---

firmed historically, that the normal tendency of high-school development was toward a restoration of the Academy as it was in the national economy of the first half of the nineteenth century, that is to say, as completion of the Common School and fulfilment of the requirements of General Education.

VI. THE UNIVERSITY IN THE NATIONAL ECONOMY

We have sought an answer to the question, "What is University and, by consequence, what is not University?" It is perhaps well to summarize the results in a description of the true working University as it might come to exist in the United States.

1. Such a University would accept no students unless they were clearly in possession of General Education, that is to say, mature intellectually, volitionally, morally, and in sense of fitness.

2. It would be founded on a complete Common School, not that the latter would be preparatory but rather that the complete University implies the existence of an adequate Common School.

3. It would set up no courses for credit but would rather be equipped for the guidance and facilitation of study in the various academic fields and professions.

Courses as we know them in American colleges and universities are in essence of the Common School or the Technical School. They are didactic. They are subdivisions of a curriculum. The Curriculum is the heart of the kind of instruction which is not only appropriate to the School but is one of the necessities of the pupillary status. In the true University, on the other hand, a curriculum is a denial of University status.

The University student would be in fact—and not merely because the president said so—a responsible adult. If he expected to attain a degree, it would be his affair in due season to bring forth evidence that he was in truth a Master of Arts or a Doctor of Philosophy, Jurisprudence, Medicine, or perhaps of Science or Letters.

4. Distinction between undergraduate and graduate would have no meaning. Every matriculant would presumably be qualified for University work in any College to which he might be admitted. While differences in interests, temperament, attainments, and health might be the determining factors in choice of College or even in admission to a particular College, there would be no question of relative demand upon the student's mentality or cultural attainments as such.

5. The several institutions constituting the University in the national economy would in large measure be foundations consisting only of the Science-Arts College, but the latter would be of Univer-

sity grade and the full equivalent in quality of science-arts colleges in the full universities. Indeed, having said so much tending to disclose the poor quality of the Science-Arts College in general, it is pleasant to be able to record the fact that in many of our independent colleges, some of the professors as matter of fact conduct seminars which seem to be of true University caliber, the equivalent in general of what is found in the existing universities at their best.

6. It does not follow that all universities would have the same professional colleges, so be it they had any at all. Nor does it follow that all true universities would make the same science-arts offerings. There is no occasion on any ground for an astronomical observatory or an oriental institute in every State. The *Full University*, on the other hand, is something more than one which has the full round of faculties. It is equipped for the fullest kind of advanced study in all its faculties. Perhaps it would have a standing corresponding somewhat to the medieval foundations to which the grade of *studium generale* was accorded. A very few such are needed in our national economy—President Eliot thought not more than four or five.

7. Degrees. It ought to be borne in mind that a true University, especially one which has come to exist under American conceptions of society, does not necessarily presume any degree at all. It is a place for the pursuit of the higher culture, regardless of extraneous motives. The moment a degree is sought as a certificate of attainment, and especially as a form of credit money exchangeable for a place of emolument, the chances begin to pile up that there will be no substance to the degree when attained. Degrees will, however, doubtless continue to be conferred. Therefore let us see what they in reality mean, especially the arts degrees.

Of the two university degrees in the Science-Arts College, that of Master has always been presumed to stand for competent knowledge of subject-matter and the qualification to teach it to others or the equivalent in guidance and direction of others. The graded-school ideology in our country has made it only a stepping-stone to the Doctor's degree, and the latter the true mastership and not a doctorate at all. Other than that, the mastership has become but a perfunctory high-school teacher's certificate. It is in truth a teaching degree, wherever the teaching is done, but only because what it signifies is the primary qualification of the teacher.

The Doctorate of Philosophy, in its very name, has rather a general personal significance, implying that the holder has not only command of knowledge but that comprehensive command which is capable of forming the basis of attainments which are rightly called Philosophy. So far as it has any vocational implications at all, it is properly the degree of those who essay to enlighten and guide the public. It properly signifies the attainments which journalists and writers in general ought to have, the higher public officials, university and school executives, and full professors. Save by chance in the cases of individuals—who, by the way, rarely hold the formal degree—we have no Doctors of Philosophy in the United States. What we confer under that name is in reality rather a narrow mastership.

8. Reduction in number of higher institutions. President Hutchins has remarked that "our ancestors sprayed colleges all over the landscape," and so they did. Some of their descendants continue to pursue the agreeable process whenever one of them conceives a "hunch" and becomes possessed of influence and funds.

In a recent edition of Marsh's *American Universities and Colleges* there are listed approximately six hundred and fifty foundations accredited by sundry associations which are more or less entitled to speak for the academic and scholastic community.

Of the total mentioned, a hundred and fifty are teachers' colleges; fifty are technical schools or colleges of Agriculture and the Mechanic Arts, and two hundred and fifty are colleges or universities which are ecclesiastically owned, controlled, or affiliated. In other words, there are about four hundred and fifty examples of the type of foundation with which we are concerned in this chapter, two hundred of which are purely secular. The list comprises only those which are recognized by the only academic authority we have. There are, of course, other hundreds, or perhaps thousands, which bear the name "college" or "university" without any substantial right to the title. Of the whole number taken collectively, at least half the scope of their course offerings overlaps some form of School, either Common or Technical.

If we count only the four hundred and fifty, the number of such institutions is from seven to ten times as many, in proportion to population, as England, France, or Germany thought necessary in their best days.

We have no figures which can pretend to either accuracy or precision as to what proportion of the students in the four hundred and fifty colleges, taken collectively, are qualified for even the work they are now supposed to be doing. But there have been many estimates, both casual and critical. I have heard a good many of the former in the last fifty years, and I cannot recall that I ever heard an estimate of better than 50 per cent qualified. Toward the end of chapter vi, some of the best of the critical estimates are cited. Inferring from the latter, it seems to be altogether probable that not more than 10 per cent of the students enrolled in our recognized foundations are qualified for true University study. Some such percentage is all there is ever likely to be in the general population and entirely enough to meet the need in the national economy.

If that be true, then there is no use in our national economy, in the well-being of the Commonwealth, for more than perhaps seventy-five of the recognized higher institutions.

The 90 per cent of the students ought to be in extended high schools until such time as they can be judged to have attained General Education, and then they should pass into regular employment; or else, if qualified, into technological training of some sort. Whereas we need fewer—and very much better—colleges and universities, we need many more and very much better technological schools. Indeed, if an adequate Common School system were erected, and the amusement-resort conception of universities were abolished, few would desire to go beyond the Common School, unless it be into the kind of training discussed in the next chapter.

The favored few in the universities indeed!

If there is a person in all the world who is not the beneficiary of favor and cannot be, it is the scholar. Scholarship cannot be bought; it cannot be inherited; it cannot be conferred politically; it cannot be received as a gift. It can only be won. It cannot be exchanged for a price; it can only be imparted freely to another. It is one of the very few things in the world which can be increased to the possessor by sharing it with another who is capable of receiving it.

CHAPTER III

THE TECHNOLOGICAL INSTITUTE

COMMON School and University are the backbone of any national system of education. Nevertheless, to leave the matter there and to ignore sundry other institutions and agencies which we commonly consider parts of the whole educational system is to fail to understand the proper scope of either School or University. Especially is it true that most high schools are diverted in part from their legitimate function as part of the Common School by what are called "vocational courses."

I. VOCATIONAL INSTRUCTION

For the last thirty-five years or thereabout, vocational education so called has been a veritable obsession with an important part of our scholastic and business community, to say nothing of the public in general—to the exasperation of scholars, the bewilderment of school-masters, and the confusion of businessmen and professional uplifters. Since what we have in mind in the present chapter will inevitably be mixed up with that whole movement, it will probably be useful to give some attention to the subject of vocations, or callings, in general.

Vocational education? All instruction may be said to be capable of leading to vocational ends. The professions are vocations. Latin has never been considered a vocational subject, but the student who follows it with a view to teaching it gives it a vocational coloring. The girl who takes an high-school course in Physiology "because she is going to be a nurse" is turning the subject, so far as she is concerned, into a vocational course. The student who seeks a college degree because he is convinced that it will improve his chances of employment is making vocational instruction out of his whole college career.

WHAT VOCATIONS?

Our people, after their habit, rushed into this whole matter with scant investigation of what they were about. Following the practice

31

of the last century, they copied from Germany, a country so essentially unlike our own in institutions, industry, and morals that we have habitually been at deadly war with her for what is now a long time. Notably, they did not pause to ask, "What vocations?" nor to consider what we already had in that field.

There are supposed to be, very roughly speaking, about a thousand different kinds of gainful occupation in this country, more or less depending on what you count and how. In the past generation we have succeeded in getting only a fragment of this whole field under instruction in the public-school system. I doubt that in any State today is it possible to give instruction in fifty vocations at the outside, and, in order to reach that number, there must be included trivial enterprises like beauty-parlor work and others in which the regular schools are incompetent to instruct, like journalism. The reason is not to be found in negligence but rather in the practical fact that it is quite impossible—and needless—to bring the whole field under scholastic attention.

One may begin by classifying the vocations according to their nature. We shall find that the following will not be very far wrong.

1. *Unskilled labor.*

Time was when this was the field from which all analyses similar to this started, and it was often called the "pick-and-shovel" field. There is, of course, some of that type of coolie labor still left. In general, we may say that this field is defined when we say that there is "no particular trick to the jobs."

Throughout the whole vocational area there is now an increasing amount of what might perhaps be called "white-collar" unskilled labor, training for which, if there is anything which can be called training, is incidental to good common schools. There is still a variant not properly to be called unskilled which is readily learnable on the job by those who are fairly well educated. Many of the household arts are illustrations.

No part of this whole extensive field is susceptible of either apprenticeship or of scholastic training. Neither of them under modern conditions is at all necessary.

2. *Apprenticeship.*

Perhaps the most substantial aspect of the agitation for vocational education thirty or forty years ago was the perception that the old craft apprenticeship had largely disappeared and that something must be erected to take its place. The principle was overlooked that Apprenticeship is an institution of universal import and that if one form disappears another will arise to take its place; and, further, that there is little in common between the crafts apprenticeship of the old days and training for employment in modern commerce and industry. "Beginning at the bottom to work up" was long the American adaptation of apprenticeship in the business world. But along with the vocational-education movement appeared and developed greatly the industrial and commercial trade school maintained by the enterprises themselves. This again is an adapted form of Apprenticeship.

Industrial and commercial trade schools.—We have seen that we cannot get the whole vocational field under Public Instruction, or anything like it; and it may be added that if we could, we could not pay the bill. If, however, we adopt the policy of locating the training in the shops or stores themselves, we find that we accomplish at least three vital things.

First, we can put the cost of training in the economic field, where it belongs, namely, as part of the cost of production and distribution, recoverable in the prices charged for goods. Cost thus becomes feasible; whereas by making it a charge on Public Instruction through tax-supported schools, the burden on the public purse is made impossible if we hope to cover anything like the whole field.

Second, where the policy of vocational training in the store or manufacturing plant where the individual is to be employed is adopted, the whole field of skilled and intelligent workmanship can be covered, since the kind of training required is automatically adjusted to the needs of the particular enterprise; and, if the policy is made universal, the whole field of the nation is covered.

Third, the possibility of securing really efficient training at once is very greatly enhanced over what it can possibly be in our obsolete system of Public Instruction, with its endless compromises and lack of incentives. Methods of training can be, and are, checked almost daily as any other industrial process is. The consequence seems to be that the industrial trade school has contributed heavily to the improvement of industrial efficiency over what it was say twenty-five years ago.

It is worth noting that in the time of the Fisher reforms in the British navy it was found expedient to adopt a parallel method of securing efficiency in the mechanical personnel. Boys were enlisted as apprentice artificers and put under training aboard ship in the engine-rooms. The result was a great improvement in that portion of the naval staff.[1]

Other forms of apprenticeship.—In the professions which are recognized in such profusion by our universities, the training in several of them is essentially modern apprenticeship, analogous to industrial and commercial training, albeit sometimes of a higher cultural type. Nursing, library work, and probably the technical side of Journalism run true to the type.

All the foregoing are Apprenticeship in their nature because they have to be learned on the job and because there is not enough content in them to justify extended technical or professional training. In all technical training, to be sure, practical experience must be a feature, but it does not bulk so high as in apprenticeship training. There is much more content in the Technologies.

The Common School has thus nothing to do with this whole immense field, save as Vocational Placement is maintained as part of administration.[2] There is, no doubt, a whole series of courses in the Practical Arts, but these are carried on as part of General Education and not for vocational ends.[3]

II. THE TECHNICAL SCHOOL

The Technical School proper was our first serious venture in this whole field. Indeed, it is one of the most ancient of organized schools. We may infer from Rostovtzeff that perhaps the most common equivalent of modern schools which the Romans ever had were

[1] See Admiral Bacon's *Life of Lord Fisher*, Vol. II.
[2] See *The Curriculum of the Common School*, chap. xiii, secs. v and viii.
[3] *Ibid.*

commercial training schools, halfway between apprenticeship and a modern commercial technical school.[4] Our technical schools were part of the movement which produced Cornell and the early colleges of agriculture and the mechanic arts. But they were little understood, and most of the enterprises were obliged to compromise with science-arts people so that many of the schools became little more than Latin schools with manual training and some commercial subjects. That process went on until, today, the tendency is for them to become a sort of dumping-ground for trades and semitrades for pupils who either cannot or will not follow the science-arts electives. But the Technical School system is an exceedingly important element in the national economy of every modern commonwealth. European countries seem to be more alert about the institution than we ourselves have ever been.

The Technical School parts company with Apprenticeship at the point at which some sort of a thought system is essential in activity and a considerable background of special knowledge. I think we can draw a useful contrast between those vocations which are properly susceptible of apprentice training and those which are not by saying that the work of the former remains much the same from day to day; it may improve in skilful performance as experience accumulates, but, after all, the job of one day is much like that of another. The work is not essentially of the problem-solving kind; if the workman knows his job, he will take minor variations in his stride. Not so with callings which either deal with matters which are always more or less new or else with matters which have so much of logic behind them that the competent workman is always dealing with ideas as well as with materials. That involves rather an extensive, specialized intellectual background. The calling is beyond apprenticeship and calls for technical training proper.

When the well-trained technician is confronted by a problem with your car or your radio or the plumbing, roofing, or wiring of your house, he acts very much as does the physician who is called in to deal with a malady. He asks questions, observes, tests, of late uses instrumentation, and finally sets up a reasonable hypothesis. He

[4] M. Rostovtzeff, *Social and Economic History of the Roman Empire* (Oxford: Clarendon Press, 1926).

remarks perhaps: "Well, so far as I can see, this must be the trouble; have to try it and see." Now this man may never have heard of a technical school in the mechanic arts, but he has the personal qualities which it is the business of the Technical School to generate. His procedure at bottom is like that of the well-educated medical man; the difference lies in the fact that the latter must have a much larger stock of principles with which to do his thinking. As a matter of inductive logic the two are on a parity; for each of them thinks straight in his own field.

The mechanic to whom we usually resort asks no questions, will not listen to explanations of symptoms, and often spends some time in exalting the capacity of the practical man as above the theorist— all who have studied their callings being lumped together in his mind as "theorists." He observes no significant facts, makes no measurements, and would not understand their implications if he did. He gives no judgment, but says he "will fix it." The chances are fifty-fifty that the machine acts as badly or worse than ever.

Thus the Technical School as such presumes a round of special study as well as of practice. It is not a College, but at its best it presumes maturity as does the University. Like the University, if it is adequately to perform its function in the national economy, it must be able to presume General Education in an adequate Common School. Moreover, like the University again, it ought not to substitute for its own important functions the social requirements of General Education for everybody, either wholly or in part. Nor is the Technical School intended to produce Engineers. The Engineer may very well be obliged to depend very largely on competent technicians, but he is not himself primarily a technician; he is planner, designer, research man.

SCOPE OF THE TECHNICAL SCHOOL

We have already differentiated the Technical School from Apprenticeship, on the one hand, and from Engineering as a profession, on the other. In general, it applies to all those activities in the Community which require a background of special knowledge in their operations and yet not the philosophy which is the characteristic of the true professions.

We have so far had experience chiefly with mechanic arts schools, commercial schools, and agricultural technical schools. But the scope today covers more fields. Among them may be noted especially aviation, charity, forestry, veterinary medicine, police work, printing, and, in short, any activity in a local community which in its nature is of technical grade. So here is another extensive vocational field with which the Common School has nothing to do, nor has the University.

III. HIGHER SUPPLEMENTARY FOUNDATIONS

In our study of the American University in chapter ii, we found that one of the chief faults of universities lies in the fact that instead of being confined in their course offerings to scholarly material, they include much which belongs elsewhere, some of it in the Common School, some in the technical schools, and much in the institutions to which we now turn our attention.

1. *The Teachers' College.*—The Teachers' College is engaged, or should be engaged, in the education and training of teachers for service in the Common School, both in respect to the subject-matter of instruction and in respect to Pedagogy and its underlying sciences. Pedagogy may here be taken to mean not only method in teaching but the whole routine involved in the administration and management of the School. Here belong most of the courses listed in the university catalogues as "credit in Education."

No doubt our existing teachers' colleges as a class are far from being the equivalent of university colleges, even of such universities as we have. The standards exacted are usually low. Even so, in my judgment, some of our teachers' colleges, in point of subject-matter taught, of essential scholarship of faculties, and of quality of work actually done, are more than the equivalent of many a recognized science-arts college, whether the latter be in a university or on an independent foundation. Aside from low standards, perhaps the greatest fault they have lies in the fact that they do not differentiate their function from that of the university college, a fault which, as we have seen, they share with the universities.

Needless to say, the Teachers' College as an institution is one of the most critically important in the whole field of Public Instruction.

We shall return to the subject in Part III with a discussion of teacher-training as a vital part of the organized State School System.

2. *Conservatory of Music.*—We have long had an institution which we call "Conservatory of Music." We have never made out of these foundations what might have been made, nor do we have enough of them.

The science of Music and scholarship therein are primarily of the Science-Arts College, since Music is one of the oldest and most vital elements in Civilization. The Conservatory deals with the art rather than with the science—although it does not eschew the latter—with the production of artists rather than with the pursuit of musical scholarship. It properly includes such kindred matters as Oratory and Dramatic Expression and such implications as Voice Training. A very considerable part of university offerings which have no place in the University belong here if they belong anywhere.

As is true of all post-School institutions, the Conservatory properly rests on an adequate Common School. Much the same principles apply which also apply to the University, the Technical School, and the Teachers' College; but the details differ. The requirement of personal maturity is common to all. Interest is also common, but in each case the kind of interest is particular. Talent is important in the acceptable matriculant in the University, but it is determinative in the Conservatory. Of all the arts and sciences, Music is so far dependent upon special talent in the prospective artist that reliance to a large extent has to be placed upon organic traits. Here is an organic temperamental endowment which makes musical artistry easy to acquire; there, an actual physiological block which makes learning impossible.

Needless to say, the Common School has no more to do with the production of musical artists than has the University. Nevertheless, the typical musical program in many if not most city school systems is laid out on the assumption that it is part of the business of the School to discover and train artists. No doubt the guidance of wise teachers of Music may now and then steer a promising pupil into the Conservatory, but that is widely different from the belief that the Common School can produce artists—even with the help of newspapers.

3. *The Art Institute.*—Art institutes exist in only a few of our larger cities, and even there the distinction between Art Institute and Art Museum is not always drawn. The latter is properly a place in which significant works of art are acquired, conserved, and exhibited for the enlightenment of the public and as material for the use of scholars. The former is properly a foundation established for the purpose of training artists, including amateurs who follow the production of pieces of painting, sculpture, or others of the fine arts as rewarding avocations. The Art Institute of necessity maintains a museum and it may also be Museum. Much of the "applied art" found in our study of college catalogues—and most of the "art work" found in the public schools—belongs to the Art Institute when it belongs anywhere. In a peculiar sense, the development of competent artists under training rests upon the personal maturity of the students.

The extent to which the ridiculous and the grotesque, especially in Painting and Sculpture, is imposed upon a gullible public, which has more money than taste, is, at least in part, traceable to neglect of competent art institutes in our national economy, backed by competent university departments of art. It is a capital illustration of the manner in which Civilization lapses when it is not continuously conserved and transmitted. The Art Institute is related to the University in the sense that art scholarship belongs to the latter and is not ignored by the former.

SUMMARY

WE COME to the close of our study of the major educational institutions, of what the School and the whole system at bottom in principle is if it be based upon a defensible theory of Education itself, upon an equally defensible theory of the content of General Education, upon a defensible theory of the University, and of the several other postschool institutions.

In the nature of the prolonged infancy of Man, of human growth from birth to adulthood, the Common School is necessarily first and the rest subsequent, not because the School is preparatory to something else conceived as the end, but because it necessarily receives children at the beginning of pupillary status and retains them to maturity. The graduate of the Common School is ideally in fundamentals much the same kind of *person* as his contemporaries, whatever his vocational destiny may be; *individually* he is, of course, what his temperamental characteristics complementary to education make him. He is in the full sense a young citizen.

The other cultural institutions of our study go on, each in its own place in the scheme of conserving and transmitting Civilization and in the national economy. Each of them is complete in itself and not merely a cog in the machine of an educational system. The latter is organism and not mechanism. Common School, University, and the rest are interdependent in the sense that dependence is upon an ordered society in which each can count on the expectation that the others will severally perform their functions.

If the body politic at any time waives reason and justification, so that the majority can follow its whim with the educational institutions, the result is always scholastic and academic futility and in the end the collapse of a society as a going concern.

PART II
SCHOOL STRUCTURE

INTRODUCTION

W E TURN, then, to the School, no longer as an institution but primarily as a working institutional enterprise, to consider how in principle it must be put together and organized in order that its institutional purpose may systematically and validly be attained.

So follows the argument of the next eight chapters.

It is, I think, peculiarly important that the reader should understand that Part II does not constitute a recipe which being followed will make all things come right. It does essay to show how schools must be organized in order that competent teaching and competent direction may achieve results which the same competency in the classroom and in the principal's office under the present system can achieve only with a waste that is a sore handicap at the best, and in most cases the achievement is not an educational outcome at all.

Nor is the organization in itself anything more than the formal side of the matter. The substance resides in a body of valid educational and pedagogical principles which must be in the mind of the effective teacher and schoolmaster.

CHAPTER IV

THE OLD COMMON SCHOOL

COMMON School has been defined, at least for our purposes, in chapter i. The definition is drawn from the function of the School as universal institution, and it contrasts the School with the University. One of the primary attributes of the Common School as thus defined is that it implies the instruction of the whole rising generation up to educational maturity, as the latter is in terms of the cultural organization of Society at any particular period of the world's history and in any particular national community. Whether or not the existing school or school system in any given period, community, region, or country will actually show the characteristic in terms of enrolment and curriculum will depend upon circumstances, chiefly economic, ethical, and familial in their nature. Can the country produce wealth enough to go round without the labor of minors? Is the population such in point of enlightenment that it can maintain a political organization capable of conducting the requisite school system? Are the families on the whole capable of an upbringing that will give the foundations for and support of instruction? The first and third of these primary conditions in our time and country have in the main been met.

I have argued the economic point elsewhere in my books, particularly in *School Revenue*, chapter ii.[1] In brief, the thesis is that enrolment in our lower schools increased but slowly all through the nineteenth century and that of the academies and high schools hardly at all, mainly because the work of children was needed in production and the children could find gainful employment, whereas after the middle of the nineties enrolment increased more and more rapidly in parallel with the installation of small labor-saving devices in the factory, on the farm, and in the home.

The rise of enlightenment in the families and the spread of enlightenment is quite another story.

[1] Henry C. Morrison, *School Revenue* (Chicago: University of Chicago Press, 1930).

44

The inveterate tendency of humans to look for a golden age in the past has led us to exalt everything connected with our formative period, so much so that a book which calls attention to historical facts which do not flatter either pride of ancestry or our prejudices stirs up wrath. It is foolish for us to feel that way about it, for the disclosure of what conditions were in the early part of our national period ought to give ground for satisfaction with the present, since it tends to show that under our institutions we have as a people greatly advanced in Civilization—even though there are times when it does not look that way.

Be that as it may, the first five chapters of Henry Adams' *History of the United States during the Administration of Thomas Jefferson* give us little ground for supposing that life in the bulk of American homes was then adequate to an upbringing of children which would support an adequate system of Common Schools. Mark Twain's portrayal of life in the Mississippi Valley as it was in his younger days supports the more historical account of Adams. The Common School has been long in filling up and becoming established, in part because there have not been enough homes of the right kind to support it.

The other principal attribute of the Common School is that it is meant to furnish instruction in the fundamentals of Civilization, that which concerns the Common Man as distinguished from the specialist, up to the point of educational maturity. In this and the chapters which follow, I trust that it will become evident that such was what the school system, unorganized though it was, attempted to do in the Colonial and early national periods.

IN THE COLONIAL PERIOD

In the Colonial period in the Bay Colony there was enjoined the instruction of children by their parents in reading, in understanding of the principles of religion and the capital laws of the country, and in industry—or else the parents must get it done. That is in intent good Common School doctrine today.

By the Massachusetts Act of 1647 each town of fifty householders must find a schoolmaster to be responsible for the task; and each town of one hundred householders must maintain a further school or schooling fit to prepare for the college at Cambridge. The further school was the Latin Grammar School of England. Now that looks like going a long way beyond Common School principles, until we see what was going through the minds of Englishmen in 1647 and of those who had launched that kind of school in the old country in the earlier centuries. In those days commerce and most skilled trades were shot through with Latin phraseology, not Latin derivatives but Latin itself. The latter was conceived to be part of the language-learning of the Common Man of the period.

So the local Colonial schools, at least in Massachusetts, were, taken together, a Common School. At least they taught what the Common Man was supposed to need to know, whether or no he availed himself of the privilege.

By the time we begin to encounter an educational literature, over in the first national period, the term "common school" has emerged as meaning the school which taught "the common English branches." Later on it meant a lower school maintained by the public in its civil capacity. It definitely did not, in the meaning then attached to it, cover the developed Latin school, nor the Academy, nor, later on, the new High School. So all through our studies we shall use two expressions as terms: "Common School" when we have in mind what is such in its social nature and "common school" when we have in mind the school which was, more or less officially, so designated. In our use Common School will be pretty nearly synonymous with School, the latter being used chiefly in the institutional sense as distinguished from University.

The common branches! There is the heart of the whole matter. They were presumably what all must learn in the existing society and culture. What are common branches today goes vastly beyond what were common in 1800, but the principle and the substance of the thing remain. When the common branches of any period have been found and incorporated in the curriculum, then the customary common school has become Common School in full institutional meaning.

Our study is centered on school structure. We are not concerned with the issue whether the school is free or a tuition fee is charged; valid structure is the same in one case as in the other. Noting that principle, and anticipating somewhat, there was nothing in the Academy or High School, and still less in the eight-grade elementary, which was not within the purview of Common School, save as professional schools were sometimes attached to academies. No doubt it is a weary road to travel before we reach the point at which all that in principle belongs to the Common School is in the Curriculum and all that does not belong is sloughed off. We have not reached that point yet. Nevertheless, by 1840 there was in effect as a going concern somewhere substantially everything which is of the Common School today, so far as it was then known. Since the academies of the day were often the equivalent of the existing colleges, and in most cases overlapped the colleges, it is fair to say that the only existing local systems which are in principle comparable with those of a century ago are those in which there is an established junior college addition to the local high school or high schools.

THE EARLY VILLAGE AND RURAL COMMON SCHOOL

It is always well in studies like this to get back, so far as seems needful, to origins and to trace from them the course of development. That helps us:

First, to understand the existing situation in which we find ourselves.

Second, to estimate how far the existing system may be composed of elements which are adaptations to conditions which have long ceased to exist.

Third, to judge what phases of development were misconceptions —in other words, where development went wrong.

It is well to bear in mind that our school reformers have seldom been distinguished for critical capacity. Pragmatists and radicals ever, they have been prone to "adopt plans." The consequence is that our school system has with difficulty developed as institution; most of the development for a century past has been through invention, often very shallow invention, or some kind of incautious borrowing. Prudent retreat is often the way to ultimate victory; salutary reaction the way to realistic progress. We turn then to the old

American common school as it often could be found in the villages
and countryside of a century and a half ago and later. Well over 90
per cent of the population dwelt in such communities.

There is no intention here of writing even a sketch of the school
history of the United States, tracing out schools in different parts of
the nation. We begin with New England, and chiefly Massachusetts,
in the belief that the structure of our schools as they are today had
its substantial origin there, however much regional culture and customs in other sections may have affected the final result, and that it
was there that the most fateful digression from the normal line of
development in the main took place.

So the village and rural common school, as it was before the villages became mill towns, is our present theme.

WAS THERE EVER A SCHOOL TYPE?

It is easy enough in works such as this to be impressed with some
particular kind of school, as I am with that old common school, and
then to make the erroneous assumption that one is dealing with
something that was once universal or, if not that, was at least
typical.

In the period of which we are writing, it would have been pretty
hard to say that there was any one universal kind of school in existence. Compulsory-schooling laws, as we know them, were unheard
of, however much in some sections it was the thing to send your children to school. Superintendents of Public Instruction and State
Boards of Education did not exist. There was no teacher-training.
Instruction was by tradition rather than by course of study. But we
can be sure of one thing: all the way westward from the New England States, through upper New York, and into the new settlements
in Ohio and presently in Michigan, there was what many of these
people and their forebears had been feeling for a century and a half,
namely, a love of and respect for learning and a missionary zeal for
the establishment of schools. Besides, there was the forthright re-
assertion of the civil purpose and necessity of public instruction in
the Northwest Ordinance and later in the uncompromising declara-
tion of the preamble to the first school legislation of Illinois. They
had, however, to combat an opposition which doubted the use of

education and enlightenment and denied that the body politic as
such had anything to do with schools.

These people had to get their own and other people's children
taught the "common English branches." They might, and sometimes did, succeed in getting the children taught more. How they
did it does not matter a great deal here. It must have been done in
an exceedingly casual way at times, and at other times such schools
as were kept up must have been hard to distinguish from ecclesiasti-
cal proselytism.

Still, it is not difficult to distinguish a conventional set-up which
was on the whole more common than any other kind. It was the
school which tended to be found wherever Calvinistic—and indeed
Lutheran—principles in Church and Commonwealth existed. We
get a picture of it, no doubt somewhat idealized, in John Watson's
Bonnie Brier Bush stories. The school in the Glen under Old Domsie,
humanist and schoolmaster, is what we find examples of in varying
degrees of excellence, all the way from western Maine to the Western
Reserve in Ohio. Lovers of the Scottish stories will recall George
Howe, the young scholar who won his way from the school to Edinburgh, and Bumbee Willie, who followed his bent and studied bee-
tles. No such pedagogical drama is within my knowledge, but I have
no doubt that something like it existed here and there all through
the region just mentioned. In the autobiography of the late Senator
Hoar of Massachusetts is described something very much of the
same sort in the Concord village school of his early days. To my
knowledge, such schools did exist over into the twentieth century, for
I visited one of them—it must have been about 1910—in South
Conway, New Hampshire. Professor Judd tells me of a similar instance which he found on a tour of inspection in Connecticut at
about the same time, and another colleague, Professor Thompson,
tells me of instances in Illinois.

Senator Hoar describes his school. He began to attend as a small
child—admission was sometimes incredibly early in those days—and
continued until he was sixteen, learning whatever there was to learn
—and what he learned was apparently about all the secondary
schools of the period had to offer. In due season his parents seem to
have judged that he had got about all out of that school there was

to get and that it was time for him to be thinking of his Harvard destiny. Accordingly, he spent a year with an accomplished woman tutor and then passed into college. He might have gone to the Boston Latin School or Phillips Andover Academy, both near by, but apparently did not need to.

Much the same had it been with Daniel Webster, a generation earlier. The Expounder went to a country school in what was then Salisbury, New Hampshire, until he had demonstrated that he was what Domsie would have called "a lad of pairts" and then went to Phillips Exeter for part of a year. Thence he went to Dartmouth. On the way the local Congregationalist minister in Salisbury helped him with the classics, very much as Geordie Howe went up to the Manse evenings where the doctor helped him with the Greek.

Other instances might easily be found, but they would come mostly from the biographies rather than from the histories.

If one delves into old volumes of State school reports, he will find that, in the Middle Period, likely boys were often going to college direct from the district schools, in townships in which by 1880 schools had so far degenerated as to be hardly entitled to the name. But two things must be remembered:

First, it was old tradition that the winter schools be kept by college students, who eked out expenses that way, and not by immature and often ignorant young girls. The Dartmouth student in *Snow Bound* is the type of many who officiated in the hill towns of New Hampshire and Vermont, on Cape Cod, and in the country schools of New York, Ohio, and Michigan. The student might find a promising boy who interested him and set to work to get the boy ready for his alma mater. Next winter the student would come back, continue the good work, and in the end "land his fish." But there was nothing systematic about it; the next student employed might, likely enough, spend the winter flirting with the big girls, while the "board of education" looked on with interest and amusement.

Second, admission to college was no such formality as it afterward became.

The school to which I have referred above, and which came under my own observation, enrolled perhaps twenty-five or thirty pupils. It was in charge of a mature and cultivated lady, in a region long known for its cultural interests. There were no grades and no promotions. If it was convenient to teach the more advanced younger pupils with the older, it was done—that was all. There was study of the natural history of the region. If and when a pupil had learned the essentials of arithmetic, he might study algebra and then geometry. I do not recall any foreign language, but otherwise I thought the school was doing good high-school as well as lower-school work.

Now the reader may be inclined to say: "Ah, but you tell us of but one school, or at most of but a few—in comparatively recent times—and you suggest the broad generalization that all schools might be like these." Nothing of the sort. I am in no sense suggesting that these schools recently seen in New England and in a midwestern State are either fair samples of an existing type of current school or even that they ought to be. But they have the advantage of being positive evidence. They prove what can be done, and a thousand negative instances do not prove that the thing cannot be done. It is inferable from even a single case, fairly stated, that contentions touching the common school of earlier days are proven possibilities. It is further suggested that if schools of today are not what they might be this is due to defects of structure as well as to paucity of competent teachers.

We are interested in the type, both factually and theoretically.

We have proceeded somewhat as does the naturalist in describing a species. He does not collect all the specimens in existence, including the runts, the cripples, and the sports, strike an average, and call that the type. On the contrary, he studies the species in the light of its evolution and identifies normality as what individuals would be and are under what can be seen to be favorable conditions. If it were otherwise, there could be no horse shows, dog shows, or baby shows. The normal is the type.

The schools which have been described probably never were fair samples of all schools anywhere. But they were a type, and most other schools were variations from the type, variation appearing mostly as relative excellence or neglect. Contrary to what is sometimes said, the type was not indigenous; it was to be found in small communities in European countries pretty much wherever Public Instruction had been established under the auspices named above, ever since the Reformation, in the nations which aspired to civil liberty under some measure of self-government and therefore had a lively sense of the importance of schooling the rising generation.

That old common school was so simple and obvious in structure that common sense would have been likely to lead men in that direction. It had the characteristics of institutional origin.

In the first place, it was Common School throughout in the sense that it was meant to be used by everybody. The discontinuous elementary–high-school setup that gradually replaced the old school was never meant to be used by everybody throughout and was not Common School in that sense until well after 1900. True enough, parents would sometimes find association of their children with evil and filthy companions and worthless teachers unendurable and set up what were called "select schools" at their own expense. Nor was that a divisive tendency on the whole. I have seen too many instances in which parents had to be defended from abuse of their children in vicious public schools to believe that occasional nonsupport of these common schools of earlier days was ordinarily anything else than self-defense on the part of parents who could afford to pay taxes and tuition as well. The erection of academies often had a similar motive, especially those which were chartered as joint-stock companies.

It was Common School, in the second place, in that subject-matter suited to public instruction (that is, subject-matter which met the common need) could be provided all the way up to pupil maturity, in so far as teachers could give it and parents desired it. It was folkway in many communities for pupils to "attend winters," so long as they thought they could learn something, up to the time they were married or had established other preoccupations. I do not say that everybody did that.

In the third place, it was continuous school. Pupils did not transfer into another school every year or half-year or two years. The old common school had little resemblance to the elementary school of today or to the current one-room country school. These are graded schools. In principle, pupils of all ages were gathered in a single room, unless there were too many of them. They were advanced in accordance with the attainment of proficiency in subject-matter and with personal growth in general; that is to say, they were advanced in terms of learning acquired and not in terms of satisfactory performance of tasks supposed to lead to learning.

In the fourth place, the old common school was terminal and not preparatory, that is to say, there was no presumption that a pupil who had finished would be going on into another school in which his standing would depend upon what he had done in the common school. To be sure, a pupil might leave the common school after a few years and enter an academy, but admission would depend upon the estimate of his qualifications made by the academy authorities and not upon what he had already done in the common school. There were no public high schools until 1821, and not a great many for fifty years afterward. There was no such relation between common school and high school as now exists between the elementary school and the high school. In the best illustrations the old common school was assumed to be parallel to high school, and not infrequently that was the case.

Likely enough, the foregoing may be contradicted out of the writings of Horace Mann and others of the reforming period. Certainly, one receives the impression from their writings that common school led to high school and high school to college. As a matter of institutional history, nothing of the sort even began to be history until after the Civil War—and then it was resisted. We are here speaking of the old village and rural common school. The city classified school, of which we shall have much to say later, in many cases embraced both lower schools and high school but not even that was an exception as compared with the severely preparatory chain in existence today. In fact, the classified system as a whole, including high school, in perhaps the majority of communities was the successor of the village common school. Indeed, it was itself a common school.

The foregoing is not to say that the terminal character of the common school was absolute and that, once entered there, the pupil was debarred from anything beyond. The school in the Glen was not in Domsie's mind preparatory to Edinburgh, but he was eager not to let the grass grow in the path between the schoolhouse and the university. Whittier's Dartmouth student did not make a district school, somewhere in the valley of the Bearcamp perhaps or maybe in Essex County, Massachusetts, preparatory, merely because he utilized the flexible structure of the school to get a likely boy ready for college. There was nothing terminal in the common school, in either its rural or its urban form, in the sense of the folk schools of Europe, mainly for the reason that there was no such thing in America as a caste system. But more of this later.

Thus we have some notion of what the old common school was in structure and in purpose. It was normal response to the schooling of citizens in countries possessed of institutions similar to ours. It was the mother lode to which our School as institution can be traced back. Our present school system bears little resemblance to it mainly because:

1. Of the incorporation of an "elementary school" so-called derived from sources which were entirely foreign to our national institutions.

2. Of the survival of a misunderstood English school in our traditional high schools and colleges.

What gave our High School its structure was the survival within its makeup of the ideology of the Colonial Latin Grammar School and of a structure founded on the belief that the High School would never become in terms of enrolment part of a common school. Thus the High School is in structure a survival of cultural conditions which became obsolete before we were a nation at all and of social conditions which were brought to an end by the gasoline engine and electric motor. The existing high schools and colleges are impossibly overgrown because they are carrying a load which it was never supposed that they would have to carry.

3. Of the evolution out of an original, justifiable school organization of a purely mechanical formalism based chiefly upon the ideology—and sometimes phraseology—of industrial enterprises.

4. And, finally, of the universal confusion between School and University and between Common School and various technical schools.

Some of the foregoing we have already met in detail; the rest we shall meet later, more particularly in chapter vi.

I am far from saying that the old rural and village common schools could advantageously be copied today, just as the best of them stood in the early part of the nineteenth century. That would be once more to copy an adaptation to a bygone set of social conditions. For one thing, we could not do it without erecting a schoolhouse in every block and in most city blocks having schoolhouses all around the boundaries. But I do say that in its essential structure it was the type of what all schools must be if they are intended to accomplish the essential purpose of the School as institution and not some other purpose. If Frederick William III of Prussia had allowed his schoolmasters to do to the *Volksschule* the equivalent of what Barnard, Mann, Pierce, Stowe, and the rest of them did to the old common school, German thoroughness and insight and competency might very possibly have imported the old American common school, refined it, and developed it. If they had done so, Prussia, and afterward, Germany as a whole would have had a School instead of an instrument of autocracy. Even so, they would have found that they were merely going back to what some of the German States were maintaining when Scotland and Massachusetts were setting up what we have called the old common school. If the Germans, between 1830 and 1848, could have done that, it would have meant the end of the caste system, and very possibly of the monarchy. There have not been wanting German students in every generation who have seen that as clearly as we can possibly see it. The imagination is staggered at the vision of what such a change might have saved this miserable world.

THE DAME SCHOOL

We cannot leave the old common school without a glance at another and correlated institution known in the books as the Dame School and a congener called the Reading and Writing School.

In the more prosperous villages and cities economically unfortunate women would set up private schools for little children, so that, when the latter reached the common school as pupils, much of the primary learning according to the notions of those days would have been acquired. Traces of that old institution could be found here and there as late as the time of the Spanish War. The school was not universal and apparently was not ordinarily recognized as part of the local school system.

It, however, and its modern descendant, the kindergarten-primary, are very suggestive as setting up actual structural distinction between primary and secondary, separating the period in which the pupil must depend entirely upon the teacher in word-of-mouth instruction, from the period in which, having the tools, he can learn from assigned study.

Here was a piece of normal institutional beginnings, originating in the common sense, experience, and felt need of mankind and inherently capable of comprehension and rational development. In those communities in which common school was preceded by dame school or reading and writing school, there was crudely what had long ago emerged in the German *Vorschule* and *Gymnasium*, the school of the upper classes, in my judgment the most rational fully developed structure the world has yet seen. If our structure had been allowed to develop in its own genius under intelligent guidance, in the end it might well have become the model primary-secondary setup for the democracies, doing for them in both commons and leadership the democratic equivalent of what the double German system did for autocracy. But in curriculum, method, and spirit it would have been as different from the German upper-class school as a Vermont farmer or Michigan lumberman was different from a Prussian *Junker*.

CHAPTER V

ACADEMY AND HIGH SCHOOL

OUR high schools, with which we are all familiar, date from the foundation of the Boston English High School in 1821. We are familiar with, or at least hear about, a few private schools called "academies," most of which are engaged strictly in the business of preparing pupils to enter college. The two taken together make a very significant chapter in the evolution of our school structure.

The High School did not come to much, outside the larger places, until after the Civil War, and it did not fully take its place as part of system of common schools until the high-school tuition acts appeared on the statute books after 1900. These acts were significant in that they made every district which did not maintain a high school liable for the tuition of children residing in the district who should attend high school in some neighboring district.

I. THE ACADEMY

But all the way back to the middle of the eighteenth century there were private schools called "academies" scattered over the country, until by 1850 one could be found in every group of two or three townships all over the Northern States so far west as the country had become settled, and southward through the Middle Atlantic States and into the South at least as far as Charleston, where one of the most famous was located.

In the first place, these academies were almost always private schools supported by tuition fees and by income from invested funds or from school lands or both. If they were free and tax supported, they were high schools under another name. Ordinarily, they were corporations, either by charter or else under the general law. Sometimes they were joint-stock companies.

The old academy appeared because something of the sort was what people who had cultural aspirations for their children believed

would be a good way to attain the latter. It was not college-preparatory, because in the minds of its constituents it was a substitute for
college as colleges then were. Bear in mind that, in the heyday of
the Academy, colleges were either one of two things for the most
part: either they were professional schools, chiefly predivinity, or
else they were very similar to the academies. The Academy was terminal; when you had finished, your General Education was supposed
to be complete.

Young George Hoar in Concord, Massachusetts, might find all
that his family could ask for in the way of juvenile culture in the village school at home until it was time to be thinking of the polish of
Harvard. If he had lived elsewhere, his parents might have con-
cluded, even as early as he was nine or ten, that the kind of school
committee they had would not be likely to provide an adequate
schooling at home, and so he would have been sent to a neighboring
academy. Not infrequently a boy might be sent to his aunt's or
grandfather's to go to school in the academy near the residence of
the relative.

A good deal would depend upon the family resources. The likely
poor boys in a country town, with some help from the minister or a
goodhearted lawyer or the winter teacher, might find their way to
college from the village school or even from the rural district school;
but bear in mind that college would not be very greatly superior to a
good academy. If, on the other hand, their folks were prosperous,
the boys would be sent to an academy, and likely enough their sisters
along with them, for the people who sent children to the academies
were prone to be progressive.

What were the academies like?

Well, in the first place, they were true institutional developments
and not mere scholastic devices as so much of our instructional
equipment has been. That is to say, they were the natural way to
get something done which was desired and which was beyond what
were esteemed to be the common branches. They were not borrowed
ready-made and then subject-matter crammed into them.

As a class, they were not the outgrowth of the Latin Grammar
schools of the hundred-householder towns of Massachusetts. The
latter seem to have given rise rather to the excellent village schools,

which some of the latter were. Neither were they copies of the Boston Latin School, but, if anything, quite the contrary. They bear a superficial resemblance to the English Public Schools, but there was no real equivalence. That place was reserved for the schools set up under the auspices of the Protestant Episcopal Church in the nineteenth century.

Finally, they were not class schools, although they are often said to have been middle-class. In truth they were not middle-class nor of any other class in the social sense. It would be hard to show that there have ever been class schools in the United States in the sense of family prestige and privilege.

But what were they in the more vital sense of their structure and pedagogy?

It is not easy to find out a great deal about them in any intimate sense. Sometimes you can get a good idea from the general literature of the period, notably from the books of Harriet Beecher Stowe, whose sister, Catherine, was one of the early feminine "educators" and whose husband, Calvin, sometimes took more interest in education than we wish he had. Now and then a more complete account can be found in the work of a competent historian. Of these last, perhaps Principal Fuess' *History of Phillips Andover Academy* is the best example. There is something, necessarily of a fragmentary character, in the general school history of the United States. But what we should most like to know, something about the individual schools that existed by thousands at the top of their vogue, is apparently buried away in town histories, and, when one of these is dug up, all one is apt to find is lists of eminent graduates.

Those of us who came on the stage as schoolmasters toward the close of the nineteenth century, however, knew some of the academies, but for the most part the good ones had reverted to the Boston Latin School type and become merely college-preparatory. Others had been founded for that purpose. Others, again, had been bought out and become town high schools. But the Academy was essentially a feature of a populous and prosperous countryside, and, when that came to an end, the academies went too. Nevertheless, we knew older people who had been graduates of academies in the days of their vigor. Their recollections were vivid, especially of some preceptor or perhaps of some rare teacher. For that matter, there are plenty of women in the generation to which I belong who completed their formal education in these terminal schools, in their cases usually "female seminaries"—for some reason our forebears seem at times to have a zoölogical apprehension of education; even now you will sometimes find a statistical report of teachers in which they are referred to as males and females, as if they belonged to a sort of educational Noah's Ark.

I recall that forty-five years ago I could see little difference in point of personal culture between these older gentlefolk from the academies and my own contemporaries from the New England colleges. I have never had occasion to change my mind.

The academy was much like the common school in structural conception. It dealt in substance rather than in form. It seldom had any formal requirements for admission beyond good character, the three R's, and little more. Admission was rather on scrutiny of each individual case; that is, if the pupil seemed likely to be able to follow the course, he was admitted. The curriculum followed that of the common-school branches above primary and went beyond. Mathematics continued to Trigonometry at least, and after that it ran out into Surveying and, in seaport sections, into Navigation.

Literature was the classical English. Brown remarks that the public for which the early school of American writers in the National Period wrote had most of it been bred in the early academies and had there acquired refined literary tastes.[1] It is, indeed, doubtful that those attempts at a national literature would ever have come to anything had it not been for the academies. Later on, another public of that same kind of educational origin was ready when the great New Englanders began to publish.

Science was to be found in the form of Natural History, which commonly embraced not only plant and animal life but minerals and the geological and astronomic stories as well. What we today call Physics was Natural Philosophy.

Logic was common, and so were Evidences of Christianity and

[1] E. E. Brown, *The Making of Our Middle Schools* (New York: Longmans, Green & Co., 1907), p. 247.

Natural and Revealed Religion. Sometimes a divinity school was attached to an academy.

Latin was of course practically universal, and Greek was common enough, and later on the modern foreign languages. The academies were as a class progressive, and there were many attempts to dispense with the ancient tongues, but usually without success—tradition was too strong.

Music was often extensively cultivated, and in one instance at least an academy long antedated the colleges in the competent pursuit of studies in the fine arts.

More exactly, Brown prints the full program of studies of Phillips Exeter for 1818.[2] I have before me a proposed curriculum for Columbia for 1810 and the curriculum of Dartmouth for 1822. Both of them are much the same in implication as the Exeter curriculum. The same thing would be true of most of the colleges of the period.

The academies had passed their peak long before the elective system as we know it came in. They had "options," no doubt, but not electives. They undertook to educate you and carried out the job according to their lights. If a pupil or his parents had proposed to lay out a course, the common-sense rejoinder of most of the academy heads would have been: "If you know what you need better than we do, why bother to come here? Better buy some books and get what you think you want by yourself."

Of course it would not be true to assert that the foregoing would be true of all of them. With the academies, as with high schools and colleges all through our history, especially before the arrival of the standardizing agencies, there were always great differences in point of excellence. Some of the academies were located on imposing campuses comparable with those of many of the colleges: most of them resided in a square colonial building, or something of the sort, with a bell tower rising above the roof and perhaps four classrooms, surrounding a main assembly room in which the principal met his classes. Dexter gives 6,085 of them as the number in existence in 1850, when the national population was twenty-three million.[3]

[2] *Ibid.*, p. 237.

[3] Edwin G. Dexter, *History of Education in the United States* (New York: Macmillan Co., 1904), p. 96.

With all its faults and handicaps, the structure which we have been describing was the normal institutional structure of the School. It disappeared because the society which made it easily possible disappeared, and, instead of developing it to meet social changes, the Germanophiles and to some extent the Anglophiles substituted something which bore no normal relation to anything in any existing society. The High School might have been the means of rapidly adapting our own American School to the necessities of an industrial society, but, first, the old New England particularist obsessions insisted on setting up High School as thing-in-itself, with strong leanings toward the English Public School; and, second, a group of reformers who had been to Europe, but who knew little of the genius of the American system, extolled the merits of the Prussian *Volksschule* and led to the adoption of that pattern as our nondescript Elementary School.

Every recent reform—junior high school, senior high school, junior college—has been a bungled attempt to get back to the original and normal American school structure. That very probably would in the end work out, were it not for a contribution of indigenous folly in the mechanical graded-school ideology, imposed upon the elective system, which has now conquered our intellectual processes all the way up to the Doctor's degree. In the end, our school resembles a department store at the entrance to an automobile factory. But all that belongs to the next chapter. Meantime, let us take a look at the High School in our educational economy.

II. THE HIGH SCHOOL

The Boston English High School, which began class work in 1821, is generally considered the pioneer of the Public High School movement. As to the reasons for establishing that high school, there is no doubt at all.

The academies were in full swing, going to college was not to become folkway for nearly another century, and the Latin School was believed to belong to a bygone day. But the academies were residential as well as local, and they charged fees for tuition. People in

Boston felt that there should be some school in their own town which would meet the needs of the "mercantile and mechanical classes," as the Latin School certainly did not—nor the needs of anybody else for that matter. Furthermore, these people had a case. It was pointed out that they were taxed for the support of the existing school but were obliged to send their children elsewhere and pay tuition. I suppose there have been few instances in which similar arguments have not been used whenever a town or school district has formally established a high school.

In the beginning, the Boston school did not bear the designation "high school"; it was called "English Classical." In another instance, the new school was called "Free Academy." Thereby, I suspect, hangs something of a tale.

Observe that the academies might receive children at relatively an early age. Pupils came from different sorts of communities, and emphasis tended to be placed upon the pupils themselves, regardless of their scholastic origins. There was no particular reason to think of the academy as "high"; on the contrary, it was another version of the old common school, equipped with better teachers, carrying pupils farther than most of the common schools could, receiving pupils early and keeping them late.

The Boston English Classical, on the other hand, and those which patterned after it, were parts of local systems in which there were lower classified schools through which it was assumed that pupils would pass before going on to the upper school. Moreover, for reasons which will appear more fully in the next chapter, even in the largest cities there would be not more than one or two of these terminal members in the classified chain. Thus it became folkway to refer to these upper schools as "high schools"; "Boston English Classical" became "Boston English High." That, and another circumstance described below, seem to me a more probable explanation of the origin of our term than others which have been conjectured.

TWO STREAMS IN THE DESCENT

Now two streams are to be noted in the lineage of the high schools which became common after the Civil War and gave rise to the unwieldy and chaotic city high schools of the present day. In tracing the development, we shall see one of the points at which the evolution of our school structure went wrong.

Independent high school.—One is the line which is most often noted, namely, that in which a high school was established by formal vote of a school district and placed under a separate high-school board. Most often that was the only thing which could be done, for no one subtownship district was large enough either to bear the cost or to furnish a sufficiency of pupils; a union district, or high-school district, had to be set up. Sometimes, special high-school districts were set up by special acts of legislatures without reference to existing town and district boundaries. Not infrequently the assets and good will of a moribund academy were taken over by contract with one of these union or special districts. In all such cases it was likely that the public would consider the high schools set up in this way as things-in-themselves, discontinuous with the lower schools and apart from them.

Perhaps it is pertinent to note here what we shall have occasion to note further, namely, the fact that until after the turn of the new century it was a commonly held belief that the children of the lower classes never would go to high school or even complete the lower schools. "Born-in-the blood" determinism was still strong, and it was seldom believed possible that families which never had sent children to high school ever would do so. All that likewise tended, especially in the larger places, to accentuate the disposition to make high school a thing-in-itself apart from the other schools. I need not here take the space to show how that whole attitude influenced the high-school curriculum as well as the school structure.

Few realize what a social revolution took place in this country between the end of the Civil War and the beginning of World War I. People came to see things in such a different light that in some respects the mores themselves were fairly overturned; but in accordance with the genius of our institutions, so far from violence and bloodshed being the instrument, very few people were at all aware that anything unusual was happening. They might now and then exclaim, "What's the world coming to!" but in their hearts they did not believe that it was coming to anything much out of the common. I cannot think of anything which has the marks of genuine revolution more than a change in the mores from a condition in which it is taken for granted that only a very few are capable of Education to a condition in which it is equally taken for granted that all shall rise to the level of educated people.

As part of the school system.—There must, however, be a preponderance of existing high schools which arose in quite a different fashion. In brief, they were set up as the fourth in a system of classification in which the others were primary, intermediate, and grammar— and sometimes a different chain which came to the same thing in the end. They were set up by school boards with or without the express sanction of the district; they had the same governing boards as the rest of the local system. They were not things-in-themselves in any other sense than were primary, intermediate, and grammar schools.

The typical structure of the local school system in townships under five thousand, let us say, as late as about 1890, ran much according to the following description.

Such a township would be likely to include several villages, one of them predominant, and more or less open farming country. If the subtownship district system of support and government was still in existence in that State, the largest village would be likely to have become a district by itself. In that case there might well be, besides the high-school building: a building housing a primary, an intermediate, and a grammar school; two buildings of two rooms each; and perhaps an outlying one-room school, or maybe several of them. In spite of the names of the schools, the whole system was in reality the old village common school conveniently classified so as to take care of a much larger number of pupils. At that time a town of that size would not be likely to maintain the *Volksschule* elementary, or "grade school." That belonged to the larger places and particularly to the factory towns.

Such a village system seldom had any regular course of study; subject-matter was traditional, and allocation to different schools was merely a matter of division of labor. So it was with the subject-matter of the high schools; Mathematics, Natural Science, Rhetoric, perhaps Latin and French, almost always Bookkeeping and a review of Arithmetic, usually United States History of an extremely jejune character—all these were traditional high-school subjects.

I do not recall that I ever heard the word "promotion" used—for I grew up in that sort of a system and afterward taught in one. When teachers thought pupils capable of doing more advanced work, that is to say, work allocated to the next teacher in order, she sent them on, and, if they survived that process, they eventually arrived in and graduated from high school. Those that did not survive simply dropped out when they found the going too hard or too uninteresting or when their parents made up their minds that their offspring was "not intellectual." There was no repeating a grade, for you didn't reckon by grades; you reckoned by subject-matter learned, or what the teacher thought was learned. You were privileged to linger until you were thought to have mastered the Arithmetic or Geography or Reading or could write well enough to go on to Miss ———. Even as late as 1890 you could get a job and drop out as soon as you could find employment or your parents would let you. There was as yet no labor surplus in most places. A job was a fascination to most boys, and, as for the girls, mother was always glad to have their help at home in an age when there were no canned foods, save what she had prepared herself, no electric light, no gas stove, no electric cookers, no telephone, no hot-and-cold plumbing, no vacuum cleaners—in short, none of the labor-saving devices which twenty years later were sending the girls to high school and now and then to college.

What in reality happened was that the survivors moved up into the grammar school and then into the high school and eventually graduated from high school—a process of natural selection. But moving into high school was no different at all from moving into grammar school, save in the fact that in the former you met new classmates from the other villages in the township. The high school was not essentially thing-in-itself.

If we look back to the description of the old village common school, it is easy enough to see that these local systems in small towns where the high schools followed this line of descent were adaptations of the common school to the conditions set up by the circumstance of having to take care of larger numbers of pupils.

How good were they as schools? The answer is that they were then, as schools always are, as good as the teachers made them, and the teachers were as good as the elected school boards were capable of finding and securing. Some of the teachers, in force of character, in cultivation, and in breadth and depth of learning were the equals or superiors of anything we have today. They were accidents, but there were many accidents of that pre-eminently desirable kind. The chief obstacle then as now lay in the fact that local people with influential family connections must first be provided with places in the schoolroom.

ARBITRARY DEFINITION OF THE HIGH SCHOOL

About the turn of the century, circumstances came to suggest that there must be some working definition of High School, and the definitions were worked out by people who had scant understanding of what a definition is and what it implies.

High School tuition laws.—The high-school tuition laws[4] in themselves lifted the High School out of its place as terminus of the classified common school, in the communities in which descent had been along that line. Administration of the tuition laws required some sort of definition of High School, even though the definition might be a wholly arbitrary one. Let us see.

In acting as a Superintendent of Public Instruction, it was perhaps my most important duty to decide what high schools and academies were what they pretended to be and what were not. That meant a definition of some sort if certification were to be anything else than the mere whim of the Superintendent. The only recognized definition at the time was "the school which comes next after an elementary school of eight grades"; and, of course, that was no definition at all. If it was acted upon officially, the officer might find that he could be compelled to certify something which was in reality mere ridiculous pretense. But nothing better could be found. The reason why I could not myself formulate a definition as the statute directed—and apparently the authors of the current definition were in the same case—lay in the fact that there was nothing to define; in logical principle, there was then and is now no such thing as high school other than by benefit of descriptive circumstance. There is a building set apart, teachers who draw pay as high-school teachers, pupils who are described as belonging to high school, and so on; but

[4] See above, p. 57.

there is nothing in either social or educational *function* which in its nature marks off what we call high school from any other school— it is part of a school system and nothing more. The Attorney-General, my official mentor, advised me that the only such school which could be recognized as being entitled to legal recognition was one in which the classical languages were taught. Not that they themselves were any part of the essence of that or of any other school, but, if a school taught them, they at least marked off that school—defined it —as being something different.

At the time, I recall, I thought the advice preposterous; and it certainly was altogether unworkable. So I fell back on the Educational Council, a body representative of the organized school people of the State, and worked out with them a sort of *modus vivendi* which at least we could all respect. Looking back over thirty-five years, which have in considerable part been devoted to the study of this and kindred problems, the advice of the law officer now seems to me singularly enlightening. A lawyer, trained by his professional practice to discriminate and define and to put the result in a form which would be a valid guide to reasonable and competent men everywhere, could find nothing in an high school which made it different from any other school, save instruction in Greek and Latin, and the latter any schoolmaster knew was a purely adventitious circumstance. The advice was equivalent to saying that there is nothing in the high school which makes it capable of definition; there is nothing about it which makes it different from any other school. If you try to define it, you will be merely talking nonsense. That is all that it need be, all that the school is anywhere today. It is part of Common School.

All the other State Superintendents had to act much as I acted in New Hampshire. We thereby helped forward the process of setting up arbitrary definitions—which we were compelled by the several statutes to do—and thereby furthered the process of derationalizing the school system, which, taken up and pushed farther by others, has led to a condition in which ideational chaos in school structure is the background and guaranty of educational chaos.

If the reader will recall the reasoning of Judge Cooley in the Kalamazoo case, upon which the validity of high schools as tax-supported enterprises rests, he will note that the decision in the end rested upon the principle that that school board, or the district, had as good a legal right to set up instruction and call it high school as it had to set up any other kind of instruction, introduction of drawing in the intermediate school for instance. That meant, and still does mean, that an high school is not in principle school-in-itself, requiring legislative sanction as such. If school districts or State legislatures set up that kind of thing, then they merely make a contribution to confusion in Public Instruction. The decision throughout rested upon what we should call Common School doctrine and, of course, upon the principles of the Northwest Ordinance.

It is an interesting and significant fact that when the Junior College appeared in the world and sought to be added to the local school system, some citizens challenged the legal right of the school board to set it up without legislative authority. The local lawyers thereupon fell back on the Kalamazoo case and the reasoning of Judge Cooley and held that, call it what you would, the departure was nothing more than extension of the common school long ago set up in the fundamental school law. Some States sanctioned the Junior College by legislative act, but they had no need to.

The Carnegie units.—A second and much more exacting arbitrary definition arose out of the necessities of the original plan of the Carnegie Foundation for pensioning college teachers. If that was to be done, there must first be definition of "College." Since in the United States the College is an integral part of the School system, one element in the definition must be a definition of that part of the School system from which it receives its students.[5]

We are not, however, concerned with the definition of "College," save as the specifications for College involved a sort of definition of High School. The latter in substance appeared as follows:

A secondary school in session for not less than 36 weeks in the year, and requiring for graduation not less than 14½ units, a unit being one course meeting not less than four days a week for one school year, and a secondary school being one which requires for admission graduation from an elementary school of eight grades.

[5] See above, p. 22.

That, of course, defines nothing save what the perpetrators had in mind. It neither describes nor specifies anything of an educational nature but only a routine of time to be spent based on other time to be spent. It made no mention of anything to be learned or of what was to be learned. The latter was left chiefly in the domain of what colleges would accept for admission requirements and what otherwise might fill up one or more Carnegie units. Nevertheless, it defined what high-school principals must do if their pupils were to be admitted to colleges which desired their professors to be blessed with Carnegie pensions. The High School in effect was described as being primarily an instructional appurtenance of the College.

The Certification Boards.—Then came the certification boards, under the name of "——— Association of Colleges and Secondary Schools." The whole country is now covered with these organizations. They exercise more real power over Public Instruction in the United States than all the State Boards of Education and Departments of Public Instruction in the forty-eight States. The power is entirely irresponsible, the use of it sanctioned by no civil authority whatever; they are not even corporations subject to suit at law for malfeasance. In effect, it is they which in the end prescribe what high schools and equivalent institutions shall be.

END OF THE COMMON SCHOOL

By the year 1900 the American common school had disappeared in most if not all the larger places, through the spread of the *Volksschule* Elementary, and that is another story. But it still remained in the classified local school system of the smaller towns which has been described. Soon after that date—and I am, of course, speaking only in approximate terms—arbitrary definition of the High School as thing-in-itself completed the process of destruction. There then followed the universalizing of the graded elementary school, even in one-room country schools.

Reverse movement.—Within a few years, however, three movements became established, all of which, properly understood and guided, were leading the structure of our schools back toward the structure of our native common school. The three movements in mind are: the Rural Consolidated School, the Junior High School, and the Junior College. But none of the three has been fully understood by those who have been most influential in its development. In the Rural Consolidated the graded-school ideology of the *Volksschule* Elementary seems to have full control. Both the others have developed into schools-in-themselves. *The gross result has come to be a wholly discontinuous school system.*

A FURTHER EFFECT OF SETTING UP THE SEPARATE HIGH SCHOOL

Before leaving the High School and its gradual and finally complete separation in administrative thought from the common school, we ought to remind ourselves how that separation has profoundly affected the pattern of our American urban communities. In a future chapter we shall have occasion to note that the typical city high school is a most serious obstacle to rational city planning.

Keeping in mind the classified common school with its apex in the high-school department, let us bear in mind that as late as 1890, the enrolment in high school for the country as a whole was less than 2 per cent of the total enrolment. In some communities the proportion would be as high as 10 per cent and in many, of course, it would be nothing at all. Generally speaking, there was little or no high-school enrolment from rural sections.

Times have so far changed that there is now some 16–17 per cent on a comparable basis of counting.

In 1890 a histogram of the distribution of enrolment would show a broad base standing for first-year attendance in the primary and a very short line standing for the number of graduates in the high school. Thus the shape of the figure would be a triangle with the apex slightly cut off. The story of changes in the distribution of enrolment from that day to this is a story of changes in the shape of the histogram from an approximate triangle to something approaching a rectangle as a limit.

The school pattern of any particular community was one of several schools, including primary, intermediate and grammar schools, and a single high school. It was a long time in our growing cities before any but the very largest had more than one high school, although elementary schools might be scattered all over town. The single high school was ample to take care of the qualified registration so long as 98 per cent of the enrolment was elsewhere.

Now observe that, as cities grew in size, the proportion of pupils enrolled in high school doubled and trebled. There were three ways to meet this overload of enrolment: the junior high school was a method of taking care of some of it; the high school itself might be enlarged (one such comes to mind in a city of moderate size which occupies a whole city block); or more high schools might be established. Curiously enough, this last method was always the one to be postponed, and the result is seen in the enormous high schools we have today in cities of any considerable size, even though many new high schools have been established.

Our nearly universal policy extending now for over half a century was never the natural and obvious one. It probably never would have been followed save for the unjustified tradition which had come to make the High School a thing apart and peculiar to itself. If we had no eight-grade system and no organic connection between High School and College, the natural thing would be to include the high-school department in the same school organization with the existing elementary, in the same buildings, and to expand the number of buildings, whenever growth demanded it, rather than expand the *size* of high-school building and the *number* of the elementaries. So far as I recall, Gary, Indiana, is the only city which took that sensible course; but then Gary had to contend neither with vested interests nor with invested school capital. After all, most Rural Consolidateds take that course.

CHAPTER VI

DISCONTINUITY AND THE CONSEQUENCES

IN THIS chapter it is proposed to trace the development of the discontinuous school system as we have it today and of the parallel substitution of the formal method of instruction for the substantial learning which is presumed to arise out of instruction.

I. SCHOOLS FOR LARGER NUMBERS OF CHILDREN

In chapter iv the old village and rural school dating from an early period in our national history is described, with perhaps considerable enthusiasm for the better examples. That school was of necessity continuous, for pupils of all degrees of advancement were gathered in the same room and under a single teacher and stayed there as long as they were thought to be learning anything or until "common-school education" was thought to be complete. It was terminal in the sense that it did not in itself imply a later school for the completion of what it had inaugurated.

Similarly was the Academy continuous, although there might be and was division of labor between the principal teacher and his assistants, and it was terminal in the same sense as was the common school.

ORIGINAL GRADING

School people possessed of orderly habits of mind turned naturally toward some sort of logical organization. Hence grading, but that originally and for long afterward meant *following a course of study*. An ungraded school was not a one-room country school but rather one in which successive teachers taught whatever seemed good to each of them. An organized course of study would have been Horace Mann's notion of the sign of a graded school.

CLASSIFICATION

Certainly, as villages increased in size and the school population grew to city dimensions, a local system of one-room schools such as suited a village or an intelligent and energetic countryside would hardly suffice. And yet the formal set-up must have lingered in its appeal or else the Lancastrian movement would hardly have attained the vogue it did. The Lancastrian monitorial scheme envisioned a large room accommodating several hundred pupils, with pupil-teachers, or "monitors," assigned to small blocks of pupils. It "swept the country," perhaps the first of many such "movements" which have been scattered through our history.[1] The small one-room school wouldn't work in a city; therefore, build a larger room. Much the same as the descendants of these people a century later, when they found that there were a good many children coming to high school, built larger and larger buildings.

However, the normal variation was under way, and that spelled the classified school system which we have encountered in the last chapter. So there were primary, intermediate, grammar, and high schools as perhaps the most common classification. Cubberley lists twenty-five cities, from Portland, Maine, to Madison, Wisconsin, and south to New Orleans, and tells us how they divided up their school systems in the period 1820–50;[2] but to my certain knowledge the idea was common down to the end of the century.

There were several other descriptions. In Hartford and New Haven it was common school and high school. In Philadelphia we find primary, secondary, grammar, and high schools; and in Harrisburg, primary, secondary, and high. In Cleveland appeared primary, intermediate, senior, and high; and in Toledo, primary, secondary, intermediate, grammar, and high. In New York City the arrangement was primary, grammar, and college. In passing, it is worth noting that Cubberley gives time allowance in years for each of the divisions in fourteen of the cities. Below high school the time varies from six to eleven years—eight years in six of the fourteen.

Now these classified schools might be graded or ungraded as the term was used before the arrival of the *Volksschule*, but they were not graded in the sense of the eight-grade elementary, which was destined to become universal. Whatever may have been the general practice in the classified schools—which nobody knows—it is certain

[1] See E. P. Cubberley, *Public Education in the United States* (Boston: Houghton Mifflin Co., 1919), pp. 90 ff.

[2] *Ibid.*, p. 228.

that in some communities at least, and probably in most of the smaller places, there was no real discontinuity save in change of teachers at intervals of perhaps two or three years. The pupil did not "finish the primary school"; rather he was judged proficient in what that teacher had to teach and was sent on. This may seem like a distinction without a difference, but, when we come to trace the eight-grade elementary, I think we shall see that the difference is substantial. Grading was in subject-matter assigned to the teachers, whereas in the succeeding type of grading, discrimination came to be in terms of years and half-years—"third-grade reading" instead of "reading," "fifth-grade arithmetic," "second-year French," and so on.

It is, of course, quite possible that the classified system would in due season have become transformed into the further stage in which pupil progress is a matter of time spent rather than a matter of advancement in learning. In the schools with which I was familiar in the closing years of the nineteenth century, as pupil, college student, teacher, and schoolmaster, it certainly had not done so. If a pupil under my charge in the year of the Spanish War had been asked what grade he was in, in most cases he would have hesitated and then answered, "I am in Miss Reed's school" or "Miss Knight's," or "in the high school." The names of the old classificatory divisions had been given up, but the graded school ideology had not become established.

II. THE PERIOD OF THE COMMON SCHOOL REVIVAL

The vigorous development of our present schools and school systems began in the thirties and forties of the last century in what is known in the books as "the Common School Revival," before all others with Horace Mann.

By the end of the first third of the century, the common schools nearly everywhere had fallen into a disorganized and neglected condition. The method of government, supervision, and support was through the subtownship school district, as it still is in many of the States—a "little republic" at every crossroads. There were no organized systems of teacher-training and no State Departments of Public Instruction of an enduring and positive character. In the Middle Atlantic States free schools as a system had scarcely been set up at all. The year 1833 may be taken as a sort of nodal point at which an era of provincialism and particularism struck bottom.

It was, on the other hand, the early part of an era of intense and militant liberalism throughout the Western world.

For many years in the United States able and patriotic men had been calling attention to the fatal consequences sure to ensue on the neglect of schools. The antislavery movement was growing in intensity. Labor was becoming organized for betterment of working conditions. Democracy had recently passed into another phase. There was bound presently to be an era of reform in public school matters.

In England the first Reform Bill had just been enacted into law, the anti-corn-law agitation was gathering force, reform of the brutal criminal code and of the ridiculous chancery procedure was under way, and extension of the franchise was becoming an issue.

On the Continent the revolutionary year of 1830 was just past, and the next revolution would be fifteen years in the future.

The factory system, which is the old name for the Industrial Revolution, was developing rapidly in America and converting villages and small cities into large mill towns and great trading centers, with many school children. States were being stirred toward public instruction, and early school-attendance laws were being enacted. Confidence in the Lancastrian movement was evaporating.

The times were ripe for doing something about it, and the fateful step was taken of copying from Europe. They were looking for a *plan*. Then, as now, our people were infatuated with the idea that some kind of a device could be found which would make it possible to have good public instruction and still keep amateur and negligent teachers and incompetent government and management. They already had a sound structure in the old common school and its derivative, but they sought a better structure. What they needed was better government and support, qualified supervision, a rational pedagogy, and trained teachers; but nobody knew it save Horace Mann and his followers.

THE EUROPEAN VISITS

Visits to European schools and reports thereon stirred up the American mind, in so far as it was capable of being stirred up by

anything of an educational nature. Now, in the midst of World War I
there arose among us a suspicion of all things German. Attention
was called to the mischievous work of the school reformers in copying the Prussian system. Since then almost any proposal looking toward the real betterment of our school system has been stigmatized
by the intransigent, and by those who fear that they may be compelled to work and produce results, as "Prussianization of our
schools." For that reason especially, I think it worth while to devote
some pages to those fateful visits and to what actually came out of
them—and what did not.

Cousin's report.—In 1831, Victor Cousin, French philosopher and
writer, had made a study of the Prussian school system and had prepared a report thereon for the French Minister of Public Instruction.
It was widely read in French and presently translated into English
and still further read.

Stowe's visit and report.—In January, 1836, Calvin E. Stowe, then
a professor in the Lane Theological Seminary in Cincinnati, made an
address at an educational gathering at Columbus on the Prussian
system, about which he had read. The address is worth reading as
throwing light on the author's frame of mind. It attracted a good
deal of attention at the time. The following summer he was visiting
Europe on a book-purchasing errand for his seminary, and he carried
with him the commission of the Governor of Ohio, in accordance
with a resolution of the State Legislature, to investigate and make a
report upon elementary public instruction in Europe. So he did. His
report was published late in 1837, and by order of the Legislature a
copy was sent to every school district in the State. Massachusetts
extended a similar compliment. Well, Stowe described with enthusiasm the Prussian system, both in form and in content, being especially impressed by the intelligent humanitarianism he saw everywhere. But he was particularly interested in the *Volksschule*, or
school of the common people. Very likely he supposed that was
what the Governor and Legislature were interested in.

Mann's visit.—Mann was broken in health and planned a recuper-
ative trip to Europe. The State Board of Education seems to have
expressed a willingness to have him report on educational matters
and, in the true spirit of the Pickwick Club, to have cordially in-

dorsed the principle that he should pay his own expenses. The *Seventh Annual Report* (1843), contains his observations on the schools of England, Scotland, Holland, Prussia, and Saxony. The Prussian schools especially claimed his admiration.[3]

GERMANY IN THE 1830'S

What impressed both Stowe and Mann was the amazing spectacle of an absolute monarch like the King of Prussia who could be, as they saw it, consistently liberal. I do not know about the liberalism, but at all events Frederick William III was one of those infrequent members of the House of Hohenzollern who was essentially a refined and cultivated man.

At the time of the visits, Schiller had been dead but a generation, and Goethe and Hegel had passed on not long before. Mendelssohn was still composing. The German universities were well launched on their great career. It was less than a generation since Prussia lay prostrate under the feet of Napoleon. When the Napoleonic scourge was past and gone, it became policy to rely on the German schoolmaster to rebuild Germany. Besides, the Protestant part of Germany had taken much the same view of the civil purpose and function of public instruction as that taken in the Massachusetts acts of 1642 and 1647.

In the historical controversy which was precipitated by Bunker's monograph[4] and especially by Judd's *A Democratic School System*[5] a great deal was made of the *Seventh Annual Report*.

[3] It is worth while, perhaps, to have before us a simple bibliography of the visits. The Cousin report is included in E. W. Knight, *Reports on European Education* (New York: McGraw-Hill Book Co., 1930). If the reader is interested in sources, he will find laid away in at least some libraries the *Report on the State of Public Instruction in Prussia*, trans. Sarah Austin, (London, 1834).

Stowe's Columbus address is available only as a rare book. The title was: *The Prussian System of Public Instruction and Its Applicability to the United States* (Columbus: Truman & Smith, 1836).

Mann's report appears in Vol. III of the complete works, *Life and Works of Horace Mann* (5 vols.; Boston: Lee & Shepard, 1891). There is an English reproduction laid away in collections of rare books, entitled *Report on an Educational Tour, etc.* (London, 1847).

[4] F. F. Bunker, *Reorganization of the Public School System* (U.S. Bureau of Education Bull. 1916, No. 8 [Washington, D.C., 1916]).

[5] C. H. Judd, *Evolution of a Democratic School System* (Boston: Houghton Mifflin Co., 1918).

The case against the importation of *Volksschule* ideas comes in part from a later period, upon which we shall presently comment. Other than that are, first, the rigid eight-year structure and, second, the arbitrarily terminal character of the school. This latter meant that, as soon as you had reached confirmation or first communion, you were out—go to work or go to a trade school.

HOW FAR WAS THERE AN IMPORTATION?

Was there an importation of structure? The answer must be that there was, and the importation was the most unfortunate thing we have, namely, the new conception of grading which gave us the Eight-Grade Elementary School. But when we come to the responsibility for that, it is clear enough that Mann cared little about it. If one will read the *Seventh Annual Report* through and think of it as a whole, he will see that Mann was chiefly impressed by the humanitarian discipline which he saw, by methods of caring for dependent and delinquent children, by intelligent methods of teaching, descriptions of which fill many pages; by a teacher-training system; and perhaps, above all, by State organization of Public Instruction. He was certainly much interested in what he called "the method of *classifying* children," but in the 170 pages of the report as it appears in his complete works, he speaks only twice of classification and then only on parts of two pages. He seems to have regarded it as something to be taken for granted and adopted out of hand "in our larger towns" but not as being nearly so fundamentally important as the other things noted above.

Mann must have been familiar with the early stages of the classified school systems, as we have been calling them in this work. He must have been aware of the "hoorah" over monitorial schools and have foreseen that they were not destined to prove to be any solution. The classification of the *Volksschule* in terms of years instead of in terms of a curriculum seemed much like that of American classified schools and probably a better plan.

But Prussia was very much in the air. Our international relations with her had always been pleasant and even cordial. The eight-year *Volksschule* was tangible and appealing and "business-like." Moreover, it could be "adopted," whereas methods of teaching have to be learned. At all events, the Prussian system was more and more adopted in the larger places, and in the end it drove out the native structure. The *Volksschule* structure was here by the route of the air rather than through Ellis Island, and in due season it became *the graded school par excellence.* Occasionally, country school boards went progressive and said that *their schools too* must be graded. They meant that everything in a one-room school must be put on eightfold discontinuity—eight classes in Arithmetic, eight in Reading, eight in Writing, and so on. I have seen many a case in which a poor teacher was struggling with forty or more "classes" a day. Happily that sort of thing was one of the inducements which led to the rural consolidated where one could have eight grades and be happy in them.

Terminal character.—The other of the two original and fundamental characteristics of the structure of the *Volksschule* as the visitors saw it was in reality its compulsory terminal character.

Toward the end of his report Mann makes some sage observations, the purport of which is in the nature of the query, "What do they bother about it all for, since it comes to nothing socially?" The pupils were turned away for good at about fourteen years of age, with the bars up in the pathway of further learning, and were destined to have no part in the conduct of public affairs of any kind. That seems to have been incomprehensible to Mann, but he makes little comment on it.

That sort of thing was utterly repugnant to American institutions then, as now, but it could hardly be impressive to most Americans as a matter of any practical concern. As we have seen, none of our people in those days or much later dreamed that the children of the urban lower classes would ever get more than the rudiments. Large numbers of them would not accept even that unless they were driven to it. As late as the eighties and nineties the State reports are full of lamentations over the difficulty of maintaining attendance, in country and city alike. Nevertheless, there was a material difference between the cities and the country towns and villages where common-school traditions survived. In the latter there was seldom any serious difficulty in the way of an ambitious and capable boy—or, indeed, girl—going as far as he or she would. Country boys and girls who were ambitious for anything else than economic prosperity were few and far between, but in the Northern States at least it hardly ever occurred to any of us that we could not go as far as we would—President? Why, certainly; was not Lincoln a rail-splitter and Garfield a canal boy? We looked upon towering ambitions with amusement rather than contempt. When the time was ripe, the high schools perforce threw open their doors to the "forgotten boys and girls," all of whom would have considered "forgotten" a singular misuse of words. No, the *Volksschule* as a lower-class school by prescription never in the slightest degree came to America.

Improvement in methods.—In another and eminently legitimate sense the institution did come among us. The age of the visits was an age of the educational missionary. Mann, Stowe, Henry Barnard, John D. Pierce, Samuel R. Hall, and many others not only were thinkers and innovators but were tireless lecturers and writers. The visitors brought back with them from Europe, and especially from Prussia, a great deal of pedagogical ammunition which they passed around to co-workers and used upon their audiences. Improved methods, for the time at least, became fashionable.

The Vorschule—Gymnasium.—It seems to me unfortunate that the visitors remained so little aware of the *Gymnasium* and the line to which it belonged. If he had thoroughly understood that institution, it seems to me that Mann at least would not only have seen that the German upper-caste school, in spite of its social connections, had in it much more that was suited to the whole genius of the American common school and its derivatives than did the *Volksschule*.[6]

As we look back on what they saw, with light derived from further study a century later and especially from experience derived from three lifetimes of social change, it is easy to see that the *Volksschule* of the forties was admirably adapted to the purpose of thoroughly training children in elementary knowledge, in the *forms* of rudimentary thinking, and in the primary intelligence which is satisfied with *what* and *how* and does not ask *why*. In brief, it was admirably cal-

[6] See above, p. 56.

culated to shift a national mores out of a notorious dreaminess,
which found its greatest love in Music, into ideals of thoroughness
and efficiency unequaled elsewhere and to train the masses to follow
leaders set up for the folk but not to follow right leaders selected by
the folk itself.

Altogether, it is easy to see why it was that our leaders in Public
Instruction of a century ago became so enthusiastic about Prussian
schools and about Prussian methods of dealing with the dependent,
defective, and delinquent.

THE LATER PRUSSIAN AND GERMAN SYSTEM

Between the time of Mann's report in 1843 and that in which
Judd saw things in the year 1913, a great deal of water had flowed
down the bloody streams of German politics. Judd showed consequences that the earlier school men had never dreamed of.

When Victor Cousin was making his report to the French ministry,
Otto von Bismarck was rather a romantic youth, full of doubts and
philosophy, chumming with young John Lothrop Motley of Boston at
Göttingen. Twenty years later the youth was helping to prop up the
Hohenzollern dynasty. Ten years later still he was Prime Minister
and on the way to becoming *Reichskanzler*. A national policy for
Prussia had been inaugurated which, under "blood and iron," was to
lead to Prussian domination of Germany, to two treaties of Ver-
sailles, and to Adolf Hitler. In seventy-five years, prior to and including 1939, Prussia and then Germany leaped at the throat of
civilized Europe seven times. The school system which Stowe and
Mann had so much admired for its enlightened liberalism had proved
in the end to have been autocracy's most powerful single weapon. A
German mores had been created in which German rule of all mankind was a principle of life, in which anything the Government of
the day might say was truth, and in which unquestioning obedience
to the decrees of Government was universal custom.

Meantime, the American "importation" taught partial payments,
a singularly unveracious national history, the name of the President
—often with suggestions that it ought to have been something else
—and, so far from inculcating unquestioning obedience, it usually
found it something of a problem to secure any obedience at all.

III. WAS THE AMERICAN ELEMENTARY SCHOOL A COPY?

Was the American Elementary School in its eight grades of one year each, and eventually of half a year each, a copy of the *Volksschule?*

The graded structure under this new conception of grading makes it look that way. If you find a man with something that you know he did not inherit and could not make or buy, you at least ask him where he got it. A chief educational officer of Michigan said they had adopted the Prussian system. Most of the rest of such officers in the United States would have been obliged to say the same thing if they had known. By the end of the century the eight-grade school had crowded out the native school and had officially been dubbed "Elementary" by the Committee of Ten. Prior to that it had usually been called "grade school" or "ward school." There had been set up complete discontinuity within the Elementary and between Elementary and High, now erroneously called "secondary." All that was left of the native system were traces of the common school in the smaller places.

To speak of "the *Volksschule* Elementary" is justifiably descriptive so far as *structure* is concerned, and that means much, but it is not descriptive so far as *content* and *method* are concerned. In these last respects our schools developed follies all their own, but at least they were American follies. In at least two respects our lower school carried over from the old common school some essentials and kept them until the process of formalization and then degeneration had stamped out these also.

THE AMERICAN TEXTBOOK

A fundamental difference between our Elementary School and what the *Volksschule* ever was arose out of our textbook prepared for use in schools which, with all its virtues and vices, is peculiarly an American institution. German teaching was typically by word of mouth, that is to say, it was didactic. No doubt the visitors found books in use, but they were apparently what we should call supplementary reading. Mann noted their resemblance to what he hoped to get out of his free libraries. But it is doubtful that Horace Mann ever saw, to appreciate, an American textbook of the kind which began to come in with the McGuffey readers.

These were appearing from 1836 to 1857. In recent years there has been appearing a sort of public awareness of William McGuffey. Those of us who have been interested in the building of a systematic pedagogy are fond of picturing him sitting by that table at Miami University and finding out experimentally what children of different ages like in the way of reading matter. In the end, McGuffey taught the American people to read, or most of them. And he had his reward, for it is doubtful that, in proportion to population, there has ever been a set of textbooks which enjoyed a wider sale. Strictly according to schedule, thirty years after his labors were at their height the census of 1880 showed a remarkable upshoot in the amount of printed matter transmitted by mail.

In 1845 began to appear the Colburn arithmetic texts. Here again was something new in the world. A pupil could take one of these books and, provided he could read, would be able to learn independently of the teacher. They had clear-cut presentation, assimilative material, and test material, all in a chapter. Schoolmasters in my time were never allowed to forget that we did not use Colburn's arithmetics. But that was not all. Colburn was followed by Greenleaf, and Greenleaf by others of the sort. Then came the Wentworth texts in mathematics for high schools and academies, made experimentally in the classroom at Phillips Exeter Academy, much as the McGuffey readers and Colburn arithmetics had been built. In the junior-college field something of the same sort appears in Olney's *General Geometry and Calculus*, made for the author's students at the University of Michigan.

Later on appeared equivalent texts in English Grammar and Composition, Chemistry and Physics and Astronomy, and in perhaps some other branches.

Now observe that textbooks like the above were made for the old common school, for the classified common and high school, and for the academy. There was no good reason why they should not be used in the graded elementary, save for the fact that interest and emphasis were more and more diverted in other directions. The books could be really studied, which was done—more or less competently—and then came the recitation. The latter was, I suppose, a derivation from the old thesis which was "set up" to be defended. The teacher called you up on a topic, and you were expected to demonstrate in full that you had mastered at least that particular topic. The great subjects of Geography and History, however, never, so far as I know, were treated that way. Until Tarr and McMurry geography was left to be memorized.

The whole system opened the way to pupils of talent for solid discipline of an intellectual sort, but it did little or nothing for children who did not happen to catch on. Later on, these school failures often proved by their success in life to be standing reproaches to lack of perspicacity in their teachers.

THE ENRICHMENT PERIOD

Then, toward the end of the century, came the so-called "Enrichment Period," and there penetrated the eight grades a sort of phenomenology called nature study and a great wealth of supplementary reading material in the sciences, history, and geography. The old graded readers gave place to complete English classics.

When the graded school as we know it had completely displaced the old common school in its classified form, it had also traveled a long way from the *Volksschule* pattern, save in structure.

So long as the *Volksschule* remained at home, in a rigid caste system, in a militaristic nation, in a society which grew up on what seems to have been almost a national genius for efficiency and thoroughness, among a people which as a whole had learned to care little for individual freedom and were patient under severe restrictions upon civil liberty—that long it was effective in doing what it was intended to do. Moreover, the Government never cherished any illusions about born teachers; if one were going to teach, he had to know his subject-matter and how to present it—again as the Government of the day desired.

The *Volksschule* pattern in America, on the other hand, was in an alien mores and an alien set of customs and institutions, in a society which was perhaps as unlike that of Germany and as opposed to it as anything could well be. As not uncommonly happens in Nature and in Society, the transplanted school structure proceeded to abort into a sort of monstrous growth and, in doing so, contrived to involve pretty much the whole of our educational system. To that process we now come.

IV. DISCONTINUITY TO ABOUT 1900

In our use of *discontinuity* as a term we have in mind a state of affairs in the structure of a school system in which there have come to exist several schools in an hierarchy of progress, each of the schools being more or less thing-in-itself rather than a functional part of a system. Let me try to be more concrete.

Difference between primary school and secondary is functional because it is a difference in the nature of things. In the primary school pupils cannot learn by studying books, because they have not the primary tools of study. They cannot read; or write; or cypher, either by performing computations or by reading those which are written into their study material. They can learn—but not by studying. In the secondary they can use the tools acquired in the primary for study purposes.

There is a functional difference between primary and secondary ordained by nature and logic and not by the school board. Such discontinuity as there is, is normal and harmless.

But in the long period stretching from the end of the primary to the attainment of educational maturity there is no functional difference in instruction. Instruction is throughout the same in concept: it is all a matter of using cultural material for disciplinary purposes with pupils who are not yet mature. Any breaking-up of that period into separate schools introduces discontinuity, but it does not necessarily break with the Common School principle of subject-matter learning.

As we have seen, the old common school was not discontinuous for the reason that it recognized no formal division points within itself, and for the further reason that it implied neither an earlier nor a later school. Likewise, the old academy was not discontinuous, because it did not admit its pupils on the completion of an earlier school but rather took them on evidence of learning acquired, whatever its source, and because it did not imply a later school. When the academies became college-preparatory, they became discontinuous, and the College ceased to be part of a University and became part of a School system.

When the Boston English High was established, it became part of a discontinuous system because it presumed an earlier school, post-primary, as preparatory. The high schools which were established as was the Boston School were, like it, discontinuous from the beginning, since their very inception made them schools-in-themselves. The high schools which followed the other line of descent as parts of a classified system were in a system which was in form discontinuous, but, so long as pupils were advanced in terms of learning acquired, the system was not in substance discontinuous. Nevertheless, let any kind of form be set up and adhered to and the form will always tend to be separated in men's minds from the substance. Hence, unless the form is in itself valid and right, substance will always tend to be lost. It is that principle, I suppose, that makes mathematical treatment of a problem always valid, where quantity and relationship are involved, for mathematical forms are of all things the most valid and right in themselves.

But the climax of discontinuity, prior to 1900, came in the Eight-grade Elementary, the Americanized *Volksschule*. Here there were eight distinct schools, and the pupils moved into an upper grade *when they had maintained satisfactory performance on assigned tasks* in the next lower. In time, promotion by half-years came in, and then there were sixteen distinct schools below high. In the larger places that meant for the pupil a new teacher each year and often two new teachers each year.

In truth the eight-grade school never worked well save by default of criticism.

By the time when the recent critical period came in, let us say 1890, faults galore began to be noted, all of them, as we can now look back and see, inherent in the structure and its consequences. Perhaps the first in order was the dissatisfaction in the product of the eight grades which led to nine grades and sometimes ten grades, on the theory, apparently, that if you have a poor thing you can improve it by getting more of it.

Then came a long-continued series of troubles and their amendments which can be grouped together under the name "laggards in our schools." In general, human nature, at least American human nature, is so constituted that it perversely declines to slide through a machine as inorganic material can ingeniously be made to do. Hence, failure to make the grade and be promoted. For many years it was necessary to adopt heroic measures to clear out the accumulation of repeaters in the fourth grade who waited there patiently until the age of fourteen and the privilege of a child labor certificate had arrived. Many devices were invented to solve the problem, but, like the old ninth- and tenth-grade solutions, none of them got at the heart of the matter. Among the devices were fast and slow sections, the so-called "double track," and semiannual promotions. Finally, the I.Q. delusion came in and sorted out human nature into sections of pupils who were born capable of promotion, others who were partly capable, and still others who were not capable at all. In other words, the eight-grade school was assumed to be eternal verity and human beings to be relative to that perverted institution.

All that critical attitude seems to be past and gone, mainly for three reasons:

First, there are hardly any school people left who are not themselves products of the system. That is the joke which fate always plays on progress in instruction: there are none so intransigent as those who desire to be considered educated. If education means getting through school and college—and that is precisely what the graded-school ideology leads to—it is a deadly affront to suggest to such people that schools and colleges are not all they ought to be. In other words, we do not hear the criticisms which we used to hear because the graded-school ideology is self-protective when enough people have been brought up on it.

Second, a partial solution has been found for "laggards in our schools" in abolishing the possibility of laggards by dispensing with any curriculum at all. Manifestly, one cannot be a laggard if there is nothing to learn. The fact that such a doctrine must lead to widespread ignorance is met by shrewdly denying the reality of Civilization itself.

Third, the most crude of the reasons arises from the practice found in some of our politics-ridden cities of universal salvation through promotion by the decree of the superintendent's office.

So by the year 1900, or soon after, the American school system had become an involved discontinuity (1) between Elementary and High and (2) within the eight-grade system of the Elementary. *The immediate consequences may be generalized as being a progressive substitution of getting through school for the acquisition of learning in school.* We proceed, then, to discuss the process at work as it may be observed almost anywhere by almost anybody.

V. FORMALIZATION

Let us bear in mind that true learning which contributes to Education of some sort, either General or Special, is ordinarily a slow process which cannot be hurried. Obstacles may be removed, and in that sense the process expedited; but the process cannot be hurried up. Moreover, in Man and the lower animals alike real learnings arise out of real experience of some sort. In the whole instructional process the first principle of pedagogy is a necessary consequence, namely, that every teacher must be able to know the pupil well enough, and be able to observe him closely enough, to follow his mind, that is to say, to sense "how things strike him." The latter in turn means that the teacher must sense what the pupil's real experience is. All this implies two primary conditioning factors in all Common School teaching:

First, the teacher must not have so many pupils that such acquaintanceship is an impossibility. That was very likely the weak point in the monitorial schools.

Second, the teacher must have the pupil long enough to get really acquainted with him and then long enough beyond that to give the teaching a chance to take effect.

LESSON-LEARNING AND LESSON-HEARING

Now, if as a teacher you have thirty to fifty pupils whom you received in September and whom you must have ready for the next grade in succession by February, or June at the latest, there is certainly little time or opportunity for becoming acquainted with them in the pupil-teacher sense. If you do attempt to achieve that vital contact by February 1, then at the best you pass your pupils on to the next teacher in the assembly line when you have just become fairly well acquainted and before you have been able to do your most effective teaching. If you can keep them until June, then you may have perhaps a fifty-fifty chance of having done some real teaching. About the best that can be done is to make daily textbook assignments or to set "activity" tasks, see that the pupil completes the assignment, estimate the quality of his work, make a record of the fact, and repeat to the end of the time he is with you. The record to the pupil is his "mark" to go on his report card and take home to show his parents. The assumption, of course, originally was that the pupil would learn from the acceptable performance of his assignments.

Assumptions are always subject to challenge, and it is of the essence of all good scientific procedure that they should all be brought to the test of significant facts and reasoning. To anybody at all familiar with the school procedure described, and at all critically minded, any such assumption could hardly be called good. His query would be, "What reason have you to suppose that the pupil in fact does learn anything out of a lesson assignment well performed?"

Twenty years ago my students and I set up a technique designed to explore factually the validity of this assumption, namely, that by learning assigned lessons pupils in reality learn what the lessons are supposed to stand for—if anything. The whole matter is reported in chapters iii and iv of *The Practice of Teaching in the Secondary School*. The disclosure was that only a small proportion actually learned in full what the lessons implied or made actual progress in learning. About the same proportion became proficient lesson-learners and yet revealed no actual progress at all, such as, for instance, ability to read French or apply a principle in Mathematics. The great bulk of the pupils made discernible progress in true learning but nothing like full learning.

Cramming.—We find the lesson-learning phenomenon perhaps more familiarly in what is called "cramming." In that the pupil, or adult for that matter, is put through a process of drill to prepare him to take some kind of test. Of course, there is no learning in the educational sense. When that is done in the classroom as part of instructional procedure, the practice is mere pedagogical dishonesty, manufacturing evidence. When it is done by an outside crammer—rather a contemptible calling by the way—what is done is intentional and the motive is apparent to all. Nevertheless, there is little or no difference in educational principle between lesson-hearing and cramming.

RELATION TO DISCONTINUITY

What has all this to do with the subject of this chapter? The answer is that the thing arises chiefly out of discontinuity in the school structure and not merely out of perversity in human nature. Let us see.

In the old common school, even though the particular school might be a poor specimen, there was no temptation to depart from the common sense of centering attention on what was to be learned, for there were no grades to induce continuous attention to the preparatory process and no school beyond for which pupils must be got ready.

In the classified school there was a mild discontinuity, but it did not involve the substitution of *getting through* for *learning*. Teachers always had the pupils at least two years; a school was not *defined* as the lapse of a year or half-year. Attention did not center upon the school itself but upon what was supposed to be learned in that school—primary, intermediate, grammar, high, or whatever the system might include. Lesson-hearing was genuine in the sense that the recitation was, as we have seen, in reality the defense of a thesis. True enough, teachers might be negligent, ignorant even, and the pupils might not learn much, but there was no inducement for the ideology of getting through school to emerge.

Where extreme discontinuity had become developed, on the other hand, pupils became less and less individuals, especially in city schools, and more and more merely children in transit. What was before a temptation to teachers became a necessity. No wonder that in the end teachers became hospitable to any shallow device which promised to liberate them from such routine. *What has grown out of that old eight-year importation is an American assembly line with from six to sixteen stations.*

PERFORMANCE ESTIMATED

To be sure that learning is taking place requires, no doubt, a capacity for critical observation and honest judgment. There is not

time for either in a single year or in a half-year. There would not be
even if teachers were fully qualified and the whole system were reorganized so as not to throw an impossible number of pupils into the
charge of a single teacher.

In default thereof, teachers long ago began to estimate daily performance on assigned lessons or other tasks or on examination papers
of some sort. Estimates came to be expressed fundamentally in percentages of what the teacher regarded as full or irreproachable performance, or in some other mathematical symbol, without, however,
any mathematical reality whatever. At the end of a reporting period
the pupil's standing was the average of these symbols of daily judgment. Such an expression as that is not a true average of anything;
it is not even the teacher's average judgment. As a refinement based
upon a perception of the truth of the principle just stated, the pupil's mark came to be a letter signifying the teacher's judgment of his
place in a scale of relative performance, from best to that which was
deemed unacceptable. In that case there was not even an estimate
of acceptable performance; the best might be very poor, but so long
as it was best in that group, it would be awarded a mark which everywhere signifies excellence. In any case, there was no sign of an estimate of actual learning achieved. If John received 80 and James 50,
then the meaning was that James was but five-eighths as good as
John, whereas there would be no evidence whatever that either of
them had learned anything at all.

Long use breeds custom. It seems absurd that anything of the
sort could anywhere exist, but given universal custom over a period
of years and the absurd comes to seem normal and valid.

Of course under such a regimen some pupils, and indeed college
students, became marvelously skilled in making recitations. In the
end the man who had "a good school record" behind him naturally
tended to become an adept in publicity. Forty years ago, when I
was taking my first tentative steps in inducing teachers to do direct
teaching of specified learning objectives instead of hearing lessons
about them, I again and again noted that the former class leaders
were likely to gravitate toward the bottom and the despised and rejected to take their places. And, after all, it is probable that most

pupils have never been greatly deceived albeit they could hardly formulate their lack of conviction.

Standardized tests.—But time still went on. Standardized tests came in, and teachers were induced to become "objective" in substituting scores on tests for their own judgment—which was praiseworthy, provided the thing to be judged had in itself any validity. The bulk of the tests were of necessity performance measures and had to be, since the testers were hunting for something which could be "measured." Like much else in our schools which purports to be modern, scientific, progressive, that notion was three hundred years out of date, for it was nothing else than an example of the old Cartesian doctrine that whatever is exists as quantity and can therefore be measured. In truth, nearly all learning—all that is ideational, substantial, and a contribution to the maturing of personality—is qualitative in its nature. It can be *identified* on the evidence of its manifestations but it can never be *measured*. To this hour our graded-school public can be captivated by broadcasts and newspaper features which raise the issue, "How much do you know?" by proposing ten questions.

In the high school.—Carried over into high school, the teacher's judgment continued to be an estimate of performance on assignments and not of learning acquired. It could not very well be otherwise, for most high-school and college teachers, as well as those in the lower grades, are products of the system under which they have been schooled, at least ever since they left the primary. They are unaware of anything else—save by the chance that they have come out of homes in which there has been some genuineness of culture and of knowledge, or that they have encountered somewhere along the line a rare teacher who has been capable of actual teaching, or, indeed, that some rare gift in temperament has turned them toward genuineness as individuals.

We have noted that the High School is continuous within itself and is therefore hardly susceptible of the inevitable kind of development which arises out of the extreme discontinuity within the Elementary School. Under the influence of strong personalities in the principal and anong the teachers whom the pupil meets, or at least knows for four full years, he may learn much; but that kind of pupil-teacher contact is possible only in a relatively small school. Moreover, the learning thus acquired is not the systematic kind of learning and discipline which ought to come from classroom study of important cultural material.

The graded-school ideology in its pure form is applicable to high-school subjects which are continuous over two or more years, notably the foreign languages, English composition, and consolidated mathematics. So we find French I, II, and III standing for courses in each of three several years. The issue then becomes: "Is the pupil doing his daily work at passing-grade level?" and not: "Is he learning to read French?" And similarly in other subjects. Note that the process which for well-nigh a century has been producing a series of schools-in-themselves has in these high-school subjects produced a series of courses-in-themselves.

THE ELECTIVE SYSTEM AND CREDITS

The ultimate in formalization came into being when systems of credits began to be set up in consequences of the conjunction of graded-school notions and the elective system. Let us take a look at the system under which nearly everybody who is still under sixty has been schooled.

The story of the origins, foundations, applications, and consequences of the elective system would require a sizable volume; but nothing of the sort is contemplated. It is usually attributed to Charles W. Eliot and Harvard, but in truth it goes a long way back, to the "greatest liberal of them all"—because it looked liberal. When Eliot advocated it for Harvard, it must be remembered, he was reforming a college system in which the round of the Ancient Classics and Mathematics was still the core of the curriculum. Natural Science had long been struggling for a place, Modern Languages and their Literatures were still suspect save perhaps in the few colleges which could teach them, and the Social Sciences were scarcely dreamed of except for the professional study of Law. Eliot was before all else a reformer, and, like many other good reformers, he worked at times indirectly. Perhaps if the boys were allowed to choose from the modern lines, sooner or later the modern lines would find a secure place in the sun. So it was, and so it has been until subject-matter has found a place in the curriculums of various institutions which has no possible justification in any kind of a cultural enterprise.

The old system had no sort of justification save that of tradition; it had been obsolete for the most part for at least a century prior to 1869. But the new was nonetheless a leap in the dark. The only psychological basis upon which it could rest, and that which Eliot himself most often urged, was being disproved by William James, or at least called seriously in question on scientific grounds, at the very time when the elective system was being put in force. In educational theory there was involved the notion that if the pupil is reluctant to become adapted to the world, then the world must be adapted to each of many pupils young and old.

Fifty years ago college electives were either "options" or else a choice between curriculums. If you did not feel up to Calculus in Sophomore year, you had the option of an easier course in Mathematics. When you entered college, you selected a curriculum as an authorized way to cultural salvation, but, when you had chosen, you did not depart from it. In the end you received a Bachelor's degree which defined your relative intellectual status before men in a graded series from A.B. down through B.S., B.L., and Ph.B.

Now, all that implied credit for courses completed, lest the unregenerate cheat the college out of some prized degree; and "credit" was strictly a commercial term. You might cultivate some intellectual interest of your own at the college library or in one of the laboratories, but you received no credit on the college books for that sort of thing and did not expect any.

In due season the structure and administration of the high schools became precisely like those of the colleges.

But the real elective system did not come in until high schools and colleges came to offer more courses than any individual could cover in many years. It then became necessary to set up a sort of pedagogical credit money. Each course came to have attached to it the value it would have in counting up entitlement to graduation or a degree. Moreover, the credits became negotiable paper when a pupil passed from high school into college or when the family removed to another town.

In colleges credits came to be expressed in semester-hours or, in institutions which are under the quarter system, in student majors. A semester-hour is attending a class which meets one hour per week for a semester or half-year. Attending two such classes, or one class which meets two hours per week, makes two semester-hours, and so on. In the other kind of colleges a course which meets five times a week for twelve weeks yields a student-major. The normal requirement for the Bachelor's degree is 120 semester-hours or 36 student-majors. But attendance is not enough; the student must have attained a passing grade on the teacher's estimates of performance.

In high schools the standard unit is a course meeting not less than four times weekly for not less than thirty-six weeks, sometimes called a "course unit" or a "Carnegie unit." Fourteen and a half such units, with standard daily performance, in an accredited school, entitles the student to admission to college.

Thus an education can conveniently be defined in mathematical terms as: eight grades in an elementary school, plus $14\frac{1}{2}$ high-school course units, plus 120 semester-hours or 36 majors.

SUMMARY OF THE GRADED-SCHOOL IDEOLOGY

We have dealt in some detail with the evolution of what has been called *graded-school ideology* and have shown its relation to the development of discontinuity in a school system which has departed about as far as it seems able to go from its origins in a system which, however inefficient particular schools might be, was, after all, a natural implication of American institutions. The result is almost utterly mechanical and formalistic. It nowhere implies learning in any systematic form. It would probably be hard to find anywhere in the United States a school or college which can fairly say that it has a record of what pupils and students have learned; all the schools and colleges have is a record in great detail of time spent, or, to use a not inappropriate penological term, served, with performance which has proved acceptable to teachers. That is not to say that pupils and students do not learn anything; but it is fair to say that they do not learn systematically and thoroughly what every intelligent citizen must know about the world in which he lives and about the country of which he is a part.

It all seems to me to be so obviously reduction to absurdity of the whole graded-school ideology that it is hardly necessary for one to be an "educator" to see the absurdity.

VI. DISCONTINUITY SINCE 1900

THE JUNIOR HIGH SCHOOL

In the decade 1890–1900, as we have several times seen, there began an upward expansion of the enrolment which was destined to dominate the policies of the whole educational system for the next generation. Pupils began to flow into the old four-year high school in great numbers, and they came more and more largely from the less cultivated homes, since children from the more cultivated homes were already in high school. Two immediate effects were apparent.

First, the high schools passed into a state of chronic crowding, requiring new buildings every few years.

Second, pupil mortality in the first years of high school became excessive. In public high schools sensitive to popular desires the adjustment tended to take the form of lowering the standards.

The structural readjustment worked out by schoolmasters took the name of "Junior High School," although there was nothing "junior" about it. In fact in some cities it was called, much more appropriately as I think, "intermediate." The move was originally a purely practical device to meet a current situation. It was as if changing social conditions had proposed to the schoolmasters of the day the issue: "Things, you see, have become different; what are you going to do about it?" Two things must be done: first, the existing high schools must be relieved of crowding and, second, the gap must be bridged between the eighth grade, which was part of a folk school, and the high school, which was still rather a remote descendant of the seventeenth-century Latin Grammar School.

Now I point out that the junior high school was at best a makeshift in the days when my generation of young schoolmasters were setting it up. The *Report of the Committee of Ten* had foreshadowed something of the sort in 1893. Sometimes it was an interval of two years, sometimes of three, sometimes of only one, between two different kinds of schools. It was well calculated to serve a useful end until such time as the whole system could be reorganized to meet the educational needs of the Common Man in an economic structure of society which was making that possible, perhaps for the first time in all human history. Gasoline engines and electric motors were releasing labor hours on the farm and in the household, and an awakened public declared an end to the days when "everybody worked but father"—in other words, the breeding of children for profit had come to an end.

The junior high school movement seems like a singularly good instance of the way in which society becomes readjusted when people do the next thing. One can see, in the light of the foregoing chapters, that it was more or less a blundering way back to the normal American school structure through the classified school. Likely enough, John Francis had something like that in mind when he called his junior high school "intermediate school." That is what it was. Unhappily, however, the school emerged at a time when mysticism in educational theory was beginning to become fashionable and when a jargon had already been evolved. The speculative theorists more or less captured the movement and created a thing which was veritably a catchall of the extant fads. In the course of their operations they succeeded in diverting the movement from its normal end and made it the most consistently thing-in-itself in the whole discontinuous system. Incidentally, it came to require an elegant building all by itself.

Moreover, the graded-school system of ideas had become so firmly rooted that the big question was not: "How can this new move make the needed adjustments most economically and effectively?" It was rather: "*How many years* shall be devoted to this junior high school?" One would think that penological notions had crept over and added themselves to the existing ideology. From that time on the debate hung about the issue of 6-3-3 or 6-2-4 or some other combination of years. In brief, another element had been added to the sadly discontinuous system, and another station had been inserted in the production line. Here was another place where the developing school structure went wrong.

JUNIOR COLLEGE

We have seen the origin of the Junior College as an adjustment by means of which certain college work of secondary character is placed where it belongs, namely, in the secondary school.[7]

Harper's arrangement with the Joliet Township High School was no new thing, save perhaps in the fact that a university took the initiative. Eleazar Wheelock apparently had the same kind of arrangement between his school at Lebanon, Connecticut, and both Yale and Princeton.[8] That must have been about 1760. In the following century Moses Waddell in Charleston, South Carolina, was sending his better students into advanced standing in college. It is altogether probable that mute and inglorious pedagogical Miltons have been doing the same sort of thing all the way along.

Now, when the practice of adding to the work of the high schools courses which had become misplaced in college, and of extending the age of final graduation two years in the hope of gaining maturity, became common, scarcely anybody was satisfied to extend the high school. On the contrary, this "junior college" had to be a thing-in-itself, a separate organization under a dean—for you cannot have a college without a dean. The work was no different in fundamental educational conception from the rest of the high-school work, but it seemed preposterous to make the boys and girls what they were in fact, namely, immature pupils not yet in possession of General Education: they must be "college students," and to many of them that meant license to defy the statutes and shatter the whole code of good manners.

So here was a further step in discontinuity, an expensive annex to the local high school, or else a separate setup, instead of a series of courses assimilated to the existing high-school work, whereas the rational intention behind the whole movement was merely to exclude from the University something that was no part of any College in the University but was decidedly part of the Common School.

Like the Junior High School movement, that of the Junior College normally represented a tendency in social adjustment, or readjust-

[7] See above, p. 25.

[8] See L. B. Richardson, *History of Dartmouth College*.

ment, backward toward the native set-up in the old common school and its overlapping academy, or an escape from the old Prussian *Volksschule* into the line of the *Vorschule*—*Gymnasium*. Either the American or the Prussian was the normal school structure.

VII. INDUSTRIALIZATION OF AN EDUCATIONAL SYSTEM

The purpose of our system in the beginning was Education of the Masses. That was long ago transformed into Mass Production in Education, parallel to industrial mass production, our chief national contribution in Industry.

Without doing undue violence to the facts, one may cherish the suspicion that the reason why the Eight-grade Elementary so readily captured the support of people in the mill towns and larger cities may have been its resemblance to a factory. Factories were highly successful. The businessman had displaced the soldier, the priest, and professional men, in general, as Nature's last word. Business methods were the supremely correct methods, "business-like" being synonymous with "systematic," "practical," "logical." Look in on the office of the modern high-school principal, or at any registrar's office, and note the resemblance to the office of a manufacturing concern. Be all that as it may, our whole discontinuous school system, and the graded-school notions which it has generated, has produced a picture of what would be, I suppose, good organization for industrial production—but scarcely an organization capable of transmitting Civilization and generating Education.

Our supremely efficient industrial organization is based on the fact that it deals with material things which change little if at all while they are in process of manufacture. This department makes this and another that, and this and that are laid away in storage—or indeed shipped to another plant—until they are called to the assembly line somewhere. Presently a wonderfully fabricated product emerges, which, however, must make good for the purpose it was designed to serve. You can do the same thing with your school and school system, provided your formal machinery works well, but you will not get an educational result. Indeed, as we have just seen well enough, an educational result is nowhere in the administrative picture. You can "get by" with it, partly because "getting by" is the chief product of the system and partly because the public seldom questions effectively that which it has no reason to understand. After all, that is the way everybody has been schooled, save for a few old men and old women who are out of court anyway because they are manifestly out of date. The school product is seldom submitted to any pragmatic test in such form that the public knows it is being submitted; the industrial product is always being submitted to the most exacting of pragmatic tests: if the bridge will not stand up or the machine will not run, something is definitely wrong somewhere.

VIII. THE PRODUCT

Well, it is now perhaps ninety years since we first embarked on the ways treated in this chapter, in the honest expectation that they would lead us to an intelligent and generally civilized citizenry. Something has been accomplished certainly, but very little, indeed, compared with what has been imperatively required, especially in a day when the whole fabric of society is constantly and fundamentally changing. Society, like nature, will not be denied the ultimate value in all evolution and development, namely, the higher adaptability.

As one looks out over the present world in the United States, he can but marvel that the thing goes at all. The commercial and industrial system breaks down from sheer lack of popular understanding of how it must be operated. Political corruption continues on a bankrupting scale on the naïve excuse that it is not good politics to save money. In common with other civilized nations, we fall into a devastating war after the pattern of the Mongol invasions of the thirteenth and fourteenth centuries, primarily because there has not been the public intelligence about world affairs which ought to have been the possession of schoolboys.

We fight for democracy in agony and the sacrifice of untold millions of small happinesses which had been gained, and yet there is abroad in the land extremely little intelligence about the working of democracy and indeed about what democracy really is. There is abundant faith in popular sovereignty, and for that we may devoutly thank God Almighty; we certainly have no occasion to thank the educational system. But if faith without works is dead, it is equally true that faith without specific intelligence is devastatingly costly in much more than money and may be futile.

Advertisers and other literary people deal with a population which they well know and proclaim is about twelve years of age in its collective cultural capacity, in the way suited to twelve-year-olds. And that is the climax of the whole indictment.

Now, with 60–70 per cent of the children of the appropriate ages in High School and with attendance at college becoming the usual rather than uncommon thing, one would think that the process of selection would have winnowed out the obviously unfit and have left among the students in our colleges and universities at least the approximately educated. The process of selection undoubtedly has been at work and has indeed left at the top about all the education the rising generations achieve. What is the result like? We have some trenchant testimony from three of our leading universities, perhaps veritably the three leading. Let us look at it.

HARVARD

Harvard Freshmen are presumably a selected group if there is a selected group anywhere. In his report for 1923–24 President Lowell had occasion to state:

Every one who has taught a Freshman course in a subject requiring the use of books dealing with large questions is aware of the fact that Freshmen can read paragraphs, or a few pages covering a definite point, but that they can rarely read a book; that is, they have not the habit of sustained thinking needed to grasp and hold a continuous line of thought and take in its full meaning. Their comprehension deals rather with a succession of points than with a train of thought; and yet this last is the very essence of the intellectual life.

If twelve years of school life have left Harvard Freshmen in that juvenile intellectual condition, it is not likely that most others who have not reached Harvard or any other university are in any better case. It is not surprising, for twelve years of learning lessons from textbooks is just what we might naturally expect would produce what President Lowell complained of. Competent citizenship requires, above all else perhaps, that the citizen be able and likely to read serious books which present sustained arguments rather than a long series of dogmatic assertions.

COLUMBIA

I quote from page 67 of Abraham Flexner's *Universities: American, English, German:*[9]

Surely the Dean of Columbia College knows American college youth.

"I am convinced," he has recently said, "that the youth of college age at the present time are as immature morally and as crude socially as they are undeveloped intellectually."

And yet there cannot be a great many youth of college age who are more nearly educated than those who are between eighteen and twenty-two in Columbia College. But the youth cannot get into Columbia College until they have passed through the school system; and there has been nothing in the school experience of most of them which would lead them to mature morally, intellectually, or in matters of ordinary taste.

Professor Woodbridge, long the Dean of the Graduate School of Columbia: "only a fourth [of the graduate students] needs to be considered seriously in the interest of scholarship and research."

If, after all these years, this statement can be made of the students in one of our most selective graduate schools, just what is supposed to be the product of our educational system as a whole? Certainly not Education.

CHICAGO

Professor Gordon J. Laing, Dean of the Graduate School, writes: "I do not think I am exaggerating when I say that scores of Masters are graduating each year without having attained even the slightest appreciation of the higher culture. Nor do they acquire it later. Large numbers of them regard the degree as a gilt-edged teacher's certificate, and having attained it they do not pursue their studies further. They are through. If you doubt my statement, study the published output of the secondary school teachers of this country (and it is in the secondary schools that the Masters are for the most part to be found) and compare it with the publications of secondary school teachers in England, Germany and France You will find that our secondary schools make but a pitiful showing beside the others."[10]

[9] Several quotations from the same work are made with the kind permission of the publishers, the Oxford University Press.

[10] Quoted by Flexner, *op. cit.*, p. 83 (from "The Standards of Graduate Work," in *Problems in Education* [Cleveland: Western Reserve University, 1927], p. 201).

A TEACHING EXPERIENCE

For eighteen years the writer was in active service as a professor in the Department of Education at the University of Chicago, meeting almost entirely graduate students. Geographically, his students were well distributed in college origins, sometimes as many as forty different States being represented in a single course.

I studied these graduate students as well as I could, and had good opportunity to do it through the papers which they furnished me. Moreover, I had some opportunity to check my findings in short lecture courses at other institutions chartered as universities. Curiously enough, my estimate of them all through that period corresponded precisely with the similar estimate of Dean Woodbridge as applied to graduate students at Columbia. I thought that 25 per cent of them might be recognized as University students, but my estimate was probably high. What, specifically, are the remaining 75 per cent like? I believe I can describe them without exaggerating their lacks.

As a class, they have no conception that this is an orderly universe in which effect follows cause, consequent follows antecedent. They have little conception of logical coherence as opposed to sentimentality, prejudice, and expediency. They can be convinced of truth, or what they suppose to be truth, through what they call "eloquent appeal" but never through demonstration. Opinion with them is founded on predilection; hence they habitually assert opinions on matters about which they do not even pretend to know anything and on issues which are not matters of opinion at all.

They cannot learn from following an argument. They can be persuaded to a course of action that way, but they cannot learn. They can get up assignments and render an account thereof to the instructor, but it seldom occurs to them that there is anything to be learned out of assignments. Assignments are good as counting toward graduate credit and that is all.

It would perhaps not be far wrong to call them "jury-minded." That is to say, they can work in one-to-one situations, where a particular piece of concrete and very tangible evidence proves or disproves a particular assertion. But they cannot hold in mind a long thread of argument in which facts, principles, and events are shown to lead to the validity of some general conclusion stated as a guiding principle. Hence, they are helpless in the presence of the historical method in any of its forms. If Aristotle himself could come back to earth divested of the glamour of his great name and lecture on Ethics, they would universally say: "That is only this man's opinion." And yet the substance of the social sciences in which our greatest need today resides cannot be reduced to one-to-one situations; you cannot, for example, reduce the Law to an experimental science.

These people may do very well in the natural sciences, and especially in the physical sciences, but only when they are chiefly interested in purely technological purposes. They would be as helpless in a department which had to deal with Natural Philosophy as they are in the study of Education. I have never taught in a College of Law, but I should confidently expect that such students might be made into practicing attorneys or counselors but never into jurists.

They seldom read anything beyond the current newspapers and magazines and the current popular books—often not even the latter. *They never read fundamental material in any field,* not even their own field. Hence, they are singularly credulous. Any wild and sensational publication will be accepted by them as gospel, since they have not the background with which to estimate its credibility.

In class, they sit furiously making notes recording what the instructor says rather than attempting to understand what he says. Protests and warnings of the futility of the practice seldom get home. In and about the corridors you hear the query: "What did he say?" That, too, is a measure of their credulity. "What he says" looms large, but never his reasons for saying it.

It is over and again manifest that they suppose a course to be set up for their approval or disapproval. Why should they not? Most of them have been accustomed to schools and colleges in which the opinion of the pupils, their likes and dislikes, is set up in local public discussion and the local press as the all-important thing.

One of the 25 per cent, on the other hand, will come to the office out of class, or meet the instructor somewhere about the campus, in order to follow an argument into its further implications and applications, or will in class challenge the facts or reasoning of the instructor.

The farthest the 75 per cent ever get, kindly souls! is to linger after class and tell the instructor "how much they agree with what he said" or "how inspiring the course is." Perhaps it is, but that is not its purpose. On bad days they notify the professor that they "cannot agree with him at all"—now and then withdrawing from the course in protest. With them agreement is a synonym for sympathy; argument means disputation; and reasonableness is the same thing as courtesy and amiability.

Such people stand in awe of majorities. An heavy majority on an intellectual issue, composed of school children, would give these people a comfortable feeling of assurance, even though the minority were composed of Newton, Laplace, and Immanuel Kant. Hence, their predilection for the questionnaire method of research.

Finally, it is quite inconceivable to most of them that anybody can know anything for which he has not taken a course and received credit. If, in fact, one does know something without that kind of academic parentage, his knowledge is likely to be suspect as being in the nature of a swindle somewhere. *That seems to me the culminating tragedy of the whole graded-school ideology.* The pertinent query seems to be: "What is *he supposed* to know about it?"

These people are not *mentally* inferior; they have "brains" enough. They are often unusually bright; but they do not know much and are in no shape to learn more. They are the logical product of the system through which they have passed. They have never in their lives encountered such a thing as intellectual discipline.

But have not the 25 per cent passed through the same kind of system? They have, indeed, but with a difference. With the others, the system is ordinarily their whole background; with the better students, there is background apart from the system. They have come out of strong and cultivated homes in which there has been a tradition of culture if not of "education." Or they have been happy in a teacher who has given them a vision of truth and genuineness. Or, finally, in some cases certainly, some vagrant temperamental trait has led them to interests which have made for them a genuine background.

But the credit-chasers, whom school and college sanctify for the most part, get their higher degrees—and then they are "supposed to know." The public is seldom allowed to forget it. Naturally enough, for the degree is the one thing they can understand; it is much like the mark of 80 per cent which lifted their average in the eighth grade enough to save them from being kept back. What the degree is "supposed" to stand for is not within their mental vision. They go out into high-school teaching staffs and administrative positions, onto college faculties, into the offices of newspapers and other journals, where they write editorials, reviews, news columns, feature columns; now and then they publish a book. They appear in the pulpit and sometimes hold important offices. They mold public opinion, and in the end the public mind which they generate is as incapable of straight thinking as they are themselves.

Now the enrolment of the graduate schools of our leading universities is presumably an highly selected product of the whole system. If the finally selected competent product is in truth not more than 25 per cent of the whole graduate enrolment, what must be the actual intellectual character of the pupils in the nation at large as they come from the high schools?

Professors, at least the older men, are well aware of the foregoing, but they are disposed to take the easy way of calling it Nature's method, to say that Nature is notoriously wasteful and that we have to put up with the inferior in order to find the superior. But the inferior have not got selected out in the sixteen school and college years before the Graduate School. The 75 per cent were never for the most part University material at all, not because they lack ability but because they lack intellectual interest of any sort or description and because they have never encountered such a thing as cultural discipline. Their interests and real ambitions lie elsewhere. But, after all, among them there is a good deal of material which is potentially valuable to the Commonwealth in University pursuits. Pupils and college students are not codfish spawn. Anywhere else than in a school and college system, it would be presumed that there is a definite teaching obligation to be attained with each of them, and the end would systematically be sought. Pupils and students would not be left to survive under the educational laissez faire of the philosophy of the graded school.

ACCOMPLISHMENT

Let us turn the picture and look to the other side if perchance we may find something to offset the well-nigh fatal lacks which we have noted. And we find it.

In the first place, the very fact that there has been for three hundred years a common-school system in our country has undoubtedly brought about an achievement of incredible value. There has been erected some measure of a common culture, in institutions, in language, and in traditions—even though little or nothing has been imparted about the institutions. The common culture is, after all, in the stage of simple awareness and not of intelligent apprehension, but even so that is much.

Roman statesmen of the Empire's best period came to despair of the Unity of Empire because they could discern no common culture. In less than a century, the process of disintegration had begun, as they had probably foreseen that it must; the course of events proved that there was no imperial society as a going concern.

So it might have been with us.

In the last one hundred years we have admitted to ourselves and made part of our body politic scores of discordant sects, alien tongues, diverse racial origins, and different sets of mores, folkways, customs, and institutions. And yet the very existence of common schools has given us a common vernacular, common institutions, common folk heroes, and common national ideals. Our national unity has responded to every test laid upon it, sometimes under severe trial. The common-school system has not brought all that about as a positive achievement: it has rather been the very condition under which unity was bound of itself to emerge and develop. Unlike the Romans of the Age of the Antonines, we have built up an imperial common culture.

In the second place, along with this infinitely valuable incidental accomplishment, there have accrued positive accomplishments in several vital forms, so far as they go.

A great population has learned in the schools to read in a common vernacular, even though that reading is in the main but the primary learning of being able to get meaning from the printed page. It is altogether probable, however, that something less than 75 per cent of the adult population is able to follow printed directions[11] and that a very much smaller percentage is able to follow an argument in print.

There has been inculcated a widespread primary intelligence in matters of health, so much so that the mores and customs have been affected to a degree which makes it possible for the community to utilize the discoveries of medical science. Immense progress has been made in stamping out the ravages of contagious disease, a thing which an enlightened medicine could in no wise achieve without a modicum of popular sanitary intelligence.

A large part of our remarkable national talent in things mechanical is probably the fruit of the teaching of the physical sciences in the high schools over two generations. Other peoples think so, even if we do not.

But all this reading and trained intelligence is only primary in character. It is reading which follows current events that have a direct appeal to the passions but not reading which interprets and explains. It is in the main an intelligence which sees *What* and *How* but stops very soon after crossing the boundaries of *Why*. Moreover, the contribution of the system to popular intelligence is mostly confined to the field of the natural sciences. It has never yet reached the field of the social sciences; not only is popular intelligence in the latter field untutored, but universal pragmatism derived from the natural sciences would raise a barrier even if the public were tutored. When one embarks on the study of Law, Economics, Sociology, Religion, or Education, he must deal in Ideals as well as in facts, experience, and one-to-one relationships.

[11] Inferable from experience with intelligence testing in our Expeditionary Force of 1917–18.

CHAPTER VII

THE MODERN COMMON SCHOOL

THE last chapter, especially if read in connection with the section on the American university in chapter ii, amounts to an indictment of our whole system of Public Instruction and of our University Establishment as well. If a mixture of legal and medical terms be permitted, the chapters also present a diagnosis. The chapters which follow exhibit the indicated reconstruction.

Preliminary to the argument are certain principles which, I believe, we can look upon as established. They are:

First, the School in its institutional function is of necessity Common School and not in any sense class school, either in constituency or in purpose.

Second, whatever may have been at different times the views of schoolmasters, other school authorities, and the public at large, social evolution, in a country having our economic foundations and our national institutions, was bound to continue to a point at which the entire rising generation would be in school somewhere and stay there until schools in their nature have nothing more to offer—as was the case with our original common school and academy.

Third, in a country with national institutions like ours, and the implied obligations toward the education of citizens, the valid presumption must be that schools exist to put the rising generation in possession of the elements of Civilization rather than to prepare individuals for something else. See that the former is done, and the latter will take care of itself.

Fourth, rights and obligations in each of the two institutions, Family and School, must be recognized; and neither of the two may trespass on the rights or assume the obligations of the other.

The thesis of this chapter is, then, that the evolution of school structure, during nearly a century past and where not interfered with, has been in the direction of bringing the whole structure into conformity with what the old common school potentially was in the beginning of our national existence, abort the process as school-masters, school boards, professors, and the general public might.[1]

I. OFF THE TRACK

It would be hard to find instances which better exemplify the truth of the old saying that Man proposes and God disposes than the development of our present system. To put the matter in other than religious terms: when humans begin to *plan* in social matters, and still more to make the adjustments which are believed to meet empirical needs, they very rarely have light enough to provide room for future development. In not more than a very few times in all human history have they succeeded, one of the instances being the Constitution of the United States. Ordinarily, progress has always been a matter of muddling through, that is, unguided social evolution. The process works slowly toward the universally valid and right, but it does so at the cost of infinite waste and sometimes suffering. The *evolutionary principle* is quite another matter, for it yields to us about all the positive intelligence we can find anywhere in the amelioration of society and indeed of personality.

The light is contained in the principle: If things are manifestly going wrong, hunt back to the point at which they seem to have been going right and inquire where, how, and wherein they began to go wrong. To put it in more homely terms, if you find that you are on the wrong road, turn back until you again come to the marked high-way.

So it is that if we wish to find light on our present condition in Public Instruction, we should hunt back for the origins of the tendencies which have produced the present conditions. That has already been done for the most part. It is well perhaps to summarize the preceding chapter. Things went wrong at the following points:

1. Maybe with the establishment of the classified system, although that was mild compared with other forms of mischief. We do not know that it ever would have gone through the same hypostatization which was the lot of the graded school—the same substitution of getting through school for learning in school.

[1] Much of the argument of this present chapter appears in the author's Inglis Lecture at Harvard, *The Evolving Common School* (Cambridge, Mass.: Harvard University Press, 1933).

2. The introduction of the independent high school.

3. The adoption and final establishment of the structural form of the *Volksschule* in our Elementary School, so called.

4. The inauguration and development of the elective system.

5. The perversion of the Junior High School.

6. The misconception and perversion of the Junior College.

7. The elaboration of a system of credits for time spent in successful performance to take the place of evidence of accruing educational values.

As we have seen, the disastrous final result has been the universal establishment of an inverted ideology in which the securing of credits, the graduation from schools, and the attainment of degrees are put in the place of Education, until only a pitifully small proportion of the graduates of schools and colleges is composed of even partially educated people.

II. EFFORTS TO GET BACK ON THE TRUNK LINE

And yet evolution always tending toward normal reality is itself a reality. So it has been here. Sundry movements can be noted which in themselves were tending backward toward the lineage of the original national schools—the old common school and the old academy.

Let us begin with 1900, which can be taken as the approximate date at which the Eight-grade Elementary had practically driven out the last vestiges of the native schools and at which school accreditment was beginning to get under way.

The first of these movements tending to counteract the evil effects of discontinuity may be identified in the various devices intended to move pupils on at something like their normal rate of learning or in accordance with what they had actually learned. Our familiar semi-annual promotions were originally an effort in that direction. Another was the so-called "double-track system," in which there were two rates in terms of years for progress through the eight grades. The P. W. Search policy in Pueblo, Colorado, pointed in the direction advocated in this whole chapter.

And there were other similar devices. There was much reference to our "procrustean system" and to "laggards in our schools." One and all they are evidence that the graded school had become well established and was delivering its normal and natural products but that the graded-school ideology had not become established in the public mind. People still thought more or less in terms of actual learning, recognized the mechanical effects of the graded school, and tried to solve the problem in terms of movement through grades—unwitting that that kind of structure had made the problems all possible and indeed inevitable.

Second is the Junior High School which we have several times met already. In its inception, as we have seen, the definite purpose was to smooth out discontinuity as between elementary school and high school, but the theorists who had become imbued with graded-school ideology succeeded in making it separate and independent. Books began to appear in large numbers bearing such titles as *Junior High School Methods*, *The Junior High School Curriculum*, *The Junior High School Building*—and many others. In truth, junior high school methods are not different from any other methods between the end of the Primary School and the attainment of educational maturity. The junior high school curriculum is simply part of the Curriculum of the Common School. There is no such thing as a junior high school building peculiar to the purpose. Mathematics, English, and Science do not become something else than these disciplines merely because the pupils are twelve to fourteen years of age.

The glamour of the Junior High School has blinded most students to another and antecedent suggestion which was impressive to forward-looking school people in the decade preceding its appearance. The *Report of the Committee of Ten* in 1893 had proposed a six-year Elementary and a six-year High School. If that idea had been adopted, by this time we should very likely be talking of a three-year Elementary (or Primary) and perhaps an eleven- or twelve-year High School—and the old names would have been about to fall into disuse. We should, in that case, have found our way back onto the trunk line from which we strayed about 1850 in experimenting with new routes to education.

The Junior College is, of course, the next point where a constructive proposal went wrong into another thing-in-itself, the most ab-

surd of them all. We have already met it in two different connections. The important point in this present connection is the history
of the *idea* and therefore of the actual meaning and justification of
the movement.

In the last chapter I have alluded to an obvious eighteenth-century instance and to another associated with the old academy. These
were, of course, initiatives from the School side. In Professor Eell's
very useful descriptive and historical work there is abundant material showing the development of the same idea from the University
end.[2] I summarize the important incidents:

1869. President Folwell at the University of Minnesota: "Transfer of the body
of the work of the first two years of our ordinary American colleges to the
secondary schools."

Early 1880's. Edmund J. James tried to persuade the authorities of the University of Pennsylvania to transfer Freshman-Sophomore work to the secondary schools, but without success.

1902. The Chicago-Joliet agreement, which we have met in chapter ii, page 25.

1905. President Edmund J. James, in his inaugural as President of the University of Illinois, urged that the work done in the first two years could just
as well be done at any one of fifty to one hundred centers in the State.

1907. President Jordan at Stanford recommended the outright abolition of the
two lower classes to take effect in 1913.

Altogether, then, the significant thing about what came to be
called the Junior College lay in the principle that the movement in
its inception was a step toward the completion of the Common
School and toward making possible a true University in the United
States. The forward-looking university executives said that it
ought to be done; and the industrious and intelligent schoolmasters
replied that it had been done before and could be done again.

But, like all the rest of the moves tending toward restoration of
the principles of the old national schools, this move on the whole
aborted into departures which made the system more chaotic and
meaningless than ever.

1. First is the practice which has become common enough of
defining the first two years of college as junior college and the last
two as senior college. Apparently, so long as the names are in use
some corresponding substance is supposed to be present. But there

2 Walter C. Eells, *The Junior College* (Boston: Houghton Mifflin Co., 1931).

is no denotation to "junior college"; it is not "junior" and is not "college" at all. The institution owed its origin to the fact that it was in substance School and no part of any College.

2. Existing four-year colleges were reduced to two years and called junior colleges. Again, here was persistence of the delusion that academic standards are a matter of time-to-be-spent; they were not in substance colleges before, and there is nothing "junior" about them now.

3. Existing private secondary schools extended themselves and called the result "junior college." So far as the substance of the thing is concerned, these enterprises ought to be classed with the efforts to get back on the trunk line; they are movements toward the structure of the Academy. They ought to call themselves "academies" and refrain from appropriating a designation which has quite a different academic usage.

4. As was the case with the Junior High School, books began to appear prepared under the apparent assumption that certain methods, curriculums, libraries, and buildings are peculiar to junior colleges. The graded-school ideologists had found another thing-in-itself to be exploited, and the accrediting agencies another college to certify.

III. FUNDAMENTAL TERMS IN SCHOOL STRUCTURE

Proceeding, then, with our argument, which is intended to show that the fundamental problem of students, schoolmasters, and governing boards in the organization and administration of Public Instruction is to understand the evolution of our school system and then to correct the structure at the points where it went wrong, we first need to be sure about our terms.

All Thought is in Language of some kind, or in the equivalent of Language, and there is no valid thinking at all save in the logical coherence which is the attribute of civilized discourse. Precise, constructive, scientific thinking in any field is in a valid terminology, or system of terms, applicable in that field. That is what makes our leading professions what they are. They are not restricted to the employment of such expressions as "that thing" or "this gadget," nor do they talk in popular phraseology nor in poetic or semi-mystical fancy. They have terms in which to *think* man-fashion.

If those who govern our Public Instruction, those who administer it, and those who operate it in the schoolroom are to be governed by reason and not by the fads and fancies of the day, they must be familiar with a terminology in which the substance of valid thought can be framed for intercourse among themselves. The principal marks of a good terminology are:

First, that the terms must be definitive and not merely descriptive.

Second, that each term must have exact denotation and not merely vague connotation.

Third, that the terms must define structures, functions, processes, and objectives which have real existence and are not merely notions.

Fourth, that words used as terms shall be employed in their correct meaning.

In the present connection we are, of course, concerned only with terms which pertain to the structure of the Common School.

PRIMARY

We have always had the term *Primary School*. One can hardly escape that. The denotation is precise: it is *primary* of necessity, since if there is to be any school at all, there must be learning of the primary school arts and, indeed, of the primary institutions in the fabric of Civilization, namely, Reading, Written Language, and a Number System. Again, the Primary division of the School marks off an *educational status* in the pupil, that namely in which he can learn but cannot learn by study. In the use of intelligent devices in teaching, in generating ideational background, which is so much to be cultivated all through the school career, in providing for the preliminary discipline of children in the social group, the Primary School may have to do with much more than the primary school arts, but its denotation as a term is in these. It has nothing to do with a particular kind of building, nor with a particular age, nor with a particular number of years.

The pupil's educational status does not change until he is truly in possession of the capacity to read the printed and written page, to express in handwriting ideas which he is aware are his own ideas, and is in control of the number system which obtains in the culture in which he lives. Then his educational status in fact has changed.

Being promoted from the third grade does not constitute the change; he is advanced to another kind of school experience because the change has taken place.

SECONDARY

If we use "Primary" as the term which defines the pupil's first educational status in school, then the next is given to us outright. It is *Secondary*. The real question is: "Is there ever a 'Tertiary'?"

If the reader will turn to Cubberley's list of cities on page 74, he will see that the use of "secondary" as correlative with "primary" must have been common in Pennsylvania, Ohio, and perhaps Illinois, before 1850. But why "Intermediate," "Grammar," and "High" after "Secondary"? In truth, they were all Secondary.

The difficulty has always apparently been that people had no conception of educational status. It has been difficult for them to make up their minds that a part of the School which is farther along in logical array of subject-matter is not necessarily a different school. Passing into more advanced study does not alter the educational status of the pupil. He learns by study under discipline in the more advanced studies as well as in the less advanced—or at least is supposed to. We may hope that he studies more readily, but he studies in the same sense of the word.

Indeed, it is not more advanced subject-matter which marks the difference between School and University. When the pupil has reached educational maturity, that in itself constitutes change in status. If he then gains matriculation, he passes into a different kind of institution in which he no longer studies under discipline. But he usually studies in higher levels of the same subjects, for, after all, he is still in pursuit of Civilization.

What was there to distinguish the old Intermediate from the old Grammar? If the distinction were in subject-matter, then the former might as justly be called the Arithmetic-Geography school as the other the Grammar. In actuality, the latter went on teaching Arithmetic and Geography as well as Grammar. On the other hand, Intermediate might be any school which happened to come between two other divisions. The terms had no denotation. They were merely descriptive in popular usage. And so it was with High School, as we have seen.[3]

[3] See above, p. 67.

IV. NO VALID ANATOMICAL AND PHYSIOLOGICAL
GROUNDS FOR SCHOOL STRUCTURE

In the early days of the movement for the Scientific Study of
Education, the dense materialism which the last half of the nineteenth century bequeathed to the twentieth led students to interpret
their task as being one of finding physiological foundations for everything educational, including school structure. The story is a long
one, far beyond our present limitations of space.

I recall vividly the enthusiasm with which American students became aware of Flechsig's studies in the maturation of nerve fibers
and how sure some of them were that the myelinization of the tangential fibers of the cortex settled the question of the meaning and
place of manual training in the Curriculum. I doubt that any of
them knew anything about tangential fibers other than the name.
Nerve pathways, synapses, chain reflexes, and above all conditioned reflexes, were illustrations of sure roads to a Science of Education and Pedagogy.

ADOLESCENCE

Before proceeding farther with our discussion of terminology, it is
perhaps well that we should have in mind a set of theories which
thirty years ago were much used in rationalizing the school structure. They cluster about the notion of Adolescence.

All the way along, indeed from primitive stages in the evolution of
Civilization, the pubertal changes have been of absorbing interest to
all who have to do with childhood and youth. As we have seen,
puberty has at some time nearly everywhere been esteemed to mark
the age of majority. The boy had become capable of begetting and
the girl of bearing children. They were physiologically mature.
Further, the boy had begun permanently to outstrip the girl in mus-
cular development and bodily height and weight. With the savage,
since questions of economic support in the midst of the universal
communism of that stage of existence were not compelling, adolescence was the beginning of the period of courtship. The latter presumed, then as now, that the bachelor must make a place for himself
in the world, but that meant a place as victor in combat and not a
job. The scalp or head of an enemy was a great deal more convinc-

ing to the lady than a diamond ring would have been—but the latter is, I suppose, symbolically the same thing. Majority, then as now, meant initiation into full customary or legal standing in the community. Hence the commonest age of pubertal establishment, namely, fifteen, was majority, as it is known to have been among the early Romans. But when society passed over into a predominantly industrial and political organization, majority came to imply wisdom rather than muscles and prowess, and the age became twenty-five among the Romans and with us twenty-one. But tradition carried the older practice down, and the churches accepted the primitive majority in conversion, confirmation, and first communion. Inferentially, it was the terminus of the *Volksschule* of which we have heard so much.

That was pretty much the whole story until Stanley Hall.

G. Stanley Hall.—A few years before the junior high school movement got started there appeared President Hall's two-volume work entitled *Adolescence*. It took. The cult forthwith swept the country, much as does the cult of complexes, frustrations, phobias, and rationalizations today.

Hall was God's gift to the intelligentsia among the high-school people and the superintendents. Before that they did not know why the high school existed, save that it seemed to be the property of the professional and, in general, prosperous classes; now they did. Plainly it was the school of adolescence, and reasoning powers evidently emerged along with red neckties and tight boots. So Nature had decreed. Presently, Junior High School was the school of pre-adolescence. Here were schools-in-themselves founded in human nature; at least so it seemed.

Using the same kind of reasoning, the school people might well have promoted from their third grade on the completion of second dentition and admitted to the Junior High School on the eruption of the twelfth-year molar—even though that interesting anatomical event frequently delays until sixteen or later. But one thing was entirely overlooked, and with respect to another thing the school people were deceived by the enthusiasts.

First, the normal range of onset of the adolescent changes is from less than ten years of age to more than sixteen, half again as long as the whole high-school period, to say nothing of the fact that girls mature earlier than boys.

Second, the changes are no such formidable matter as the school people were led to believe thirty-five years ago. Especially was it not true that children cannot reason until then. Doubtless, in some instances problems are created, but the problems are mainly physiological in their nature and perhaps a matter of medical warning to principals and teachers. Where there is a real school problem involved, it is in personnel administration or in teaching, but in no different sense than bodily health and individual temperament create problems from the time the child enters school.

The changes are not determinative of what the pupil shall study nor of in what school he shall be placed. Adolescence is not and never was ground for setting up divisions in the structure of the School, nor is any other bodily condition whatever, save where sensory and motor and cerebral defects require a particular kind of instruction or sometimes no instruction at all. Educational status is a matter of nodal points in personal development and not of age nor of physiological development.

MEANINGLESS TERMS

Kindergarten.—"Garden of the children!" Could there well be a more sentimental designation for anything that people are supposed to take seriously? You might as well induce the medical people to stop saying "pediatrics" and adopt "baby days" or something of the sort. It should be remembered that the name was attached at a time when European schools were still likely to be brutal affairs and were usually given to meaningless drill. We may well believe that the name as selected was intended to emphasize that the new school was something different than what was prevalent, much as merchandisers sometimes introduce a new product by giving it a name which attracts attention. The term is meaningless, partly because it sins against every canon of good terminology and partly because a sane and wholesome kindergarten is nothing else than Primary School.

Elementary.—"Elementary" as the name given to the first six or eight years utterly lacks definitiveness and is, moreover, incorrectly used as an English word. In Cubberley's list of cities the term "Elementary" does not appear at all. In truth, the Elementary School as we know it cannot be defined. You can say that it is the six or eight grades above Kindergarten or above the point at which the child enters school. But that is no definition. It has sometimes been called the school which imparts the "tool subjects." The expression is inaccurate, partly because it is misleading to speak of some subjects as tools more than are other subjects and partly because the meaning which is thereby attached to the word "tools" belongs to the Primary School, which is nowhere coextensive with Elementary.

In subject-matter it is quite impossible to draw the line between Elementary and High, unless the old doctrine be adhered to that the High School is primarily a Latin School and that the pupil cannot or may not learn Latin at any lower level. Above the level of Primary, the Elementary School subjects have been Arithmetic, Spelling, Penmanship, Language lessons, History, Geography, Grammar, Drawing, Music, Nature Study. But every one of these has also been taught in High School. They are all Common School subjects.

On the other hand, Foreign Language, both ancient and modern, Algebra, Geometry, and the natural sciences have in old tradition been among the High School subjects. But they have frequently been Elementary School subjects. Again, with the exception of the Foreign Language, these, too, are Common School subjects.

Moreover, the word itself is incorrectly used. "Elementary" means "pertaining to the elements," that is to say, to the foundations of a study or pursuit. We sometimes hear it said that a person is in command of the *elements* of Law, Medicine, Engineering. That signifies that he is in command of the fundamental ideas on the basis of which he can proceed to acquire the profession. Similarly, the School as institution is concerned with the *elements* of Civilization but not with the whole content of Civilization. The elements of any cultural pursuit are not necessarily easy to be learned. Algebra, Geometry, Trigonometry, and Calculus are parts of the elements of Mathematics, but nobody would say that they are easily learned. And yet, in the minds of most school people, the name of the school signifies that it deals with the easy parts of the subject-matter of instruction, whereas fifth-grade fractions, for example, are probably as difficult to the pupils who study them as is differential calculus to the youth of twenty.

High School.—In a precisely similar sense, "High School" is meaningless as a term, either as a definition of function or as a description, save as a matter of convenience in conversation. I have referred earlier to the difficulty of finding a definition which could be made to do duty as a legal term in the administration of a statute.[4]

NO TERTIARY

There is, then, no ground whatever for setting up such divisions in school structure as are signified by the words Kindergarten, sub-Primary, Elementary, Junior High School, High School, Senior High School, Junior College, and proclaiming a differentiated educational status in each, which would not equally well justify setting up a new school and a new educational status every month. The divisions and the terms affixed to them represent fortuitous changes in the process of continuously adapting the school system to changing social structure in the community. There is nothing rational, nothing positive, about the system; nor does it in reality amount to more than blundering adaptation to social change.

There is manifestly no division founded on essential difference in instructional function between the point at which educational status passes from Primary to Secondary and that at which maturity has been established. Beyond educational maturity there is no pupillary status at all. The young person is in something else. There is no Tertiary. There are but two fundamental terms in school structure, namely, Primary and Secondary. To use more is to introduce confusion in thought.

As *names* in popular usage, "Primary" is already a good one. It has not only exact denotation but correct established connotation as well. "Secondary" is a logical and professional term rather than a name conveniently usable by the public. In the old days the Germans called their secondary school *Gymnasium*, and one of the names for the French secondary is *Lycée*. The one word in our usage which is serviceable in the same sense as the French and German names is *Academy*. That well might come to be the name for our secondary school.

4 See above, p. 67.

V. COMMON SCHOOL IN FACT

Whether or not Common School is an existing fact depends upon two issues:

First, has the actuality of class school, whether made such by custom, law, or circumstance, practically disappeared?

Second, have there ceased to be organic differences, either in substance or in purpose, within the curriculum? That is to say, are there such differences within the School as are implied by the existence of both general and vocational purposes?

DISTRIBUTION OF ENROLMENT

In 1890 and earlier the enrolment in the high schools, and equivalent schools, in the nation at large, as we have seen, was less than 2 per cent of the total enrolment. So long as that situation remained, and appeared to be permanent, there could hardly be said to be Common School in fact. The High School was not a class school in the eye of the law, but the substance of class school existed by force of circumstances.

Today, the enrolment in high schools, again for the nation at large, is more than 60 per cent of the total possible. To put it in another way: whereas in 1890 there were less than two pupils of every hundred of the total enrolment in High School, today there are some seventeen or eighteen, and the maximum possible in an eight-four system is from twenty-eight to thirty, allowance being made for actual mortality in the advancing age-groups.

With the ratio of high-school enrolment what it now is, and with the extension of the High School called "Junior College" well launched, it can fairly be said that Common School is an actuality so far as enrolment is concerned. The evidence is the more compelling when we observe that in thousands of local communities passage from the eighth grade to the high school is about the same as passage from the seventh to the eighth and when we further reflect that the same forces which caused the High School to increase as it has will cause it to continue to increase to its maximum, including what we now call Junior College.

The old common school was Common by the tests just proposed, but, with the advent of the independent High School and the importation of *Volksschule* structure, it was only the Eight-Grade Elementary which was in any sense common school. And so the name "common school" became translated into the equivalent of "lower school." Most people still think of "common school" as being the synonym of "elementary." Social change has forced that use of "common school," so far as enrolment is concerned, upward until it includes Junior College and indeed the College proper as we now permit universities to be administered. It only remains to make over our whole Secondary—and, indeed, University—structure, so that we shall have in concept as well as in fact a Common School organization.

So long, however, as there is no conception of a common content of Education in High School and Junior College, that is to say, so long as the elective system is retained, there still exists something even worse than class school, namely, a school of rank individualism. And yet a thing so founded in the nature of our society and of Civilization as the Common School can hardly be denied. Something will complete the Common School, awkwardly and wastefully it may be, even though the proponents of the something are unaware of the full meaning of what they are doing.

VI. WHAT BELONGS AND WHAT DOES NOT?

What, then, of the various schools and semi-schools which have grown up? Do they all belong to the 'Common School?

Nurseries.—In the first place, we have a number of so-called schools which are in principle no part of the School, but which belong to the Family if they belong anywhere. That is, in general, true of many kindergarten establishments, pre-primary schools, and nursery schools. All such are to be classified as *nurseries*, as extensions of the care the young child is supposed to get at home. They have appeared as responses to the desires of mothers to have their children cared for elsewhere than at home, either because circumstances make it impossible for them to be cared for all day at home or because the mothers desire to devote themselves to something else than bringing up their children. But there is also at times a motive which arises out of the day of small families; the mother is keenly aware of the

educational utility of having her child in company with other children for a good part of the day. The nurseries may be excellent as
such. They may serve a useful end. But they are not schools nor
any part of the School as institution.

No doubt there is such a thing as pre-school education, just as
there is extra-school education; but there can be no such thing as pre-
school or extra-school instruction. Education, we recall, is a natural
process which goes on anyway, for better or worse; instruction is in
principle a deliberate process which belongs to the School and is intended to see that education is adequate, normal, and right education. It is distinguished from upbringing, which belongs to the Family and which also purports to guide and direct the normal and right
education of the child. The School becomes marked off from the
Family at the point at which instruction begins, and instruction has
for its content the universal institutions. That is concretely what
makes the School social. Wherever instruction in the primary-
school arts begins, there is the essence of School, even though instruction be at the mother's knee.

BEGINNING OF THE PRIMARY SCHOOL

One may reasonably suspect that the reason for the nurseries, or
one of the reasons, has been the more or less formulated feeling of
parents that their child is ready for school. The evidence on the
whole is that such may well be the case.

Our tradition for many years has been that the Primary School
begins at age six. Why six rather than five or seven? The answer is
that six was part of the imported pattern of the *Volksschule*. Children entered the old common school much earlier than that, often
under more difficult physical conditions.

Several reasons have been assigned for keeping children out of
school until six, or even a good deal later. The most common is the
dogmatic assertion, "I think they ought to be kept at home until
six," an opinion which is negatived by the popularity of admission to
kindergarten at four or five and, in the case of the nursery school,
earlier. Probably the more or less critical scientific reason has been
lack of mental development. It has been shown in a previous work
that notions centering on mental development have scant justifica-

tion in observed fact and principle.[5] The old maxim, "We are always underestimating the child's capacity and overestimating his experience," holds good.

We occasionally meet people who learned to read by themselves. Ordinarily, in my experience at least, they seem to have learned at four or earlier. Handwriting is another story, for that has to wait on the ripening of neuromuscular control. However, well-brought-up children would probably learn about as well at five as at seven, and the waifs of the slums, quite possibly, even more readily, since they are likely to have had more sensory-motor experience. I have known children who could not manage control of a pencil at nine, but then they could not hold fork and spoon at table nor tie their shoes. The definite answer with these children was, however, that nursemaids had always done everything for them. Daily experience in the manual-training room soon set normal development under way.

Numbers are supposed to be difficult, and if cultural history throws any light on the difficulties of individuals, fraction concepts the most difficult of all. In 1929 Miss Ada Polkinghorne of our Laboratory Schools staff presented the results of an investigation of such concepts as had been acquired independently of teaching by children of kindergarten age and from that upward to the point at which they had begun to meet the concepts under teaching.[6] She studied especially the following: (1) unit fractions, (2) proper fractions other than unit fractions, (3) improper fractions, (4) identification of written fractions, and (5) equivalent fractions. Of the two hundred and fifty or thereabout tested, 53 per cent had somewhere picked up the notion of unit fractions. Between 17 and 18 per cent had clear concepts of proper fractions other than unit fractions, which is more than Egyptian culture apparently ever achieved. Very few of them had any notion of improper fractions, and identification of written fractions was beyond them. That is not surprising, since both these items are part of systematic arithmetic.

It is not important whether or not all children of these ages could or would grasp what these children did. For the most part, the con-

---

[5] See the author's *Basic Principles in Education*, pp. 112–13 and 229–32.

[6] Ada Ruth Polkinghorne, "The Fraction Concepts of Children" (unpublished Master's thesis, Department of Education, University of Chicago, 1929).

cepts in their cases arose by chance out of the childish experience of the pupils, aided probably by some casual home teaching. The evidence is positive, and it justifies the inference that young children can and frequently do pick up fundamental cultural concepts apart from teaching. If the early school period, certainly as low as the beginning of what is now kindergarten, were arranged so that pertinent experience would systematically be met and a modicum of direct teaching done, it is reasonable to suppose that mentally normal young children would acquire a rich background of all sorts of ideas, the lack of which is the chief obstacle to learning in the long Secondary period.

I have observed a young child who is probably somewhat above the average in mental capacity but certainly nothing more than human—not a "genius." It was clear over and over again that he conceived antecedent and consequent in a cause-and-effect relationship before he could talk. At about four-and-a-half he identifies in a flash every State in the Union by its shape. But he has had the experience and family interest in his doings which would readily explain these things. We are constantly hearing of similar achievements in other pre-school children, and I have no doubt that the stories are mostly in substance true.

Putting all this sort of thing together, the meaning, I take it, is that for seventy years past American mothers and school people have been anxious to prolong babyhood far beyond the limits of infancy and, of late, to extend it indefinitely. It would be well if they abandoned the eighteenth-century fads of Jean Jacques Rousseau in favor of something more valid and more in conformity with common sense. If the Primary School were to begin at four or thereabout and the kind of experience arranged which would be found in a cultivated home, learning in the primary-school arts might as well begin then as later. Time would be made available to see that all actually did learn, and the all-important matter of a rich ideational background might be better attended to.

SCHOOLS FOR THE HANDICAPPED

The term "handicapped" is used in order to avoid "defective," which should perhaps be reserved to the mentally subnormal, "delinquent," and "predelinquent." It includes the blind, the deaf and dumb, the crippled, the normal children who have to be removed from the regular school for sanitary precautions of one sort or another, and those who require special hygienic care.

It follows from our whole argument that these children are in the Common School, just as they are certainly in pupillary status in the School as institution. Education with them is the same as it is with children who are not handicapped; the content of their education is the Curriculum of the Common School, save in those particulars in which sensory and motor defects block the learning process. Instructional method has to differ from what it is with normal children, but that is not enough to create with them what would in substance be a class school. They are all to be viewed as extreme cases of the instructional problems which are recognized and provided for in all good regular schools. Indeed, most regular teachers would be the better if they would take on the scientific spirit of those who deal with the handicapped.

We place the handicapped in separate school organizations because it is administratively convenient to do so. Aside from sanitary and hygienic precautions to be observed with some of them, there is no good reason *in principle* why the unfortunates should not come under special instruction within the organization of the regular schools.

THE DELINQUENT

With the Delinquent the logic is more complicated.

All civilized countries have long held to the principle that children are legally incapable of crime below some age arbitrarily determined by statutory enactment. That, however, is pure legal fiction unless criminal jurisprudence rests on the retributive theory of dealing with crime—as indeed some jurisdictions manifestly do. If you send the thief to prison or the murderer to the gallows in order to wreak vengeance upon him for his misdeeds, then it is manifestly unfair so to punish one who presumably could have had no idea of the difference between right and wrong or of the criminal nature of his acts. If, on the other hand, penological theory is deterrence, prevention, cure of the malefactor, then the premises take on quite a different color. Socially, a crime is a crime, whether committed by a child, by a feeble-minded adult, by an insane person, or by a drunken man. The victim is just as dead if he has been killed by one of these as if he had been killed by a normal adult.

When a child has committed a crime, especially if he has contracted the criminal habit, then he has become delinquent and subject to judicial notice, it matters not whether he comes before a juvenile court or some other kind of court. He is subject to incarceration, or custodial care, or police supervision, lest he keep on doing it. Doubtless, the court will observe equity according to circumstances.

The establishment having him in charge will engage not in Public Instruction alone, and certainly not in measuring out vengeance, but in personal rehabilitation. But the child is no longer in normal pupillary status; he is not in the Common School.

THE TROUBLESOME CHILD

There is a long distance between the delinquent status and the condition of being a troublesome pupil. Between the two comes the whole field of misdemeanors, within which I suppose all of us have at one time or another trespassed. The troublesome pupil is in the beginning an ordinary problem in instruction. The school can no more renounce its obligations to systematic, constructive discipline in his case than it can rightly neglect a problem in Reading or Arithmetic.

Troublesomeness at school may include and probably imply misdemeanors in the community, which sooner or later may become delinquency. If the police will use judgment and work with the school, then the latter, if it be at all competent, will commonly work a cure. In fact the old-time officer on the beat was often one of the most useful citizens in the community for the way in which he dealt with such boys—and sometimes wayward girls. In the days of the old common school the schoolmaster was given great latitude in taking cognizance of mischief committed off the school grounds by his pupils. I suppose the old Vermont case of *Lander* v. *Seaver* may still be the classic, but I judge it is no longer a ruling case.

But all that is past and gone. The old "cop" is lolling in a cruising car, and a new Pharaoh hath arisen which knoweth not the old schoolmaster. Irate citizens looking for vengeance on the small boy who has perhaps broken their windows; and school boards under the domination of self-willed parents who will brook no discipline at all if they can help it and of sentimentalists who oppose discipline at school, even as they oppose martial resistance to the aggressions of savage nations, have left the schoolmaster with little or no power to discipline his school, either externally or internally.

The outcome is that the troublesome pupil becomes a delinquent, and the average age in criminals, even in homicide, steadily falls. The public gets just what it has asked for—just as the little girls and blind women who are the victims of brutal rapists get what women and girls in general have solicited for them.

But, in principle, the troublesome pupil who is not yet delinquent is still in pupillary status in the Common School.

THE INCORRIGIBLE CHILD

There is a further broad field in which flourishes the incorrigible child, long known to the canon as well as to the civil law and now largely confused with delinquents or else forgotten altogether. Such children do not turn out to be amenable to the discipline of the regular school and must be excluded because of their demoralizing influence. They commonly, but by no means always, come from vicious or incompetent homes or from homes which are both. They are not subject to incarceration as is the delinquent proper, and by definition they are not delinquents. The appropriate solution has in some of the States been found in a custodial school, sometimes called a Parental School. The children are pupils still; they belong to the Common School—in short, their actual status is parallel to that of the blind, save for the fact that the latter are not essentially custodial. The incorrigible are custodial cases, for the very reason that they must be put in some place in which they can be brought under control. In all probability the appropriate treatment is in many instances medical in its nature. Custodial care implies some kind of commitment, unless the parents can be got to consent.

Many years ago, at a time when I was actively engaged in this side of school work, I became convinced that in this whole class of cases there is a twilight zone between the functions of schoolmaster and those of the judge and policeman. The former is presumably competent in the field of instruction, but the two latter seldom have the instructional point of view—and would have no means of carrying it out if they had.

The juvenile court was set up as the instrument for dealing with this class of cases and the delinquents as well, and then the whole question begged by introducing a category known as that of the "pre-delinquent." Delinquency is delinquency; you cannot introduce a sort of junior status into which those fall who, you think, are going to be delinquent. While no doubt our juvenile courts have been an immense improvement over what went on in the days when children were always to be found about police stations waiting to be dealt with by the same courts which dealt with burglary and murder, nevertheless the needed thing is to keep children who are not delinquent out of any court at all.

Moreover, when commitment to a custodial school is an issue in court, it is in the nature of things very hard for the judge to keep his mind clear over the principle that such commitment does not imply conviction, either present or prior. The teacher or principal who is before the court as complainant is expected to prove that the pupil is incorrigible—and, of course, there can be no *corpus delicti*. The commitment is for the pupil's good and that of the school, and the school people are the judges of that issue, subject to review by a court on proper petition. Indeed, that has always been in substance the procedure with incorrigibles when the school authorities have been forced to fall back on that form of repudiation known as expulsion.

To this end, I have never had occasion to change my early opinion that the school principal should be clothed with quasi-judicial powers, at any rate be made competent to commit an incorrigible pupil to parental school. After all, the process ought not to be so very different from transferring a pupil from the Grant School to the MacArthur. If it be argued in opposition that the schoolmaster is not a lawyer, then the pertinent rejoinder is that neither is the judge a schoolmaster; and admittedly the whole thing is a matter of public instruction and not of criminal jurisprudence. Moreover, the heads of parental schools ought in principle to be schoolmasters, men of special aptitude and training no doubt, but still schoolmasters and not penologists.

MENTAL DEFECTIVES

The remaining class to be considered is that of the true mental defectives. Contrary to popular notions, they are few in number, but they nevertheless constitute more or less of a problem in every sizable local community. I have dealt with the issue, as the authentic revelations seem to me to justify, in chapter xi of *Basic Principles in Education*.

Actual organic defect in adaptive capacity is an inborn trait or, perhaps better, is traceable to such a trait. The individual is either congenitally defective or he is not; the trait is a unit character. What is usually mistaken for mental defect is rather retarded personal development, traceable either to a culturally negative home or to incompetent teaching and discipline or to both. The true defective cannot learn anything which contributes to the fabric of educated personality. True enough, the reports sometimes show cultural amelioration of the condition, but, where that is apparent, it is altogether probable that the subjects were never mental defectives at all but only ordinary problem cases in school. The trait is genetically transmissible; hence it is one of the most critical of the social problems involved.

The Defective is, then, clearly not a subject for public instruction. He can never be in pupillary status in the Common School. It is a waste of time and money and energy to set up special rooms and teaching in the Common School for defectives. As social problems they fall within the field of the Department of Charities and Corrections. In so far as they are submitted to educational treatment of a sort, the problem is one in medical psychiatry and not in pedagogy.

VII. SCHOOL A SINGLE COMMUNITY

The old rural and village common school was prevailingly a single school community housed in a single room. That was an adaptation to small populations rather evenly distributed. In practice it was sound, inasmuch as it made instruction, however poor in itself, necessarily continuous. The same principle applies today. There is no good reason in principle why a Common School as a whole should not be a single community housed under a single roof or in adjacent buildings. That, however, is a matter which can hardly be settled offhand. There is involved: first, a consideration of the school as in itself minor community; and, second, of the school in the local community.

CHAPTER VIII

THE SCHOOL AS COMMUNITY AND
IN THE COMMUNITY

HITHERTO we have been dealing with the School and the Common School as institutions and then as made concrete in a structure which has a history. The social milieu in which any particular school must operate has for the time being been left out of account. To that we now come, and first of all to the individual school as in itself Community.

A. THE SCHOOL AS COMMUNITY

Doubtless the actual function of instruction has often been carried on in the home, either because there were no schools available, or because the parents distrusted the schools that were available, or for any of a multitude of other reasons. Instruction has been in the hands of the parents themselves or perhaps in the hands of tutors and governesses. But home instruction on the whole never worked well. Since the early Renaissance at the latest, the School has increasingly been the administrator of instruction. If you ask "Why?" you will very likely have had the answer many times in the common sense and experience of parents who have said: "Children need association with other children." And so they do.

I. SOCIAL FOUNDATIONS OF INSTRUCTION

If Education were limited to knowledge of the three R's, to familiarity with the Classics, and to learning in Mathematics, the ideal instruction would perhaps be that administered in the Tudor family by Roger Ascham, a qualified scholar and expert teacher employed to teach the children.

But, despite the persistent delusion of many who ought to know better, Education is not limited to the things of the Intellect. Fundamental to normal, civilized personality is that fabric of moral and volitional and aesthetic attitudes which we call Moral Character and Taste. To that pretty much all else that contributes to Education is in one way or another referred, and about it is integrated the whole body of personal traits which in the broadest sense constitute *sanity*. Especially is it true that even the most intellectual of learning products has in it a volitional element if it be genuine.

It is the most social thing about us, and it cannot be learned altogether out of books; it can be fully learned only out of experience in the actions and reactions between many individuals which are everywhere the basic materials of developing societies. Specifically, the child in his experience of things social acquires friends—and makes enemies—and in the give-and-take of the school he tends to find himself as part of a community. He tends to complete the sloughing-off of his cruder egoisms, conceit, and impertinence, a process which began in the well-ordered family circle. In varied intercourse with many children of all ages, egoisms which would not have become apparent in the small family do emerge in the school and tend to get knocked off—unless teachers are so obsessed with mock kindness that they will not allow it.

Such experience of ordered society as is valuable in the education of the young can arise only in communities, which communities are themselves made up of children and youth of different ages. I do not say that children can be put in communities of their contemporaries and that moral character will forthwith be secreted. There must be government of the parental type, for government is a major essential in all communities, and the constant guidance and example of mature persons who are themselves individuals of ripened personal character. But neither government, guidance, nor example will mean anything vital and concrete to the pupils, except as they have had a wealth of experience in a school community which has come to take on the fundamental characteristics of all true communities.

In general, we may say of school communities (1) that there is an optimum size at which all sorts of varieties in the intercourse of individuals will be likely to arise, and the individual still not be swamped in the mass; and (2) that the presence in the school community of children of all ages will always tend to economize educational progress, as the young children learn from the older children. The large family is the type of the normal minor community, but no family was ever large enough to provide adequate social foundations for the instruction required in the advanced stages of Civilization.

So the school as School must always be a company of children and youth organized into a minor community as well as a body of pupils under instruction.

II. THE SCHOOL COMMUNITY

Now, no community of adults actually comes into existence as a community until the primary social forces have produced a society as a going concern. There is no society save in terms of common expectations, and these are found in folkways, customs, and mores which have become so firmly established that individuals follow them as matter of course. Then and then only becomes possible that co-operation which transforms a mere population into a working community.

So it is with a school, which is a minor community. If the school is of some years standing, there will probably have emerged sets of school ways, customs, and, above all, a school mores, which in truth enable the pupils to get along together as young human beings. We sometimes call these things the school traditions. Certainly, a long-established school is almost certain to have become more truly a community than is a new one or one which is little more than a barracks in a rapidly-shifting city population.

Given such a real school community, in which society within the school is allowed to have its way under a wise and firm school government, there will ordinarily have been met the primary social conditions of effective instruction—not only in character building but intellectual instruction as well. The primary relations are being made ready to be assimilated by the pupils, not that the pupils themselves are ever aware of the process. Moreover, the pupils will be taking their first steps in the art of self-government—not by setting up artificial "school cities" but rather by getting rid of infantile self-conceit and by becoming adjusted to the ways of the group.

In that case the school is genuine, so far as it goes, something which grew up almost in the order of Nature. For sundry reasons, government is required, as it is required in all communities, but the

Head governs by influencing the elements of the school society, especially the mores, rather than by regimenting the pupils. There are, I suppose, many such schools in the United States, made such by a succession of wise heads who probably never did formulate their philosophy. At any rate, I have seen a good many of them in many different States.

Genuineness can be spoiled in more ways than one, but two stand out as conspicuous.

First, *regimentation*. Here the school government refuses to assume that pupils will under ordinary circumstances tend to do right of themselves and in their own way. In the sound and healthy school, by contrast, the usual charge for misdeeds is: "You knew better than that, didn't you? Then why did you do it?" That is in conformity with the spirit of the Common Law in adult life. In the regimented school, however, there is set up a multitude of rules and regulations for the guiding of conduct; these are enforced in the manner of the drill sergeant, and faults are checked in the manner of the cross-examining district attorney who takes for granted the guilt of the accused to start with. The outside appearance of things is often admirable; but the moment school government of that type is removed or relaxed, good order and good morals alike collapse, for there has never been any school community, never any school society as a going concern. The school inspector who knows his job commonly estimates the morale of a school by noting the natural behavior when the presence of teachers is removed.

Second, the school community may easily be rendered spurious through substituting for the school ways, customs, and attitudes which have grown up naturally artificial slogans, clichés, and sentimentalized ideals. Many of our colleges, which are, after all, nothing but schools, are peculiarly subject to that kind of emptiness. The time comes when the unfortunate pupils hardly know what to do next unless the slogan factory is running full blast. I suspect that if a census could be made, it would appear that there is a good deal more of this kind of spuriousness in our country than of that which arises out of regimentation. On the whole, if one must have the thing at all, the latter is to be preferred, for it, after all, leads only to a sort of negative emptiness, while the other generates that positive kind which appears as some form of pietism and gush even among the unregenerate.

III. EFFECTIVE SIZE

Given any group of pupils living together under school conditions, there will normally tend to grow up pretty much the kinds of social experience which are normal to Education, again provided there is firm and sound and constructive government. But much depends upon the size of the school community, and upon that there is little of a positive nature to guide us. We are certainly unable to say that thirty pupils is the lower limit of the effective school and that twenty-nine pupils is no school; but we can set up some guides for our reasoning about the matter.

If we take the maximum number of pupils which ought to be assigned to any one teacher, commonly set at from thirty to thirty-five, as a basis, then we can observe and note how much social experience is likely to arise in the group. Not very much evidently, especially if only one or two age-groups are included, but certainly a great deal more than there will be where there are only ten pupils or less.

Now there is no community except there be the necessity of co-operation in enterprises—and, above all, in enterprises which have a universal appeal. Perhaps the most striking example in school is to be found in co-operative games. Let us take baseball, by all odds the best of them all. A full-fledged game requires at least eighteen players and an umpire. Realizing that not all boys will play, and assuming for the moment that it is a boys' game, and further assuming that the girls will have their own games, there is implied from games a school of perhaps fifty, including both sexes.

But baseball is certainly not the only game, nor would a school founded on baseball alone be a normal sort of thing, nor games the whole story. If the teaching is what it should be, a good deal of cultural interest is stirred up, and that may well eventuate in sundry clubs devoted to photography, aviation, engineering, dramatics, woodworking and ironworking, radio, and many others. There is a large field to choose from. Such things are community enterprises, and they tend to intensify the experience that perhaps most naturally arises on the playing field. Finally, under good teaching, every course is more or less an enterprise in a community. We might then reasonably conjecture that a school of a hundred would not be very far from the lower limit of the fully effective school community, if children of all ages above Primary be included. From that point, how far upward in the scale of enrolment might we go before we reach the point at which the individual is lost in the mass and the pupil has become merely a card in the office files?

Pupil acquaintance.—Evidently, it is largely a matter of acquaintanceship, for there is scarcely any primary social experience among people who are merely different units in a count of population.

How many can an individual know? That, of course, depends upon the individual, upon his temperamental peculiarities, upon the conditions under which he lives, and to a considerable extent upon previous social experience.

If you will take the trouble to observe the acquaintanceship of people who live in fairly permanent dwellings, in not overlarge communities, you will find that, young and old, their circle of acquaintanceship is likely to be classifiable as (1) more or less intimate friends; (2) neighbors more or less remote; (3) those who are not known but are known about. Translated into school terms, the three main groups are chums, classmates, and schoolmates. The feasible school community cannot be larger than the total number of such acquaintances belonging to the typical pupil. How many is that in non-residential schools?

Of course, the answer is, That depends upon conditions. The favorable conditions would seem to be the following:

1. That the school is Common School, that is to say, pupils of all degrees of advancement are within the same school community, so that the older ones have been together a good many years, and the younger have long been looking up to their elders until they themselves have become elders.

2. That they come from homes which are within "calling distance," that is to say, true neighborhoods.[1]

3. That school conditions are such that pupils are meeting or seeing each other about every day. This last in turn depends upon:

[1] See discussion of the Neighborhood Unit in Section B of the present chapter.

a) Whether a common curriculum is followed, or the curriculum is so elective that not many different pupils ever meet in the class-room.

b) The number of wholesome clubs and similar organizations in the school community.

c) The elimination of fraternities and similar divisive clubs.

d) The extent of playground activities, whether all are expected to take part in games, or there is devotion to school teams alone.

A check-up on schools themselves, especially on our Laboratory Schools, where all the conditions are met save the second, makes it fairly evident that pupils can have the kind of acquaintanceship described, which can reasonably be expected of people who do not make a business of getting acquainted, up to an enrolment of about twelve hundred, and perhaps that could be expanded to fifteen hundred. The feasible non-residential school community probably does not, however, exceed the latter number. The number itself is merely a working basis. The ideal may be somewhat less and possibly somewhat more. The number itself is not important; the principles used in arriving at the number are important.

The principal's knowledge of his pupils.—If the foregoing is a reasonable estimate, we need only to inquire whether fifteen hundred is too large a number for the Head of a school to know sufficiently well to make it possible for him to know his pupils personally and not merely as identifiable names.

In the first place, it is his business to know them, much as, let us say, the competent politician knows his constituents. All the experience of the present writer, as well as observation and a scrutiny of the experience of others, leads to the conclusion that from twelve to fifteen hundred is well within the capacity of men and women who are personally qualified to be principals at all and provided they are not mere birds of passage from one job to a better one. But certainly not five thousand or anything like it.

Anent the last statement, perhaps the reader may be inclined to remark that the author cannot know much about modern methods of school organization. The rejoinder is that modern methods of school organization belong not to the School but to Industry. For a principal to know a thousand pupils as they are in school is to know a thousand different individuals and not a thousand different pieces of material in process of manufacture where there is but one individual, namely, the pattern. More than that, the principal does not know the pupils at all save as he knows them as individuals in a community of individuals. Not a little of the personal deviation found in a given population today, ranging from chronic shyness to actual mania, is without much doubt attributable to the neglect of school principals to know their pupils, neglect to know what is going on in the school community, and especially to the weakness of those principals who commit their duties and responsibilities to committees of teachers. Perhaps there should be added to the list of neglects that which arises from the preoccupation of some principals with the intellectual and academic side of their duties.

How about the teachers?—If a given teacher has a group of pupils for a year or half-year, and then the pupils move on to the next grade or half-grade, the teaching force collectively knows little about the pupils severally. The latter are merely children in transit. If, on the other hand, the teacher is meeting every day, let us say, four different groups of pupils, one of which is new to her this year, and the others she has known in one, two, or three different years in the past, and if that is typical teaching experience in the school, then the chances are that the teaching staff collectively knows the pupil body individually fairly well. But it does not follow that the several teachers know all the pupils individually. After all, a teaching staff cannot know the pupil body as the principal can and should know them. In the one-room school the teacher in charge, of course, combines in one person functions which have to be distributed in the large school.

Finally, let us take the school, usually an high school, which has become larger than many a sizable town. The teaching force has to be so large that it is doubtful that the teachers themselves know each other save in small groups. Teachers meet perhaps 150 pupils each in the course of a year, or 600 in the course of four years— with some overlapping. Meantime annual classes come and go, so that at the end of four years, in a school registering 5,000 at any one time, there have been perhaps 8,750. No one teacher can have had the slightest acquaintance with more than about one-fourteenth of the pupils at the outside, and that means that the staff in general can have known them only in a similar proportion. And yet these are still *in statu pupillari*, subject to disciplinary instruction.

Altogether, then, we may say with some confidence that a school of less than a hundred pupils is not likely to show variety and intensity of social experience enough to be worth much *as a school community;* and that in a school which ranges above fifteen hundred the individual pupil is more and more likely to be lost in the mass, a supporter of school teams and the pawn of the embryo intriguing politicians whom the school breeds.

IV. WHAT IS INVOLVED IN THE SCHOOL AS COMMUNITY?

In the first place, there is involved *Government*, and Government means *Control*. A school is not a debating society, nor is it a democracy; it is rather a parental absolutism under the law of the land. The body politic of the school is not the pupils but the citizenship of the Commonwealth wherein the particular school exists. Even so, Government does not involve regimentation as an army is regimented. As Montaigne once remarked, the competent schoolmaster has to be a competent politician, that is to say, one who is versed in the theory and practice of civil rather than martial government.

School government exists in any school as part of the process of instruction, that is to say, as discipline. But we have in mind here that government which would exist if there were a community of minors without any thought of instruction. Any such group brought together within the larger community creates the responsibility of group government as a subordinate phase of civil government itself. The responsibility is there without regard to, or at least antecedent to, school-board regulation, statutory enactment, or court decision.

There is involved in government, first of all, the keeping of order, perhaps the primary function of all government. There is implied, in the second place, the establishment of justice as between the pupils themselves. The miserable brutality and not infrequent bodily injury meted out to the younger and weaker pupils by bullies of both sexes in the not remote past is a sorry tale. It existed either because the management was so incompetent that it did not know what was going on, because the head was himself a product of the system and knew no better, or, perhaps as often, because the management justified such behavior as an excuse for its own inability to put a stop to it—much as some moderns decry good order in school because they know that they cannot keep order.

In the third place, the school community is part of the larger adult community, while the children in pupillary status are of necessity more or less outside the ordinary police control. But that creates in the school an obligation to keep children out of mischief in the wider community, so long as directly or indirectly they are presumptively under the school control.

Pastoral relations of the school.—Analogous to the responsibility of Government created by the fact that a community exists is the responsibility of the pastoral relation which, of necessity, exists between the head of the school and the homes from which the children come, although the responsibility is moral rather than legal.

It must be borne in mind that while the pupil is not merely a piece of goods in process of manufacture, neither is he merely a receptacle for the curriculum. He is in the nature of things a member of the school community, and the latter more or less interpenetrates the larger community of which it is a part. An ill-fed child will respond but feebly to instruction; but it is equally true that the home atmosphere to which he is exposed may easily outweigh the influence of instruction. These things are universally recognized, but what will you do about it? It boots nothing to assert, "It is all the parents' fault! Parents should do their duty!"

Some of these defects in the homes can be reached by the law and are reached. The greater part of them are not reached by the law and never will be. Some of them are reached by organized charity, but that does not reach anything like all of them, partly because it never learns of the existence of even all the cases which fall within its own purview, but chiefly because most of the home problems which affect the children in school are not within the purview of charity at all.

Most of these problems are in their nature pastoral affairs. They have always existed, and the pastoral care of the churches which understand the matter has always been the natural response. Failing that, people write to the newspapers for advice, or they organize a Parent-Teachers' Association, at the meetings of which they can discuss the shortcomings of both children and schools. There have grown up and become extended numerous organizations which exist wholly or in part to supplement the work of the schools and to take over work which the schools perhaps neglect. Such organizations as the Y.M.C.A. and the Y.W.C.A., in their activities with minors, Boy Scouts, and Girl Guides—and many others—are in reality responses to this need of the pastoral relation.

But all such are volunteer, casual, and diffusive in their effect and are far from reaching the heart of the matter. They assume a function which in reality belongs to the schools, and the latter apparently feel glad that somebody else is willing to be responsible.

Now the public school system of the United States, supplemented by the parochial and private-school systems, literally reaches nearly every minor between the ages of six and sixteen in the whole nation. There has been nothing like it since the days of the universal Church in the Middle Ages. Most things which the organizations above named intend to reach can be reached better, more comprehensively, and more systematically by the schools. What the latter have to do is to recognize and set up the pastoral relationship between home and school.

All through our school history there have been many instances, and there still are, in which a principal has felt a concern for the well-being of his pupils which has led him or her out into the upbuilding of a position of trust and confidence and reliance, first on the part of parents, and then on the part of others in the neighborhood of which the school is the center.

I recall one high-school principal in a great city who came to be looked upon as about its most useful citizen because of the talent which he brought to the exercise of the school's pastoral function among his people. And yet, I profess, the one type of school of which it can hardly be said that it has any pastoral function at all is the large-city high school, the reason being that it is not a neighborhood school.

In serving upon a relief committee in the early stages of the recent hard times, I recall the amazement of the committee when it discovered the efficiency with which a woman elementary-school principal had organized her whole constituency for relief purposes, and yet she had gone about the task as part of the day's work without noise or publicity.

In a third case, there comes to mind the principal of a small four-room building who concerned herself not only with the well-being of her pupils at home in health and disease but with the problems of the families themselves, until she became guide, philosopher, and friend to a whole neighborhood community, rescuing their children from tragic injuries by invoking the charitable interest of great physicians and surgeons in a neighboring great city and rescuing their mothers from the poverty imposed by saloons. And she, like the others, did it all without requirement or compensation and with very little recognition.

What some have done of their devotion and generosity, the heads of schools in general ought to do as part of their obligation. After all, the obligation is created by the sheer fact that there is a community of which the school community is an integral part and that of this neighborhood community the school principal is by force of circumstances the pastoral head, for there is, and can be, no other. Naturally, such work requires tact and the ability to avoid the gross impertinence of the ways of Meddlesome Matty. The American principal, let us hope, is schoolmaster as well as pedagogue.

Obviously, I have no reference to sacramental visiting. If the churches cannot take care of that, it will have to go uncared for.

SANITATION

Every community creates problems of *sanitation* which do not exist for individuals who live separately. The latter involve hygiene no doubt, but not sanitation. This is not the place, of course, to go into the whole problem of school sanitation, and it would not be necessary if it were the place; there have long been accumulating excellent treatises upon the subject. Indeed the schools have made a good deal more progress in that direction during the past forty years than they have made in instruction.

But it is worth while to remind ourselves that the necessity of sanitation is an aspect of the school community which is one of the conditioning factors which determine school structure. It makes part of the load, and, like most burdens which arise out of social conditions, the cost increases faster than the population affected—in this case, the school enrolment. It is typical of the factors which impose a limit on the economical size of a school.

There are two allied· issues with which sanitation should not be confused: (1) there is the menace of contagious diseases, about which the school management is certainly concerned, but which is primarily the responsibility of the local Board of Health, and (2) the Health program in instruction as part of the curriculum.[2]

RECREATION

Perhaps the fundamental responsibility which arises out of the fact that the school is, or should be, a community is Recreation, fundamental because much of the evil that arises in schools is due to lack of recreation and because a sane and well-ordered recreational regime contributes heavily to the material with which instruction deals.

Physical recreation is not only an organic necessity, especially with growing children and youth, but it makes by all odds the most effective community-organizing enterprise. In school it is normally the chief source of constructive social experience. It would not be so were it not for the fact that most of our good games are institutional in character and, as such, in themselves parts of normal organized society in the community of youth. They are Athletics. Out of them rightly administered come, as perhaps from no other source, ideas of courtesy and fair play and the equity which lies at the foundation of our whole conception of justice.

We also take cognizance of recreation in the program of health instruction. That is another and, of course, related matter, but it arises in our thinking as an inference from a defensible theory of Education and not out of the sheer fact that the school is a community.

If we have not in mind recreation solely as part of the health program, we still less have in mind athletics as a public-entertainment enterprise and a medium for the gambling proclivities of Main Street. Legitimate athletics in the school community is intramural

[2] See *Curriculum of the Common School*, chap. xiv.

athletics, with interscholastic games only as incidental, and that not as an occasion for the attendance of gladiatorial throngs and exploitation in the newspapers.

The school, of course, does not meet its responsibilities unless there are not only games for everybody, boys and girls alike, but athletic participation by all as contrasted with participation by perhaps fifty selected youth out of the whole pupil body, no matter how large. It follows that the placing of the school in the physical community implies enough adjacent vacant land to make possible not one diamond but many, not one football field but several, and space for other games in proportion. The principle is that everybody plays something daily unless exempted for good reasons.

The principle in itself evidently limits the size of the feasible school community, that is, of the school. Experience running over many years with Jackman Field, the playground of the Laboratory Schools of the University of Chicago, has made it evident that an area approximately 600 by 375 feet is none too large for a Common School enrolment of about twelve hundred. Even so, the primary-school pupils are accommodated in an interior court, and for some girls' games the Midway, a public park, is utilized. Manifestly, the legitimate recreational, and especially athletic, needs of an overgrown school of five thousand or more would require the area of a large city park, and at that the actual playing ground for many would be so remote as not to be accessible within the school day.

B. The School in the Community

I. UNCONTROLLED CHANGES IN COMMUNITY PATTERN

Not only is a school in itself a community but it is conditioned by the fact that it is within another community.

In the United States the pattern of the local community, and that of the national community as well, have long been changing so rapidly that we can fairly say that the only constant thing about either of them is the facility with which pattern changes. Not only the physical pattern of the community but the society which exists therein. That fact may be conceded by all, and yet in the minds of most no sort of relation to school structure and school system will be seen. Nevertheless, lack of adjustment between the school community and the larger local community is the parent of much of our increasing lack of efficiency in the School as a civil institution. In chapter vi we studied the development of the internal school structure and saw that it went seriously wrong at several places, largely because our native institutions were consistently ignored.

In much the same sense we have a prevalent physical community pattern which is in part the product of intense individualism and in part the outcome of the mathematical conveniences of the land survey. In order to see how our present typical community pattern has come about, to understand the reasons which make it subversive of healthy community development, and especially development in effective public instruction, we must take another backward glance in order to see why we are what we are in these respects.

FRONTIER LACK OF PATTERN

It is still hard for our people to escape out of the ideology of the frontier and especially out of the intense individualism and particularism which were partly the reason for the advance of the nation across the continent and partly the consequence of frontier existence. Especially is the idea deeply embedded in our mores that individualism is the same thing as civil liberty and synonymous with democracy, whereas it is perhaps the chief reason for the ineffectiveness of democracy in generating true civil liberty. Democracy, be it recalled, is *Government* by the People and their representatives and nothing else. It implies a rich social experience in well-ordered communities if it is to be effective as Government.

In general, after the menace of Indian raids was conquered, first in the East and then successively as the Western States were settled, the most characteristic thing about our national community was that it had little or no pattern. Homesteads were established wherever title to a farm was acquired, in such fashion that the farmer could get to work on his fields with the greatest economy of effort. That was fundamental, and schools, churches, police, trading centers, and eventually railroads and highways had to adapt themselves to this lack of pattern of which the individualism and particularism of the isolated farm home was the determining factor. In brief, the individual camped down wherever it suited his convenience, and all else came after. Let us see as concretely as we can how it all came about.

THE ISOLATED FARM

On the eastern seaboard, especially in New England and then in New York, the original farming community usually centered on the stockaded village and its defensive works. The cultivators went out to their fields in much the same fashion as had been common European practice for centuries. On the raising of the alarm of an Indian raid, the field hands legged it for the stockade at their best gait, not invariably with success. For perhaps seventy-five years, beginning with the wars of King William III, the history of the Colonies, from what is now Maine to Virginia, was one long story of such raids, led by able and ruthless Frenchmen and directed from Quebec. That came to an end, save for a brief return in the Conspiracy of Pontiac, with the final conquest of Canada in 1760. Forthwith, the stockaded village came to an end, save as a trading center, and the farmers moved out upon the land. It is interesting to recall that by far the most particularistic institution in our whole national economy, namely, the local subtownship school district, was sanctioned in the Massachusetts Act of 1789, thirty years after the Battle of the Plains of Abraham. A little more than a generation later Horace Mann, who was a lawyer, called that act the most unfortunate ever placed on the statute book of the Commonwealth. What it sanctioned is still the basis of the political and fiscal organization of several of our greatest Northern States. Forthwith began the degeneration of Public Instruction. The all-comprehending village school of early national days tended to give place to the meager, scattered district schools with which we have long been familiar, and the strong village church with its significant semicircle of horse sheds gave place to the crossroads meeting-house. Farms were isolated not only from the village but from each other, and there was typically little in the way of neighborhood or any real community. In some cases, no doubt, topography required small farms and homes within walking distance of each other. In such cases there often grew up what were very wonderful local communities, especially in respect to neighborly helpfulness. These have been extolled

in literature so much that we are prone to suppose that they were
typical of the whole nation.

Let us cross the Alleghenies.

Here we encounter the land survey, with its square arrangement
of county, township, section, and quarter-section. The geometrical
pattern adopted enforced maximum distance between neighbors,
although it did make possible maximum accessibility of all parts of
a farm to the homestead dwelling. New England and New York
particularism moved West and became geographically sanctified.

Again, over the vast rural area as a whole, the important institutions—Church, School, and State—had little normal and vital existence. Meeting-houses became scattered about, their congregations
throve for a time and then gave up, leaving behind the burying-
ground as the only vital social reminder. The school was the more
and more meager one-room country school, valuable chiefly as making jobs for generations of inept young girls as teachers. I have
known these girls to fail miserably to qualify for high school and
then turn up as teachers, according to local custom.

Finally, the body politic thus generated was no body politic, as
that of municipalities often would be, but merely a collection of individuals with the voting franchise.

II. THE URBAN COMMUNITY

In some of the older States you will occasionally come upon old
cities which still enjoy a prosperous existence, in which a central
square, often laid out about a central park, is the determining factor in urban layout. The main streets *radiate* outward in all directions. Crossing the main radial streets are minor streets which on
the whole make a circular pattern. That means that internal communication is along the shortest lines. Such places are sometimes
continuous, historically speaking, with the stockaded villages of the
seventeenth and eighteenth centuries and have apparently kept a
strong community existence all through the years. Where that is
true, we can be sure that there was good geographical reason for the
community in the first place. Indeed, the city square is itself the
symbol of community. Well, Washington is in a sense a great city

laid out on very much the motive of central square and radial streets, but it took a professional city planner to do it.

But for the most part, our American cities, large and small, follow the ideology of the frontier. Laid out in rectangular co-ordinates, they are very understandable if you desire to go somewhere; but it may take you a long time to get there if your direction is diagonal to the scheme.

What is worse, however, all through the period of their growth, true to frontier individualism, residences, factories, railroad yards, and shops were dropped down wherever individual interest happened to decree. The net result has been that "rugged individualism" defeated its own ends; the *community* in such places has seldom had much more than a struggling and ineffective existence. It takes time for a community to become established and for salutary folkways, customs, and mores to grow up. It is extremely difficult to get anything like community feeling out of a population the individuals of which are here today and gone tomorrow. The typical attitude toward social evils of one sort or another is: "What can you do about it?" In brief, individualism passes on into a second, third, and fourth stage, until there is not only little or no community but little or no ordered society. This last, I take it, is to an alarming degree very much the stage in which we now are; continuous normal betterment gives place to the frenzied activities of pressure groups which arise, make a good deal of noise, and are then forgotten.

ZONING

In due season it became manifest to the thoughtful that all this amounted to nothing more than continuous destruction of capital values of sundry kinds. Here a valuable residence section became ruined by the invasion of mercantile enterprise. There another was turned into a slum because factories had been set up. Elsewhere a beautiful water front must have somewhere in its length an image of the old-time levee because a railroad terminal or steamship docks had secured a foothold. Fashion decreed tall office buildings, and these not only made other office property valueless but created traffic problems.

Finally, the bane of our cities, the apartment house or flat building, makes the Home little more than nonexistent and valid public opinion as well. There is no normal public opinion on local matters unless there be a community, and there is no community except there be enduring acquaintanceship. But it is notorious that millions of city people so dwell that they have no neighbors, even those who live under the same roof. Acquaintance stops pretty much with: "I believe they live on the fifth floor." Such people may individually be very attractive examples of humanity, but they are only in a dictionary sense social beings.

All this has led to *Zoning*, which has sometimes been defined as "putting things in their right places and keeping them there," and to the launching of a new profession as a branch of Architecture. We need not follow the subject farther. Suffice it to refer the reader to an authoritative work on the subject.[3]

What has all this to do with school structure? Much, for in some ways the existing urban school pattern makes sound city planning difficult if not impossible. It is exceedingly difficult to integrate the existing graded-school system including the independent high school into any kind of a well-ordered plan. Let us see.

High school and constituent elementary schools.—We recall that in 1890 and earlier, less than 2 per cent of the total public school enrolment of the nation was in four-year high schools and more than 98 per cent was in the eight-grade elementary or its equivalent. That meant that for every city high school there must be several elementary schools. In those days one seldom had occasion to speak of the Lincoln High School or the Emerson High School. One knew only the high school which bore the name of the city, since up to about 150,000 of city population there was probably but one high school, and that school enrolled on the average perhaps six hundred pupils. It was still the period in which the institution was by force of circumstances a class school. In some of the large cities there were no public high schools at all; but that fact was offset by the further fact that here and there a city of much less than the population named was presently to begin to differentiate between science-

---

[3] E. M. Bassett, *Zoning: The Laws, Administration, and Court Decisions during the First Twenty Years* (New York: Russell Sage Foundation, 1936).

arts, commercial, and technical high schools and to erect specimens of each.

So the pattern got set up—a single high school for several elementary schools—and that became almost the universal American city pattern. It is still the pattern. As a larger and larger proportion of these elementary-school graduates entered high school and persisted to graduation there, the high schools grew to utterly unmanageable size.

On the basis of an eight-year elementary feeding into a four-year high, there will at saturation point be nearly half as many pupils in the upper four years (the particular high school in mind) as in the lower eight years (all the elementary schools concerned combined). The high school must, of course, grow enormously, even though all the elementary schools remain stationary in enrolment. Old high-school buildings must constantly be enlarged, and new ones erected, even though the city is growing in neither population nor taxable wealth.

If now the elementary schools are reduced to six grades, and junior high schools made available for all, then the combined enrolments of junior and senior high schools at saturation point will tend to be equal to the combined enrolments of all the constituent elementary schools, but the enrolment of any one of the upper schools will be half of the combined elementary-school enrolment from which pupils are derived. The typical elementary school may, so far as the pupil body is concerned, remain an entirely manageable school of perhaps fifteen hundred at the outside, while all the junior and senior high schools will be on their way to impossible enrolments of twenty-five hundred and more.

Old ideas die hard. It has occurred to few school authorities, indeed, that if the high schools were all discontinued, their enrolment distributed back to the elementary school buildings, and the high-school studies completed there, the enrolment in each of the elementary schools would be increased but 50 per cent at saturation point—at the present ratio in the United States as a whole by about 35 per cent. The result would be entirely manageable schools, which would be common schools.

"Occurred to few school authorities?" It did occur to the late

William Wirt, superintendent of schools in Gary, Indiana. Perhaps the reason why it occurred effectively to him was in the fact that Gary was a city which sprang full-armed out of geographical circumstance in the sand hills at the southern end of Lake Michigan at about the time at which high schools began to grow. Thirty years ago Gary was the Mecca of all the schoolmasters who wished to see something new. To them the impressive things about it were devices in school management and in instruction which were far less fundamental than the erection of a new school system without high schools but with high-school instruction carried on within the same buildings as all the rest of the instruction. The schools were called community schools. They might accurately have been called single-community schools. Actually, so far as structure is concerned, they were common schools, a return to the original American structure in a brand-new twentieth-century city.

Bear in mind that we still have the elementary–high school pattern because we still adhere to what was legitimate and normal adjustment in 1890—an adjustment which for fifty years past has been becoming more and more a maladjustment. Specifically, what of it? Where does the maladjustment appear? All maladjustments in society appear in many ways, and so does this, but it appears especially in three manifestations which are economically and instructionally disruptive.

Disused schoolhouses.—The elementary-school building has to be within easy reach of the homes of the children for the reason that most of the latter cannot be conveyed to school. There is the further reason that in cities of any considerable size there are always children enough within reach of the school to fill a large building. Hence, elementary schools are sensitive to shifts in residential population in a nonzoned city, so much so that any given building is likely to be wholly or in part deserted.

Here a factory has been set up, and for a few years the enrolment dwindles and leaves rooms unoccupied, while another building becomes congested. Or, quite as likely, something suddenly changes the trend of city growth, and the families all move over to the other side of the city. Perhaps the street running past the school becomes part of an arterial highway, and many of the parents desert lest they lose their children altogether. All this means continuous loss of school capital in deserted and semideserted schoolhouses and the borrowing of additional capital for investment in schoolhouse replacements elsewhere in the city. Be it noted that school capital is likely to be the most elusive term in the management of the school money.

Conversely, custom accepts the distant high school, and since the high-school building is central to a number of elementary schools, it must continually be enlarged. The enlargement process goes on until the building may be an anomaly in the community and the school system, but the abandonment of so much capital staggers even a reckless school board.

Effect on city planning.—The one thing that is likely most to impress a foreign visitor in one of our cities is the multitude and elegance of the school buildings. I suppose we all have a feeling of pride in the remarks which he makes. Nevertheless, when the problem of zoning and properly organizing the city community arises, the school buildings seem not unlike the stumps in a large field which it is proposed to lay down as a park. The high schools are much the same kind of a problem as that presented by a railway terminal or a privately held cemetery. You cannot organize about them, for the reason that they cannot be made integral parts of a properly organized community; they grew up as physical entities to suit the needs of the very conditions which the zoners and planners are trying to eradicate.

Instruction and morale.—In the preceding section of this chapter there has been emphasized the effect of permanency of pupil body on the growth of the school community which underlies so much of instruction. The pupil body of city elementary schools is obviously anything but permanent when so large a proportion of the parents change residence every May and October. That is only another way of saying that there is no school community when there is so little of a city community.

In the larger cities the high school is part of no neighborhood, and its community connections are few and remote. The consequence is seen, in part at least, in certain untoward tendencies which have been emerging amongst high-school teaching staffs in recent years.

High-school teachers become inclined to insist on freedom of teaching, which has no possible reference to high-school teaching, and then to translate freedom of teaching into freedom to proclaim their own opinions about men and things without reference to teaching. The conception comes to prevail that education itself is a long-drawn-out process of considering all sorts of opinions instead of acquiring the fundamental knowledge and culture which presumably lie at the basis of any possible valid opinion. Even if teachers were all qualified to play Socrates, which they are not, the office to which they seem to aspire would be out of place. We are not told that the Athenian sage gathered the children about him in pursuit of truth. The evil has grown up under conditions in which direct administrative control is about as difficult as is the control of similar evils in publications by censoring them.

Now high-school instruction located in close neighborhood relations is not likely to fall into such decadence, for the simple reason that public opinion restrains it and there is a public opinion. The latter usually acts as does any other manifestation of the mores, that is to say, without organization of pressure groups or outward action of any other sort. Most of us conform merely because we are social beings. Teachers who are meeting the parents of their pupils every day are likely to be kept somewhere within the bounds of sanity and common sense, the latest nihilistic best seller to the contrary notwithstanding.

Overhead.—Returning to the economic side of our problem, the cardinal economic principle involved is *overhead*.[4] The term itself may be explained as meaning that portion of the cost of an enterprise which does not vary materially with increase and decrease of the load. For example:

A rural county in which all the schools are one-room schools is ordinarily a very uneconomic method of school organization, no matter what the cost in money. The reason at bottom is that each school requires at least one teacher and one building, no matter whether the enrolment be six pupils or thirty. For either the cost is much the same. If there are a hundred of these schools in the

---

[4] I have discussed the principle at some length as it applies to schools in *Management of the School Money* (Chicago: University of Chicago Press, 1932).

county, the total cost to the county, at any given standard of unit costs—at any given standard of what people are willing to spend on their schools—will be the same whether the total enrolment be six hundred or three thousand. If, now, steps are taken to organize so as to make the teaching force required vary more directly with the size of the enrolment, usually through the erection of consolidated schools, then overhead is said to have been *distributed*, and the economy is much better, even disregarding the superior quality of school work made possible.

A somewhat similar situation always exists in independent high schools of small and moderate size, on account of the departmental organization of teaching and especially of the elective system. Up to a certain point in enrolment, there is always a large overhead factor due to the fact that teaching sections do not fill up. How so?

Let us assume thirty pupils to a teacher to be the maximum load which ought on instructional principles to be assigned to any one teacher—any other figure would do as well provided it is an assumed maximum. If now all sections automatically had that number, there would be no overhead—save the cost of administration perhaps—and any increase in enrolment would be met by providing one extra teacher, or several such, in proportion to the amount of the increase. The teaching cost would vary with the load.

But that is not the case with the small high school. There teachers enough must be provided to carry the advertised program, regardless of the number of pupils in each course or section. Here will be a section with the normal enrolment of thirty; here one with twenty; here several with ten; here two or three with but two or three pupils each. Evidently, the organization is very uneconomic, no matter what the actual cost in money, since the existing staff might carry an enrolment of three hundred as well as one of perhaps a hundred. As the school grows larger, the tendency is, of course, for fewer sections of very small registration to exist, that is to say, overhead is distributed.

As the school continues to grow, the overhead factor becomes less and less until overhead has been entirely distributed, and optimum economic size for that kind of school has been reached. Beyond that point diminishing returns from increase in size appear.

Now throughout the economic world the maintenance of enterprises which are past the point of diminishing returns is as uneconomical as is maintenance of those in which there is a large overhead. The high school which has gone far beyond that point is as uneconomical as is a rural county school system composed of six-pupil one-room schools. The oversize high school tends to show the following characteristics.

1. It has gone beyond the point at which an effective school community is possible.

2. The universal principle in public finance is encountered in terms of which the cost of effective organization and control has increased much faster than increase in population, in this case faster than enrolment. That is especially true of ancillary services and staff work, the reason being that all the way from janitorial service to psychological testing there must be superstaff, that is to say, staff to control the staff. Unhappily, the staff work tends to fall behind, while a desperate effort is made to accomplish what trained staff alone can do by the familiar mass-production devices administered by clerks.

3. The supervisory function has become so extensive that an hierarchy of supervisors has to be set up, and the Principal who is the key to the whole school becomes more and more remote from what is going on in the classroom.

4. The capital investment required in buildings of the most expensive type has become enormous, the annual debt service has become a larger and larger item in the budget, and presently the fateful steps of funding operating debt and refunding due bonds are taken.

5. Numerous pupil services, of which lunchrooms are typical, must more and more be organized, by reason of the fact that larger and larger percentages of the pupils live at a distance from the school.

The foregoing are but illustrations of what happens in schools whose enrolment has gone beyond the point of diminishing returns from increase in size.

Combined overhead.—Assuming now that Common Schools as we now understand them were established so that the whole School from the beginning of Primary, or at least the end of Primary status, to the end of Secondary were made part of the same school community—although not necessarily housed in the same building—then there would be total overhead. But, since it would apply to a wider area, both in respect to enrolment and in respect to studies, it would always tend to be distributed. In brief, the combined overhead of a local school system found by adding the several overheads of elementary schools, junior high schools, senior high schools, and junior colleges would be consolidated into a single overhead factor, so much so that important features of a valid school, such as auditoriums, workshops, and playing fields, would become possible where often at present they are not possible. Let us see.

A good illustration is in auditoriums. Every modern school of any size, elementary as well as high, requires an assembly room. The older high schools, before the era of rapid growth, always had a main room in which the school was normally seated. Of course, the one-room school is all assembly room. Certain exercises in their nature belong to the auditorium, and the latter may be a chief factor in producing a school community. But auditoriums are very wasteful at best in a discontinuous school system, for the capital involved is large, and they are not used much. In a Common School, on the other hand, the same auditorium can be used daily by as many different sections of the school as seems desirable.

The most important contributory factor in overhead, however, arises out of inflexibility. So it is with a large number of one-room schools in a rural county. The schools are fixed and immovable on account of the buildings. So it is with eight-grade schools and the discontinuous system in general, where instruction in a given subject is confined to a particular grade and school. So it is with the departmental system in a separate high school.

But in the modern Common School properly conceived and administered, the essence of the structure is movement of pupils according to proficiency in the subject-matter of learning over perhaps fourteen years. Moreover, the meaning of instruction under discipline is that pupils are the subjects of instruction and not subject-matter primarily. In other words, subject-matter is the material of instruction and not the objective. Hence, while undoubtedly in the higher reaches of the secondary school subject-matter specialists are required, in general teachers are not confined to particular grades or departments.

But, even so, shifts in the character of what have been residential sections in nonzoned cities may leave many rooms unused or partly used even in the Common School. Nevertheless, that leaves only a capital overhead in the local system and not a teacher overhead, since under Common School conditions the migration of pupils carries the teachers along with it instead of leaving teachers to preside over half-empty rooms.

We are thus brought to one of the most important, and indeed fundamental, features of modern city planning.

III. THE NEIGHBORHOOD UNIT

There is one phase of city planning as a whole which is not only directly related to the school pattern of the local community but which is, I suggest, intimately tied up in mutual relations with the structure of the School itself. I refer to the *neighborhood-unit idea*. In general, the neighborhood unit is a plan or series of plans under which a whole area in a city is taken over and physically reorganized to meet the community needs of people dwelling therein and to serve as a motive in construction of the city community itself. It is familiar to many in recent years through use in slum-clearance projects; but in principle it is as applicable to high-grade residence sections as to the slum areas.

In such an area, in the first place, the existing street plan is abolished altogether—and ordinarily the dwelling houses as well. The street net is then written in to serve the projected area plan, instead of making the latter conform to the existing layout of streets, established perhaps when there was nothing but open country in the whole section.

Second, the rectangular layout is as far as possible avoided, so that the area before building on it may be bounded by perhaps two straight streets at a right angle and otherwise by curved lines.

Third, residence lots and the residences thereon are located near the boundaries of the area, leaving one side to servicing enterprises, and the whole interior to recreation, church and school, and com-

munity house. The servicing enterprises furnish services and com-
modities in daily use, leaving other shopping to be done downtown.
The unit can perhaps be more precisely described by citing the principles which are supposed to govern its construction.

1. *Size*
   A residential development unit should provide housing for that population
   for which one elementary school is ordinarily required, its actual area depending upon population density.

2. *Boundaries*
   The unit should be bounded on all sides by arterial streets, sufficiently
   wide to facilitate its by-passing.

3. *Open space*
   A system of small parks and recreation spaces, planned to meet the needs
   of the particular neighborhood, should be provided.

4. *Institution sites*
   Sites for the school and other institutions having service spheres coinciding
   with the limits of the unit should be suitably grouped about a central point or
   common.

5. *Local shops*
   One or more shopping districts, adequate to the population to be served,
   should be laid out in the circumference of the unit, preferably at traffice junc-
   tions and adjacent to similar districts of adjoining neighborhoods.

6. *Internal street system*
   The unit should be provided with a special street system, each highway
   being proportioned to its probable traffic load, and the street net as a whole
   being designed to facilitate circulation within the unit and to discourage its
   use by through traffic.[5]

Observe that the first principle makes the size of the residential
unit that population for which one elementary school is ordinarily
required. The principle is undoubtedly at bottom sound, for it recognizes, as has seldom been done before, that the point of departure in
the design of any physical community, in a country which rests on
free institutions, is the schooling of the young generation, and the
schools thus made necessary. The statement of the principle, however, seems to me unnecessarily lacking in flexibility in that it lacks
the generalization which would be justified.

[5] C. A. Perry, *Housing in the Machine Age* (New York: Russell Sage Foundation, 1939).

What is one elementary school? Well, a single eight-grade or six-grade layout, enrolling a maximum of 280 or 210 pupils, is an elementary school; and duplications of that up to the maximum agreed upon. The authors of the Regional Survey of New York, however, fall back on the estimates of Strayer and Englehardt for New York City. The enrolment 1,000–1,500 is given, and that is what is meant by "an elementary school"—in New York City, at least for the purposes of the survey. It corresponds very well with our estimate of 1,200–1,500 as the enrolment maximum, and probably optimum, for any school community whether discontinuous or Common School.

But why leave the issue on the indefinite "elementary school" or at a maximum enrolment? Even if 1,200–1,500 is perhaps the optimum, other things being equal, it is certainly not the only workable enrolment. As we have seen, a workable school can be set up within the enrolment limits of 100 and 1,500. It would seem to me that the principle might be generalized by recognizing that there are three variables: first, the desirable population density; second, the probable birth rate for the kind of population intended as occupants; third, the limits of the size of the *single school community* for the unit. In practice, the planner must fit the variables together, the third being, of course, the ultimate determining factor.

In the great cities we can doubtless in most areas start with an enrolment of fifteen hundred and fit everything else to that, but only because one of the problems in a great city is to distribute the population so that excessive enrolment will be avoided.

But how about the small village and the middle-sized city—indeed, urban communities of all sizes? City planning and the neighborhood-unit idea are a matter of principle and not merely clever devices. Not only are they socially of critical importance but I profess that the latter especially is critical in the erection of a school system which can do what we want of our schools in the education of the Common Man. The difference between the larger and the smaller local community consists chiefly in the current fact that application of the principle in the former is urgent, and in respect to slum clearance more or less fashionable, whereas in the village it does not seem urgent. On the other hand, if the village be a growing one with good reason to think that growth will continue, then application of planning is there also urgent, since the sooner community planning is put into operation, the less will be the growth of vested interests which commonly prove to be the greatest obstacle to community reconstruction.

If one will observe the sketches of unit plans and, better, photographic representations of projects in actual operation, he can hardly fail to see how truly they suggest skilled refinements of the way in which some older villages and small cities grew up, all the way from the Puritan beauty of a New England example, with its central common, to the Spanish beauty of homes clustered about the village plaza which one sometimes comes upon in the Southwest. But these were before the factory system destroyed most of the beauty, comfort, convenience, and decency of many a local community.

We might well have a village Common School of a hundred pupils in regular attendance. At present ratios that would mean on the average a village population of five hundred. The planned village layout would itself be a small neighborhood unit instead of a prospective village slum allowed to spread over several square miles of other than farm dwellings and make any kind of true local community impossible.

ELEMENTARY SCHOOL OR COMMON SCHOOL

Using the elementary school as the basis of estimating population, an enrolment of fifteen hundred would imply a residence population in the unit of about nine thousand at current city ratios. If, instead of an elementary school as the basis, the Common School were used, then at current ratios for the country as a whole—varying, of course, from place to place—an enrolment of fifteen hundred would imply a residence population of seventy-five hundred, and at school saturation point one of six thousand.

But to use the elementary school as the basis leaves some of the larger community problems not even touched—and out of sight of being solved. And yet these are intimately related to the ultimate success of the whole city-planning movement.

In the first place, by no means all the cities are on the traditional eight-four basis. Many of them are organized as six-three-three systems. If the elementary school is accepted as the neighborhood basis, then, in the cities last named, children above the age of twelve are left to seek distant junior high schools and then senior high schools far outside the community influence, which it is a cardinal purpose of the neighborhood-unit scheme to further. Every one of those high schools becomes a problem by itself in ultimate community planning.

In the second place, in the eight-four cities, it leaves the long-obsolete separate high school in existence as one of the most serious of city problems, one which if left unsolved bids fair to demoralize the youth of the community and to bankrupt the school system. But let all that go: probably some of my readers will be skeptical of the statement. Be that as it may, another generation of city planners will find out that they have the work of their predecessors to do all over again, because the latter had refused to recognize that an integral part of every community pattern of their time belonged to a society which was moribund in 1890 and had long ceased to exist.

Basing the neighborhood unit on the Common School, on the other hand, the children and young people are kept within the neighborhood influence up to the end of their General Education. Not only are they in a school community abiding enough to become more and more genuine from year to year but they and their teachers are in a neighborhood community. The two institutions which are about equally concerned with education, the Family and the School, are intimately related in everyday life.

IV. THE RURAL COMMUNITY

The United States is laid out in an hierarchy of natural communities, centering upon cities, all the way from great continental centers like New York, Chicago, New Orleans, and San Francisco, down through the great regional centers, to a multitude of rural trading villages. Hitherto, we have been concerned with urban communities, the local communities of first instance. We now come to these rural communities.

Each of these trading centers is itself an urban community, sometimes a sizable city with some industrial equipment. But it is also part of a natural community which extends outward so far as there are surrounding farmers and other rural enterprisers who find it advantageous to drive to the center to market or store their products and to buy goods. But trade is not all. Several nights a week, perhaps every night, cars may be found parked about the streets while their owners attend the cinema theaters. Or it may be lodge night, or the night of some entertainment. Likely enough, some of the rural people are parishioners of the village churches. And here is the site of the consolidated school.

We need hardly take the space to investigate the interesting tale of the manner in which the automobile has extended the limits of this rural community and perhaps drawn people away from the next or another. Above all for our purposes, however, is the fact that the automobile has made the modern rural consolidated school a possibility and a permanency—a school community.

Now, it is easy enough to see that these consolidated schools, with all the rigidity of the discontinuous system which they have taken over from the industrial city, are after all in their community relations the lineal descendants of the village common schools of early days. It only remains to break up the discontinuity of the graded school and high school to find in them perhaps as near an approach to the structure of the ideal school community in the midst of the larger community as can be found anywhere. Certainly, none exists more naturally.

There are left few parts of our national territory in which there is any longer need of the meager, isolated, one-room school. Conveyance of children to the community center is nearly everywhere possible and is held back chiefly by inveterate objection to change and by the political self-interest which keeps alive the antiquated district system of school government and support.

But there are still sections which are too isolated to belong to any community. For them the one-room school is the only possible school. So be it. There is no good school, even where school structure is everything that it should be, without intelligent, competent teaching at the hands of persons who have cultural background enough to be teachers at all. Given a group of children large enough to be a school of some sort and that kind of teaching, there is no reason why the isolated one-room school should not be Common School, at least in part. That it could ever lead to real educational maturity in these days is hardly to be expected. The excellent rural common schools which were sometimes to be found a century ago could hardly teach the full curriculum demanded by modern cultural conditions. The isolated small one-room school under a competent and cultivated teacher could, however, take its pupils far on the road of General Education, even if not to the end.

Scattered groups of children in typically inaccessible sections, such as remote coves in the mountains, islands in the Great Lakes and off the Coast, more or less temporary lumber and mining camps, and the unpopulated open plains, cannot be made into schools. For them the problem of Public Instruction must be solved otherwise than through regular schools.

CHAPTER IX

THE PRACTICAL ISSUE

THE Common School has been defined as, first, an organized school in which is pursued the course of instruction from the beginning to the end of formal General Education, in a single school community, as contrasted with a series of separate schools which are either externally or internally discontinuous or both.

Second, a school which advances pupils in terms of learnings acquired rather than in terms of successful performance on lessons or other tasks assigned or of scholastic credits of some sort accumulated.

Third, a school which recognizes a common curriculum for all pupils and refuses to tolerate free choice of studies among immature children and youth.

Fourth, a school which is predicated (a) on the ethical principle that all normal children ought of right to reach full General Education and (b) on the social fact that school enrolment is evidently tending toward the point at which all normal young people will ordinarily be in school up to the age of legal majority.

The argument of the preceding chapters has developed the thesis that the Common School has the structure which is presumed by common sense in a world of varied activities, holding that there are some things that the whole rising generation must learn; that such a structure is in the large that which was developed in the Western World after the Reformation of the sixteenth century, when the idea emerged of General Education for everybody as a social necessity and particularly as a civil necessity for free men; that it was singularly applicable to the project of the American Commonwealth; and that, as a matter of fact, it was the form which our early schools in the national period followed in the old rural and village common school and in the old academy.

It has also been shown that the American common school gave

place to a discontinuous system, partly as the result of the establishment of the separate High School; partly as the consequence of the
importation of a lower terminal school for the masses from a country
possessed of political institutions as unlike ours as possible; and partly as the outcome of the decadence of the old American science-arts
college into an admittedly higher school.

It has been shown that the discontinuous system thus created has
become more and more mechanical and that within the structure
thus set up premium is so placed on getting through that actual
learning and valid education have become in large measure lost concepts.

Finally, it has been argued that the junior high school and junior
college movements are rightly to be interpreted as responses to social
forces which are tending slowly to restore the whole system to the
structure which was native in this country.

In the preceding volume there has been worked out on both factual and rational grounds the cultural content of General Education
which is appropriate to instructional use in the Common School. All
the above, however, is still theoretical analysis, valid theory in our
belief, but still for the most part abstract. It remains to make a picture of what a modern Common School might look like under operation and so far as possible to consider its feasibility.

I. FROM THE THEORETICAL TO THE PRACTICAL

The task is difficult. There is no existing model to which we can
point and say, "Here is what ought to be. This is the way things are
done, and these are the results. Go and do likewise, and you will get
the same results." If we were describing such a model, we should be
describing an educational factory and not a school. Even so, the
results would not be what we might say they would be. Education
and Instruction are simply not in that kind of a logical category.
Many times departures in the field of public instruction have thus
been described and much claimed for them, pilgrimages of school
people have been made and acclamations shouted—and in a few
years it is all forgotten. The reason is not obvious, but it is identifiable.

In the long run most of our people look for tangible results, but, save in school subjects like stenography and typing, spelling, penmanship, and ciphering, there are no tangible results. The only identifiable results are those implied by some theory of education—and there has commonly been no theory, at least no positively defensible theory, on which men's minds could meet. The public, including the school public, tends to see no results, at least no desirable results, other than custodial care of children outside the home, entertainment, and jobs. Whatever yields these things is remembered; whatever does not is forgotten.

A given school enterprise, whether it be a method of teaching or a school as a whole, is not a positive entity to be identified, described, measured, and found again in the same characteristics. It is not a machine, nor a chemical compound, not a plant or animal species—nothing like any of them.

The method may be sound in educational conception and sound in its psychology of learning, but when it appears as a matter of visible form in a school, it is only what the teacher's conception of the method, plus the latter's skill in operative technique, plus the principal's conception of school organization have produced. Methods, plans, and organizations in schoolcraft never "work" of themselves, according to a book of instructions, and "produce results." It is only our materialistic industrial ideology and inveterate pragmatism which make us think it must be so. School people sometimes succeed in "working" plans, methods, and organizations so that there are produced the educational outcomes in individual personalities which are intended. But that implies pedagogical and cultural background in teachers, insight and skill, beyond what we commonly get.

We are always, in the presence of issues between the theoretical and the practical, confronted with the age-old dualism of form and substance. The form, that is to say, at the best a body of principles, may be indubitable, but it is not the form which produces the substance. It is rather the worker who implements the form by applying the principles. Beside, the form may be no body of principles whatever but only a traditional technique like lesson-hearing. In that case, results appear, but they are not valid results as contributing to the education of individuals; and that issue can never be met on empirical grounds. One cannot wait thirty years to check an experiment. It can be met only by appeal to reason resting on defensible theory. The pragmatic test, "Anyway, it works," is always fallacious, even when it is reassuring.

The practical issue in our present concern is not whether the reasoning which has given us our theory of Education, of the Curriculum, and of the Common School is sound reasoning or not. We have a right to assume that it is, unless the contrary be proved. The issue is rather: Can the ends implied in the theory be achieved under modern conditions in the school structure which is proposed? Here we are reasoning from principles to practical conclusions in the light of what we know about schools.

Again, we remind ourselves of the principle that failure to obtain the indicated results in any particular school or many schools—or all schools, for that matter—is not evidence that the proposals themselves are founded on error. A thousand negative outcomes never in themselves prove that a thing cannot be done; a single positive outcome proves that it can be done.

Nor is evidence drawn from the failure in college of graduates of any school or series of schools evidence of the soundness or unsoundness of the principles which the schools profess. To cite such evidence is to beg the question, since the existing college is a gross instance of the very things which the principles condemn. Even if it were otherwise, we cannot infer success or failure of schools from success or failure of their pupils in college without assuming perfection in colleges as a class. Valid adverse evidence on any kind of empirical test of a principle must be of a kind in which it is shown *why* the proposal failed in operation and, further, *why on the evidence* the whole body of principles is in some major or minor essential feature false. When that is done, the evidence ceases to be empirical alone and becomes rational as well.

So far as instances of the whole program of instruction being placed in a common school are concerned, we have historical evidence that not only has it been done but further that it was a common way of doing things, not only in our own national economy but in that of other nations possessed of institutions and aspirations similar to our own. We have further seen how and why and when it went wrong in the United States. There is, however, so far as I know, no instance as yet in which the whole program suited to modern cultural needs is so being carried out.

We have, however, a respectable body of evidence touching ways and means derived from the schools set up and operated under laboratory conditions at the University of Chicago, in which for a matter of ten years the principal interest was working out the consolidation of schools and the administration of junior college as part of the existing high school. Reference will be made here and there to that experience without particular citation. The purpose, then, in the present chapter is to exhibit an analysis in concrete terms of what must and can be done and, in general, the way of doing it.

II. SYSTEMATIC INSTRUCTION

First of all, the modern Common School requires a systematic instructional procedure.

In chapter vi we have seen that the failure of the existing school and university system as a whole to produce an educated citizenry is to be summed up as failure to conceive and apply the same kind of systematic procedures which are found everywhere in the modern world save in public instruction alone. The connotation of the word "systematic" may be taken to include "scientific," "rational," "business-like," "orderly." It implies a series of learning objectives and then teaching which assumes that the objectives will be attained rather than that which merely observes pupil performance and records the results of observation. The conception rests at bottom on the principle that the well-being of the individual and the well-being of the community in which he lives are conditioned by a logic which has no relation whatever to the desires and aspirations of individuals, save the aspiration to find and follow the logic; that validity in all things is objective and not subjective.

So there is the statement of a fundamental implication of the modern Common School. Is it likely to prove feasible? The answer is that it is, in general, the program of all the professions, of industrial enterprises, even, in a superlative degree, of modern martial operations. To assert that something entirely different is true of instruction alone is merely to stultify the capacity of everybody connected with schools. They could if they would.

The point of departure is, then, found in the Curriculum, for without a series of objectives to be taught and learned there can, of course, be nothing systematic about the school, and such a series is a curriculum, whatever its content may be found to be.

Apart from a curriculum there is no school, Common or other, any more than there are building operations without some kind of plans and specifications. Moreover, if there is to be Common School, recognition must be given to the principle that the world in which we live is in its fundamentals common to all mankind; that the Culture which has grown up in the ages is in the nature of an adjustment to the three primary conditions of all existence, the physical, the biological, and the social; that the adjustment to be acquired by the individual is at bottom that common cultural adjustment; and that, while the individual can be adjusted to the world, it is absurd to suppose that the world can be adjusted to each of many million individuals. If it is to be Common School, we may further rest in confidence in the principle that the human nature which does the learning is in its fundamentals common to the whole species of Man which now occupies the planet and has been ever since the species emerged.

Moreover, if the appropriate curriculum cannot be reasoned out by the methods which are common to all intellectual endeavor, then nothing can be reasoned out, and we are left to make what we can of a world of whim and caprice. Any curriculum so derived no doubt is only as good as the reasoning of the maker is good, but that applies equally well to any court decision or to any statement of scientific principle.

TEACHING

Teaching becomes possible only when there is cultural subject matter to be learned, and from the earliest days teaching has presumed, in the first place, knowledge of the subject-matter with which pupils are to be taught—*docet magister*. If the subject-matter is Life, as an eminent writer has recently suggested, then the most eminent philosophers of the day must be drafted into the schoolrooms from the beginning of the Primary. Needless to say, there will not be enough of them to go round, and most of us would have little confidence in them if there were.

Teaching presumes, in the second place, an active enterprise which starts with objectives to be attained and then sees to it that the results are registered in the fabric of the pupil's personality. The irate parent who is disgusted with a series of poor report cards which accompany his hopeful homeward at periodic intervals sometimes cries out, "I send my boy to school to be taught; why don't you teach him?" The parent is right about it. He reasons as he does about everything else in his world. Teaching is about the only activity in the world which is allowed to "get by" without delivering the service for which it is paid.

There is thus implied organizing the Curriculum into a series of objectives, good for the school, the time, and the place, which objectives constitute a *program*, subject to change as experience demonstrates that others will serve the curricular ends better. They are definite units to be taught and, from the pupil's standpoint, definite learnings to be acquired.

There is implied, in the third place, continuous testing to see if the objectives are registering with the pupil and, if they are not, finding out why and reteaching until learning is evident.

Thus, the whole procedure is one of continuous problem-solving, which of itself makes teaching, rightly conceived, a learned profession, kindred to the practice of medicine more than to anything else. In a very true sense, every pupil is always a problem, but we commonly restrict the term "problem pupil" to the persistent nonlearner. To analyze his case and find out why he does not learn is also systematic teaching, even though in the end it is disclosed that the pupil is in truth subnormal and cannot learn cultural material.

The general technique of dealing with such cases has been explained in chapter xxx of the revised edition of the author's *Practice of Teaching in the Secondary School*. The method followed in the Laboratory Schools is illustrated, with specific cases, in the following publications:

WILLIAM C. REAVIS. *Pupil Adjustment in the Junior and Senior High Schools.* Boston: D. C. Heath & Co., 1926.

ELSIE M. SMITHIES. *Case Studies of Normal Adolescent Girls.* New York: D. Appleton & Co., 1933.

IDEATIONAL BACKGROUND

We have met this subject before and shall meet it again. Suffice it to say in the present connection that the systematic upbuilding of rich and wholesome ideational background in each pupil is not only part of systematic instruction but that it creates one of the conditions which make the latter possible. Those children who come from cultivated homes have the background already; the problem is to see that the others are built up to parity.

For more than an hundred years past, say since the coming of the factory system and the mill towns, our people have been hagridden by the notion that there are lower classes made what they are by inescapable organic inheritance. Such beliefs are tantamount to surrender of one of the cardinal principles of the fabric of our institutions and a return to a caste society. We have seen in chapter vi how powerfully the idea found expression in the building of a school structure which has finally become reduced to its destined absurdity. It is scarcely to be doubted that there are lower classes and all kinds of classes in any kind of a community, but to say that is far from contending that such have any indefeasible, organic, "born-in-the-blood" foundation. Book after book has been written to give the sanction of science to the caste proclivities of humanity, but such books have been fallacious in their reasoning and in their comprehension of the significant facts. In due season the lower classes did send their children to high school and then to college. Nor have they as a class ever shown evidence of lack of wit. They have commonly shown evidence of miraculous lack of culture, that is to say, of organized ideas.

To achieve an actual higher level of *mentality* would require eugenic breeding. Even if an all-powerful autocracy should ultimately succeed, so much so that its totalitarianism were extended to the conversion of a nation into a human stock farm, still it could never produce an higher general level of normal mentality, for, of all animals, the human is the most mongrel. Nor even if it could succeed, would the result be of any value, for the product could be no more than a normal specimen of the genus *Homo sapiens*. The product would still have to learn, and it would never become anything more than it had learned. Human mentality as such became good enough fifty thousand years ago, perhaps an hundred thousand.

But ideational background organized into culture can be acquired by any normal person in the course of his minority. The fact that it has never been done on any large scale is no evidence to the contrary; the schools have never tried. No doubt, numerous individuals, some of them of great eminence, have arisen out of culturally meager homes and, usually by chance, have come into possession of the culture of the race—but they had to learn it.

DISCIPLINE

We have already met the term *discipline* and have considered its true meaning. There is, however, a specific application to systematic teaching.

There is meant primarily the inculcation of ideas of oughtness, ideas of effort, ideas of self-restraint, and ideas of application. They operate as internal compulsion so that the individual comes to be governed by them. Now it ought to be borne in mind that there is always a volitional element in all true learning in which the idea of coherency, of logic, is involved; but we usually call that "intellectual discipline."

The ideas which are the content of discipline are themselves a part of culture. In so far as they are a part of Morality, they are curricular material in the same sense as that in which Mathematics and Literature and Science are parts of the Curriculum. In another sense they are part of systematic instruction, for only as they are progressively built up will pupils listen to the teacher or, in the secondary period, show capacity to learn by studying. The latter requires the volitional capacity of sustained application, regardless of initial-interest appeal.

MASTERY

If systematic teaching is thoroughly carried out, and no pupil learning recognized which is short of actual learning, more time is required than is the case when pupils are advanced on a dubious 70 per cent of perfect performance. Nevertheless, the lag in time is more than made up, both by the rate and thoroughness with which pupils later learn and by the amount which they can learn. Half-learning and spurious learning as the typical basis of advancement of pupils mean less and less than half-learning as the pupils go on through the discontinuous system. There are few pupils, indeed, whose graduation from high school means anything of importance in terms of the education presumed.

Systematic classroom teaching, correction of problem cases, maintenance of wise and firm discipline, and continuous development of ideational background mean that pupils improve in learning capacity as they move upward. Our experience with the Laboratory Schools in the ten-year period to which I have referred left much incomplete, but three statements of fact are, I believe, significant as bearing upon the principles urged in this section.

First, after a time it became noticeable that there were scarcely any laggards left.

Second, it became common for one section in Mathematics in the eleventh year—not the twelfth—to be doing all the junior-college Mathematics offered in the University. Much the same was true of Modern Languages and History.

The school system as a whole established in eleven years the conventional standards which are commonly reached in twelve years, despite the fact that the school refused to permit the annual organization of a section in preparation for college-entrance examinations.

III. THE PRIMARY SCHOOL

We may remind ourselves that "Primary School" is properly the name for an educational status as well as the name for an integral division of the Common School. It is not part of an elementary school. The Common School as a whole deals with "elements"—of Civilization; that is one of the characteristics which make it Common. Nor is the Primary School a certain number of grades, for "passing" any number of years, or half-years, of schooling can never yield the substance of Education at any level.

CHANGE OF STATUS

The fact that change of status does occur at the end of the Primary means that the administration of pupil advancement has to be somewhat different in the transfer to Secondary than is ever necessary throughout the whole Secondary career.

There are four unit learnings, or sets of learnings, in the Primary which determine status: Reading, Handwriting, Number concepts, and the primary moral and volitional learnings. The building of ideational background is not peculiar to Primary. Primary status is not at an end until the pupil is secure in all of the four. In other words, change of status implies a definite node in personal development, and no similar node again occurs until the emergence of maturity. Hence it is that the individual pupil cannot be advanced into Secondary School and standing until he is in full status; there can be no advancement in some respects and not in others. On the other hand, individual pupils or sets of pupils can be advanced when they are severally at that stage, leaving slower pupils to come along later. Nevertheless, as Primary teachers get more and more into the swing of systematic procedure, they will find not nearly so great a spread in pupil learning rates as they might expect.

THE PRIMARY AS SEPARATE SCHOOL COMMUNITY

Since the old Dame School and the old Reading and Writing School disappeared, it has been American practice to include the Primary School in the school community which is called Elementary —with complete forgetfulness of the peculiar condition which we have called Primary status. In the classified school Primary status was at least implicitly recognized, and the whole Common School was put together as Primary, Intermediate, Grammar, and High, commonly with the last organized as separate school community, although not always. In the Rural Consolidated the whole sequence is ordinarily in a single building.

European practice seems to have tended much more toward making the Primary School a separate community.

Is there a principle involved? I think there is, although it looks two ways.

In the first place, the children who are of the ages which necessarily belong to the Primary School usually tend to flock by themselves, save as an occasional ambitious lad seeks the shadows of the big boys. It is to be observed that where Common School exists,

housed in a single building or a group of buildings, with ample playground, it seems necessary to set up a separate playground for the
little children. They are not yet at the stage of co-operative games.
And, of course, there can be no instructional community between
those who are in Primary status and those who are in Secondary. In
short, there is real and normal discontinuity between Primary and
Secondary. It follows that there is nothing offensive to principle in
locating primary schools at various points about the city nearer the
homes, when convenience would thus accrue. That is the way it was
often done in our early period.

On the other hand, there is undoubtedly an administrative as well
as an educational advantage in having the pupils of the Primary
School more or less in association with older pupils and, indeed, familiar with much older pupils. They learn much informally in that
way and especially are time and energy and grief saved through their
not being obliged to become habituated to strange surroundings
when they are transferred to the Secondary School.

IV. THE SECONDARY SCHOOL

The critical difference between Primary and Secondary is in the
principle that the pure didactics of the Primary gives place more and
more to the semi-independence involved in learning to study and in
learning by study.[1] Systematic teaching comes to include the supervision of study and, perhaps even more, the organization of material
for study. It is difficult for lesson-hearing teachers to see what is
meant by true study, for to them the idea is deeply implanted that
study means the preparation of lessons.

STUDY

We have already seen that American schools have carried the use
of the school textbook farther than has been true elsewhere in the
scholastic world, and a sort of variant of the Treatise as a literary
form has emerged. But the art of textbook-making has followed the
pedagogical fashions, and, moreover, it is under the doubtful blessing
of having become, in successful instances, profitable. The outcome

---

[1] For a discussion of the whole matter of study under instruction see my *The Practice
of Teaching in the Secondary School*, especially pp. 283–85 in the revised edition.

is, at least as it appears to me after some weeks of examining texts in an important collection, that textbooks designed for study in the hands of pupils have well-nigh disappeared. Instead of textbooks, with a few conspicuous exceptions, we have, at the best, handbooks and, at the worst, mere volumes of indiscriminate, and sometimes unreliable, information.

The textbooks which saved our schools from utter futility, in the period in which the old common school was giving place to the classified school and then to the graded school, were commonly arranged so that the diligent pupil who had learned to read could almost dispense with teaching. The principles to be taught were arranged much as we arrange units today. The body of each chapter was then made up of: a brief introduction connecting the new with the old; presentation of the new principle with illustrations; and a large body of "examples" to serve as assimilative material. Perhaps there have never been more skilfully organized pieces of expository treatment of subject-matter for children.[2] Of course, I am speaking of textbooks in Mathematics and the Sciences particularly. The foregoing does not apply to schoolbooks for use in other fields.

Even with the most excellent of textbooks, however, the purpose is more than likely to go astray, since it is easy to hypostatize the books and come to suppose that learning consists in getting through the books rather than in acquiring solid grasp on principles which the books seek to elucidate. After all, the heart of any school, whether or not textbooks are used, is in the competent teacher and probably always will be.

Further, inadequately supervised textbook schooling has long had the disastrous effect of setting up the notion that learning is conning a particular book rather than learning how to use books. Hence the expression, "He knows his book." The consequence certainly is that only a chance few of our people have ever learned to read in its most vital sense, namely, the ready use of expository books and ready and critical following of the whole argument contained therein. At the best, they read editorials in their favorite newspaper—provided the latter are well displayed—and highly *ex parte* arguments in their favorite weekly or monthly periodical. Opinion is thus bought ready-

[2] See also above, p. 83.

made. Hence it is that learning by study requires not only suitable supplementary books in use from age nine or thereabout but, as time goes on, familiarity with and use of the regular treatises which anybody might read, graded in point of availability from those written as popular science to those which are made to be used by educated people who are not specialists.

All this involves appropriate supervision of the study of pupils and seeing to it that they do learn how to study, with mastery in view rather than examination and a passing grade.

The whole principle of the Common School calls for advancement of pupils in accordance with what has been learned rather than in terms of satisfactory performance on tasks assigned. Let us trace out illustrative examples showing how it can be done.

Systematic teaching presumes that (a) is a curriculum; (b) that the curriculum is organized in a program of courses; and (c) that each course is organized in one or more units according to the psychological nature of the learnings proposed.

Now the pretest on an early unit of a course may well suggest that certain pupils are already proficient in the course as a whole, and a few out-of-class meetings with those pupils may verify the suggestion. I once met a student who told me that she had "had" "The Industrial Revolution" no less than five times—as I recall it. I have known college students who never had to work much, for the reason that they encountered little or nothing new in the whole college career. Well, these proficient individuals are transferred from that course to the next in that field or to one in another field. That is in substance just what would have happened in a good village common school, or in an academy, in the year 1800. Instead of wasting a year and getting an "A," they are permitted to go on.

Another illustration is found when several pupils draw ahead of others on their way to mastery and do so consistently. If the school is of optimum size or near it, the number of these pupils will be likely to justify resectioning, so as to transfer the whole group either to a more advanced section of the same course, to a more advanced course in the same field, or to a course in another field. Again, this is exactly what a good teacher in the old common school would have done, only he would have advanced individuals.

The practical and critical schoolmaster will at once respond that there are such things as room and hour assignments to place limits on ideals. That is true. However, Dr. W. C. Reavis, when he was acting as principal of the University High School, found that in a school of five hundred and fifty he could and did adopt a policy of continuous resectioning, that is, of resectioning whenever the situation described above came to exist, provided he could have two spare classrooms. In recalling to him this experience of several years ago, Dr. Reavis informs me that reports of the procedure as actually carried out are on file in the school archives.

If the skeptical principal is historically minded, he may well say that all this is old stuff, that it has been tried again and again with sundry devices, and that no special benefit ever came of it. That is also true. But observe that all such devices were attempts to escape from the procrustean bed of the graded school into another bed just like it. The pupil in instances of devices like the double-track system, for example, was deemed to be advancing when he was transferred to another grade or half-grade rather than to advanced subject-matter on the basis of learnings acquired. Pupils in the high-speed lane learned lesson assignments faster, and that was all there was to it.

A third illustration, perhaps the most common of all, is found, especially after several years of systematic teaching, when a given section has become fairly homogeneous, not in terms of mental capacity but rather in terms of cultural attainments. Learning capacity of the mental, organic type may in actuality differ among them a good deal, but cultural capacity has so far accumulated that it overshadows the other type. The section keeps together fairly well in terms of the rate at which successive units are mastered and in the end moves into a more advanced part of the field, or into another field, together, regardless of time restrictions.

If the school is thoroughly well administered, advancement at the end of the year, or of any other subdivision of time, will come to be incidental rather than systematic. When that tendency has had time to work out its full length, we shall perhaps become able to see that the long summer vacation is an anachronism, descended to us from a day when it served the purposes of adjustment to haying time. I was once city superintendent in a seaport town, which in my time had followed the fashion of ten or twelve weeks' vacation in the summer. And yet in earlier days its schools had kept open forty-eight weeks in the year. I was destined to discover that for most of the children, especially those who were not endowed with parents able to "go away for the summer," the summer vacation was a time of utter boredom. Some good people gave me money to set up a vacation school, and throughout its term the children hung about in a waiting list, hoping for a vacancy.

THE VOLUNTARY PROJECT

Under ideal conditions in which organization, administration, and teaching in a Common School have reached an high degree of excellence, the situation just described may be common enough. Progress in working through an adequate program toward the goal of maturity in General Education is made possible. Even so, however, there will be pupils who either outstrip the others in the rate at which they learn, or else do not work up to capacity. They are likely, in rather a shallow fashion as it seems to me, to be rated as "geniuses" or at least as "gifted pupils," whereas they are rarely anything of the sort.

In the lesson-hearing school they are often only expert lesson-learners, while the real learners become more or less submerged. In nearly all cases in the Common School they are pupils who have acquired some special or general intellectual interest, and that is likely to have led them into an unusual cultural background. They may or may not also be unusually bright mentally. On rather a superficial view of Common School principles, such pupils can often be rapidly advanced and run through school at a rate which attracts attention.

In truth, these pupils who move at a rapid rate and often do very substantial work on the intellectual side have learned the art of study unusually early and unusually well; but the primary social traits which cannot be learned out of books are likely to have suffered. They may be moving too fast toward a sort of spurious maturity.

Now, one of the marks of the educated person is the reach of his or her avocations, the spread of varied cultural interests. Something like that was seized upon to meet the situation just described. We called it the "Voluntary Project." Perhaps that is not a very good name. Be that as it may, the device itself seems to have had systematic value.

Provision was made for rather serious special study and report on some subject which fell within the range of the pupil's special interest and was still germane to the course. In substance that meant that instead of getting an high mark—marks of the common sort were not awarded—the pupil worked up to mastery in the course and learned something more beside. In form, there was nothing new about it all, for high-school pupils have long made assigned outside studies and reported thereon. These projects were not, however, assigned; they were volunteered. They were not accepted from all pupils but only from those who had interest, time, and energy to work them out. The pupil might work at one of them throughout the whole period during which he was meeting daily with other pupils in the regular course, or he might finish and file his report in a week or two. There was nothing assigned and no credit. In intrinsic value the reports varied from trivial exercises to something that would compare not unfavorably with many a Master's dissertation. In instructional effect the practice broadened and deepened capacity to study, took the pupil's mind off the idea of credit for work done, served as a useful source of evidence touching real superiority, and gave the pupil time to mature in the fundamental social traits. Nor were these projects confined to pupils in the upper ranges of the school; they were occasionally worked out by pupils in the old fifth and sixth grades, or the equivalent in point of pupil age.

EXAMINATIONS

The essence of examination, I take it, is that it is a method of collecting evidence touching the presence of learning in the pupil—or older person for that matter. If that be its essential purpose, then as commonly used it is one of the most indefensible instruments in existence.

Workers in the laboratories of the exact sciences, in the search for evidence bearing upon some moot point, deal with entities in which constancy and uniformity is a proverb. They use instruments of marvelous precision. They carefully eliminate all attendant circumstance which would render the meaning of their data ambiguous. They are not content with a single observation but check their results by repeated observations.

In the ordinary examination the observer is dealing with the most inconstant and variable thing in the universe, namely, the human being and his personality. No examination paper is an instrument of precision. The candidate in examination is utterly subject to influences which have no constant relation to his ability to display his knowledge. His bodily condition, the physical condition of the examination room, an abnormal emotional state inherent in the fact that he is being examined—all these are circumstances which completely invalidate the data secured, be they good or bad.

Instead of using the mean of several observations, the individual's whole career is often made to depend upon the results of a single examination. And yet men of distinction in scientific careers, who would never dream of subjecting a current of electricity or the fluids of the body to the kind of investigation which they give their students, complacently violate all their principles the moment they find themselves in charge of an examination. It is not strange that such methods in one way or another are carried downward through the school system until they reach the pre-school child.

Finally, be it observed, the examination system, both in this country and still more elsewhere, is the consummate instance of the substitution of form for substance. The examination in the minds of nearly everybody connected with it becomes the supreme purpose of instruction. To pass a final examination is to feel assured that education is complete. Hence it is that teachers, parents, and pupils alike go through the frenzied period of cramming characteristic of pre-examination days, blissfully unaware of the fact that they are merely engaged in the nefarious business of manufacturing evidence.

On the other hand, the pupil who is under systematic instruction is revealing evidence of himself every day throughout his whole course, not only in one aspect of his developing personality but in many aspects. The competent teacher might well say, "If after having had these pupils for several months, I do not know more about them than any examination can tell me, you would do well to find a more competent teacher."

It may well be rejoined that the foregoing would not be true of most teachers. I profess that it would not but assert that it is still true that teachers who cannot observe daily work and draw just conclusions therefrom are not enlightened by examination. An essential part of the training of teachers is training in pedagogical observation and the weighing of evidence. Training in the use of standardized tests is anything but training in the weighing of evidence; education is not so much an exact science as all that would come to. It would hardly be expected that any college graduate picked up at the club could be put in charge of an investigation of cosmic rays.

"But," it may further be said, "there is nothing objective about the observations of such teachers as you describe." The answer is that objectivity is worthless unless the instrument used is reliable and the data obtained valid. The ordinary examination is scarcely reliable, for no two readers can be depended upon to record the same score; and, as we have seen, it is not valid at all. But the teacher's judgments about pupils are entirely objective when they are recorded in plain English and supported by facts similarly recorded. They are valid only in so far as the teacher is in possession of a sound theory of education and a competent knowledge of educational psychology; but that is equally true of all other methods of arriving at educational judgments.

So, all in all, the record upon which pupil advancement is made must in the end be a record of well-supported teachers' judgments.[3] That is about as far as we can go; but when we go even that far we are at least on the solid ground of what we can know. Instruction is not a technology of precision and probably never can be—certainly not unless some future totalitarian regime can reduce human beings

---

[3] For discussion of evidence of learning see *The Practice of Teaching in the Secondary School*, chaps. viii, ix, xi–xiii, xix–xx, xxii, xxiv–xxvi, and xxix.

to such a state of uniformity and constancy that mathematical formulas can be applied to them.

V. CAN THE CURRICULUM BE CARRIED OUT?

The question resolves itself into the more precise query, "Can the Curriculum of the Common School as developed in the preceding volume of this series, under that title, be carried out between the establishment of the child as pupil in the Primary School and the completion of pupillary status, approximately at age twenty-one?"

We have no direct empirical evidence that it can, so far as I know, but, on the other hand, there is certainly no evidence to the effect that it is inherently impossible.

In the first place, the standard program commonly in use to the end of junior college, under the elective system, has been done experimentally for the most difficult subject, Mathematics, in eleven years after age six, and for several of the less difficult subjects.

In the second place, in other years and long ago and under different cultural conditions, it was done by the old academies not only for the first two years of the colleges which then existed but for substantially the whole college program.[4]

In the third place, in recent years in numerous instances, the whole program up to the junior year in college has been carried out in junior colleges attached to local high schools with not only satisfactory but superior results in the work of graduates in a leading university. Such instances are positive and tend to prove what can be done. Ten thousand failures do not prove that it cannot be done; they only prove that it has not been done in the schools concerned.

But all this in recent instances has been under the elective system, reckoned in artificial high-school course credits and equally artificial student-majors. In the experimental cases it was certainly not done for all pupils; but, on the other hand, what was done was completed in three years less than the time presumably available.

But the Common School Curriculum, such as that with which we are dealing in this volume, on a nonelective basis, has never so far as I know, been completed in a single school community. Moreover, as a whole, it could not at present be carried out, for lack of ade-

4 See above, p. 61.

quately-prepared teachers, save perhaps in a few local systems or private schools. On the other hand, the Curriculum has been compared in point of time-allowance estimates, assuming competent teachers, with the traditional allotments up through the first two years of college, with the result of finding that it would probably require less, rather than more, time.[5]

TIME NOT OF THE ESSENCE

We become concerned about the time allowance because our whole ideology is that of the graded school, and we find it exceedingly hard to get a different point of view. In truth, learning acquired is the substance of the School, and the time required is merely circumstantial. The School is defined as subsisting between the beginning and the end of pupillary status. In terms of age, Primary status may be established at four, or five, or in practice scarcely later than six. Maturity may have been achieved by age eighteen, nineteen, twenty-one, twenty-five, or it may never be achieved at all. Maturity is of the essence, and the age of emergence is not of the essence. Indeed, a pupil who is educationally mature at twenty-one might well mature earlier if we could conceive it possible for him to start all over again.

ARRANGEMENT OF THE PROGRAM OF STUDIES

We are thus brought to what is the principal administrative problem in instruction, namely, the Program of Studies.

The Curriculum in its nature is constant and universal. In substance, it is an outline of the fabric of Civilization, as the latter subsists in its universal and major institutions. The Program of Studies, on the other hand, is the arrangement set up in a particular school as the method of achieving the Curriculum, or so much of it as the personnel and equipment of that particular school, at that particular time, make possible. If the school assumes that it is in effect proceeding with the full Curriculum, then the program arrangement may be called "Standard Program."

Many schools are under limitations of material equipment, but that is altogether the least important limitation. Many more are overequipped. Most of them are under limitations of the existing

[5] See *The Curriculum of the Common School*, p. 666.

cultural background of pupils, but, as we have repeatedly seen, limitation is removable in any school. Most of them are further under
the limitation of qualification in procurable teachers and principals,
and that can be removed only through an immense improvement in
teachers' colleges. Nevertheless, per contra, there are a great many
teachers and principals indeed who, having once been led to see the
nature of the problem before them, can begin and learn to build up
an administrative and teaching technique adapted to the solution of
the problem and capable of being improved from year to year.

It has been said that qualified teachers capable of carrying out
the Curriculum as a whole are not available, save perhaps in a few
local systems and schools. But well-qualified and fairly well-qualified teachers and principals do exist in large numbers for all the Curriculum as found, saving in the four major social subjects, namely,
Civics, Politics, Commerce, and Industry. For parts of these there
are some well qualified, and the teachers' colleges could, if they
would, in a few years train up a force well qualified for the whole
Curriculum.

Certainly, if the programs of various schools were shaped to put in
operation as much as is in each case possible and were carried out in
accordance with what we have called Common School doctrine, then
the educational effect on the pupils would at least be genuine. Pupils
might well come to substantial maturity in all save the intellectual
phases of social adjustment, and even there great gains might be
made.

CLASSIFICATION OF STUDIES

Any schoolmaster of experience and observation knows well
enough that people actually learn only from experience. They may
take on information through recalling what they have read or have
been told, but no change in attitude—which is the crux of learning—
ordinarily comes that way. Moreover, they learn the new in terms of
the old, the remote in terms of the less remote. Hence it is that the
subject-matter of study must always be arranged with that principle
in view rather than in the strict logic of sequence.

Mentality and ability grouping.—A fallacy to be avoided is the dogma of fixed mentality in the individual as being determinative of
what he can learn. It is a well-worn subject, especially in my own
writings, but in the present connection, namely, the feasibility of the

Common School, I venture to ask the reader to bear with some further notes. If the dogma is well established, then the Eight-Grade Elementary or less than that as terminal school for the masses is part of the Order of Nature. Let us first see just what it is that we are talking about.

If a given pupil is consistently superior in sensory capacity, in span of attention, in readiness of recall, in imaginative capacity, in quickness of perception, in naïve judgment, then we say that in truth he is *mentally* superior. He is bright. Moreover, we have good physiological bases for our opinion. Other things being equal, he will learn more readily than his somewhat duller schoolmate. But other things are seldom equal; and, after all, bright or dull, he must learn. Nevertheless, mental superiority as such is real and is not affected by educational development, for it is organic.

Learning capacity is conditioned in part, it is true, by the quality of mentality; but it is further and much more vitally conditioned by what has been learned, including moral and volitional attitudes. For example, Reading is the most effective of all learning instruments. If we were to imagine a superlatively bright pupil who has nevertheless never learned to read, and a duller contemporary who has learned, we should hardly hesitate to say which of the two will make the better progress at school.[6] No doubt, cultural attainments

[6] In 1928–29 Dr. Wilbur Beauchamp subjected the details of the study-learning process in a General Science course to daily observation over a period of seven and one-half-months. His report contains a great deal touching upon the results of his observations of pupils at work. It records measures of sustained application, ideational background, I.Q. on the Stanford Revision of the Binet-Simon scale, and study-reading ability on the Thorndike-McCall scale. The intelligence-quotient notion was then generally accepted as a measure of relative *mental* capacity, and for that reason it was included in the comparisons to be made, although I deny that it is any such measure.

These four qualities in the several pupils were compared with *rate of learning* as measured by (a) time elapsed between pretest and mastery in the several pupils and (b) the number of attempts made before the results of study were accepted.

It is significant that rate of learning on both measures showed the following order of correlation with the test results: (1) sustained application, (2) study-reading ability, (3) ideational background, (4) I.Q.

Now all these traits are improvable under instruction, including slow improvement of the I.Q. The most important trait, with that class at least, was volitional application. One notes that the histogram of sustained application changes from a picture scattered along the abscissa line to a bunching-up at the upper end toward 100 per cent (Wilbur Lee Beauchamp, unpublished doctoral dissertation, Department of Education, University of Chicago).

being the same, superior mental capacity will yield superior learning capacity, but mental superiority is no guaranty of cultural superiority. Especially is it important that that child of caste preconceptions—the notion that there is an absolute organic ceiling to what can be learned in school by a particular individual—should be avoided. The reader is invited to consider the chapter entitled "Educability" in the author's *Basic Principles in Education*.

In truth, this whole long chapter in our school history which has been so shot through with an assumed exclusively native learning capacity is very likely due in the main to confusion between learning and adult achievement. The conclusion seems to have been hastily drawn that learning in school and adult achievement are the same thing, whereas they are very different things.

The nib of the foregoing is the warning that principals should be critical over the whole matter of ability groupings.

The basis of the whole doctrine of the Common School, both ancient and modern, is that pupils advance in accordance with their proficiency in accumulated learnings and not in accordance with either time spent or abilities which, it is assumed, ought to enable them to learn. As we have seen in considerable detail, those pupils who in fact outstrip their fellows in what they have learned move into a more advanced section or course. Those who learn but slowly give rise to the question, "What is the cause of their apparent sluggishness?" If the cause is identified and is removable, then systematic instruction requires that it should be removed. Nevertheless, it is quite true that the old story of the hare and the tortoise told at a thousand school prize-givings has truth in it. The slow learner is not infrequently, as every experienced schoolmaster knows, in the end the best learner.

The principal ought likewise to be very critical over much of current psychology which seems to have passed on from the dogma of fixed learning capacity to that of fixed personality. The very essence of human individuality and personality is in its lack of fixity, in its lability. Any pupil may actually be somewhat a different person this afternoon from what he was this forenoon. If he has really learned something over the lunch hour, his personal pattern will be somewhat different and his learning capacity different. If he is the same in learning capacity and personality at legal majority that he was when he entered Secondary status, after the fashion of his finger-prints, then there has been no education.

VI. COMMON-SCHOOL STRUCTURE IN URBAN COMMUNITIES

The rural consolidated school doubtless furnishes the best opportunity for transforming an existing discontinuous system into a Common School, for there is already in most instances a single school community—high-school upstairs and grades below. So it often is, or might be, in small villages.

IN LARGE CITIES

In the large urban community the problem is far from being so simple, largely because of the capital tied up in huge high-school buildings. Doubtless, few city people will be hospitable to the adjustments implied in the following analysis. But let us see.

Let us take a typical large-city high school of five thousand. Some of them are a good deal larger than that, but such a school will serve as an illustration. Some of them are a good deal smaller, but for these also the illustration will serve in principle. The school is far beyond the limits of a working school community, and it is part of a mechanical discontinuous system.

At saturation point, that is to say, the enrolment which would exist when literally all the educables were going to high school and staying through, an high-school enrolment of 5,000 would imply an underlying elementary-school enrolment of something over 10,000, in an eight-four system. If the elementary schools enrol not to exceed 1,200 each, then a single high school of the size in mind would have probably nine contributing elementary schools. If the high school were discontinued, its enrolment distributed back to the elementary schools, and each of the latter made into a Common School, the enrolment of each of the latter would be increased by about 550 to 1,750. Presuming the enrolment to be kept at 1,200 each, about thirteen buildings would be required, four of them new. The high-school building would probably be abandoned, scrapped, or else converted to other uses. The great need of city technological schools might account for the use of some existing high-school plants.

But that is not the whole story. Common School implies the extension of high school which is now called junior college. At the theoretical saturation point, that would add something less than 2,500 to be distributed back into the elementary buildings, let us say 2,000. It would mean two more common-school buildings, or fifteen in all. That would appear to be an outside limit. If the enrolment in each of the Common Schools were allowed to increase to the probably workable school community of 1,500, then the total number of buildings required, old and new, would be fourteen.

But the school system as a whole is not at saturation point and perhaps never will be. For the country as a whole the high-school enrolment is about 35 per cent of the elementary-school enrolment. On that basis our high school of 5,000 has probably an underlying enrolment of 14,300. Following the same method of computation as before, we should need sixteen buildings if the new common-school enrolment were kept at 1,200. If we include the junior college, as, of course, we should, then the saturation point moves still farther away, making a single additional building for that purpose, or seventeen in all. If we assume 1,500 as the standard enrolment of the new schools, then the total enrolment up through junior college would require but fourteen buildings.

The foregoing estimates are made on the basis of an 8-4-2 school system. If the system is 6-3-3-2, or any other combination of years, then the estimates must be changed accordingly. The chief difference would be in the fact that junior high school buildings would not have to be abandoned, save where they are designed for an enrolment beyond the working conditions of a normal school community of, say, 1,500. In other words, it would be a much simpler matter to pass from a 6-3-3-2 system of discontinuous schools to a Common School basis than to pass from an 8-4-2 basis. The reason, of course, is that the former is already a good deal nearer Common School than the latter.

It ought to be borne in mind that all the foregoing computation rests on the familiar graded-school structure and separate high school. The Common School once consistently in operation, laggards would tend to disappear and the enrolment relative to population to decrease.

It requires not much exercise of imagination to realize how "radical" the proposals implied in the foregoing must seem. No proposal is made but only an analysis of what transition from a discontinuous system to a Common School would mean in large cities in terms of material structures. Probably most people will resent the idea that high schools as such be given up. And yet the reason for that view of things is to be found in the fact that in two to four generations we have become so familiar with things as they are that we take it for granted that high schools are the next thing to a part of the fixed Order of Nature, whereas in this country they are at the outside only about a hundred and twenty years old—say forty to sixty years as generally established—and, at that, an adaptation to a society which has long since disappeared.

Nevertheless, are there not features of standard high-school design and instruction which are appropriate and necessary to what goes on in High School and which cannot be carried on below that level? Let us see.

Laboratories.—I suppose that the first item which would be cited is the provision of laboratories and similar equipment.

Nearly, if not quite, every critical study of the utility of laboratories anywhere in the secondary school including junior college has shown they have no utility over and above what can be achieved in lecture-table demonstrations. The reason why the facts as found are what they are is not far to seek. In brief, laboratory work belongs to the University and not in the field of General Education. Here is another of the points at which things went wrong.

In the last quarter of the nineteenth century there was a widespread "progressive" movement on, and, like their kind in all the ages, the progressives took little thought of analysis. The Pestalozzian notions of instruction had been with us long enough to have more or less permeated the pedagogical community. The heart of the movement was reformist, in that it sought to get away from the utter meaninglessness of verbal memorization of books without clarity of concepts. One of the big expressions was "object teaching," and that applied especially to the sciences as they were coming to be known in schools, and especially to Physics and Chemistry. As late as the eighties, we seldom had either demonstration table or laboratory; but in most high schools the books were conned and the results yielded up in question-and-answer recitations. If the boys had imagination enough to sense a meaning in terms of their own experience, they learned something. Otherwise they did not. The girls "just hated it," since few of them had ever had any common experience in the field. Here and there a teacher accumulated a few pieces of apparatus with which "to do experiments." These, of course, were not experiments at all but only exhibitions of "the wonders of science" as manifested by Geissler tubes, marvelously changing colors in test tubes, glass-plate electric machines, and holding hands while the "ponk" from a Leyden jar traversed the circle—and the girls made themselves as delightful as possible by screaming.

But along with it all came the reforms of Charles W. Eliot and then the University Idea movement, of which college laboratories—and by implication high-school laboratories—were an important feature. Note that, when these laboratories came in, the professed purpose was derived from mental discipline; they were to train the "faculties" of observation and inference. I doubt not that to this day cut-and-dried laboratory notebooks can be found in many a high school in which after every "experiment" is a blank space headed "From this we infer———." Of course, nothing ever came of all that and never could.

But certain academic foundations were struggling to become true Universities, and therein science laboratories in the hands of trained specialists and their neophytes had rightly a critical place. So had they in engineering and medical colleges, but it was still a long time in the latter before there was much more than perfunctory routine. Finally, the present purpose in the University came to be seen. In the Faculty of Philosophy it is training in firsthand fact-finding of a particular sort. In the Faculties of Engineering and Medicine it is training in the use of laboratory facilities for fact-finding in professional practice. There is no mythical mental development about it. But these are practices and purposes with which neither high school

nor junior college has anything to do. A building designed to provide for laboratories is no good reason for a separate high school according to tradition.

Gymnasium and stadium.—I suppose gymnasium and stadium
would come next. The former in any legitimate use belongs to the
Elementary School as truly as to the High School. It is of the Common School. In its illegitimate use, that of a public-entertainment
place for basketball exhibitions, it belongs to no school at all. The
same thing can be said of the stadium.[7]

Libraries.—The only other query of the sort that I can think of,
touching the High School as thing-in-itself, has to do with school libraries. But not only is it true that few high schools have libraries
worthy of the name but that the library is as critically useful in the
Elementary School as in the High. From the beginning of the secondary period, learning how to use books is, as we have seen, an essential of the learning-by-study process. Moreover, in the all-important
matter of building background, libraries are one of the most important resources. In the Common School at least two separate libraries
will always prove useful; at least so we found it in the Laboratory
Schools.

FORCE OF CIRCUMSTANCES

But, after all, the foregoing discussion of the large-city situation
is academic. The mere course of events will inevitably bring about
something of the sort. Once let a great city grow up, and you will
find that it will keep on growing in ways never dreamed of. A re-
cently-observed phenomenon, for example, is the surprising way in
which large retail establishments located in the outskirts bid fair
more or less to obliterate the downtown retail district—to the con-
sternation of real estate owners.

In the first place, the Community-Planning movement, now preoccupied with slum clearance, must come to see that just as it centered its neighborhood units on the Elementary School, so if it would
deal with the city as a whole, it must center them on a different kind
of school, namely, the modern Common School.

In the second place, junior high schools are already becoming
rather dubious high schools, and elementary schools are beginning to

[7] See *The Curriculum of the Common School*, p. 648.

do some junior high school work. It has been one of the contentions of this volume that the social forces which produced the Junior High School and Junior College will persist until little by little our communities will find themselves back on the pattern of school structure with which we started our national history. What is greatly important is the issue whether the whole movement shall continue to run along in a laissez faire process or shall be guided by some rational control. One way means waste and many false steps; the other means steady progress with a minimum amount of waste of time, capital, and energy.

In the third place, near-in suburban communities, and what are sometimes called new divisions in our medium-sized cities, are likely to learn that the economy and potential efficiency of the Common School near at hand is greatly to be preferred to driving high-school children daily to a distant city high school, of dubious influence.

IN THE SMALL CITIES

In the small cities, with high schools of fifteen hundred or less, the problem of reorganization is much simpler than it is in the larger cities, mainly for the reason that high-school buildings would not necessarily have to be abandoned. Each of them would probably be suited to the housing of a Common School.

In many of the smaller cities and larger villages, any sort of effective school organization is well-nigh impossible, because of the sprawling, characterless community pattern. But what is true of the schools is true of nearly all other social functions. These meaningless communities in which anybody can stick up any kind of house, shop, factory, railroad track, slum district, anywhere, are not only unbeautiful things, but they are as inefficient as a small boy's playroom which has not received maternal inspection since a week ago yesterday. Nothing is in its place. Before there can be any wholesome community life of any sort, they will have to be more or less rebuilt.

Frontier times are gone forever!

CHAPTER X

THE HEAD OF THE SCHOOL

THE School is an institution. Any particular school is normally a community of teachers and pupils and, in its instructional purpose, an enterprise. As a community, it requires regulation as do all communities; as an orderly enterprise capable of attaining an end, it requires a responsible head. Whether as community or as enterprise, it behaves like all organisms, whether natural or social, from a plant in the garden to a great nation, in that it will not function without head dominance of some kind. If there is at the moment no head, it will presently grow one. If the duly appointed principal is not in fact head, then some teacher or even pupil will become head. Hence it is fatal to the organized purpose of a school that the individual who is set to be principal cannot be head.

So Headship is in a manner institutional in character. Let us consider it in that respect for the moment, avoiding for the time any personalization whatever, and ask ourselves the question, "What has to get done through Headship and cannot otherwise get done?"

These five things have to be carried on from day to day: *government* of the school community; *supervision* of the instruction; the *pastoral relation* between the school and the homes from which the pupils come; *control and care of the materiél* used in the school functions; and the *financial administration* in which the school is necessarily involved. Thus is Headship instituted, no matter what the size of the school.

So it is with the Common School. All that has been written down in the preceding chapters concerning the natural and logical character of that institution, concerning the potential efficiency of its structure, concerning its adaptability to our civil institutions, is mere preachment save as it is all integrated in the present chapter— and that for which the chapter stands.

I. THE PRINCIPALSHIP

In American usage the head of a school is most often called "Principal." He is sometimes called "Headmaster," following an English usage. Either term carries the connotation that the Head is simply the leading teacher, but he is much more than that. In the Scottish usage he is "Rector," and that is more definitive.

In my judgment, having had experience in all the major positions found in the regular schools under our system of public instruction, the Principalship is not only the most critical of them all but the most attractive as well to the person whose interests are the most distinctively professional. I do not say that it is the most important; doubtless, that distinction belongs to the City Superintendency and to the office which is correctly as well as legally called the Superintendency of Public Instruction. But it is critical, much as the command of a working army unit, or of a ship at sea, or the superintendency of an industrial plant is critical. No city superintendent can achieve fit results unless he can have a body of competent principals. Such a corps can function without a superintendent in certain types of small cities; it could conceivably do so in the largest cities in the event of emergency. Moreover, the thoroughly competent principal is not even dependent on his teachers, for he can train them—indeed, in most cases he has to train teachers in practice.

THE PRINCIPALSHIP AND THE COMMON SCHOOL

Now, one of the numerous sins of discontinuity and the elective system has been the degradation of the Principalship. The Principal in such a system is not the head of a school; he is rather foreman of a department. He has scant professional function of any kind. True enough, he is still vested with the government of school children and can, if he will, exercise the pastoral function. Educationally, however, he is but an humdrum secretary devoted to administering performance tests, solemnly tabulating and graphing the results, and keeping things running smoothly.

Foreman of a department? Yes, just that; for under the discontinuous system a principal never sees intimately the education of youth as a process; he sees it only as a matter of keeping records of passing marks and accumulating credits. It is not surprising that "education" has become but little more than a cant expression.

On the other hand, when a principal becomes Head of a Common School, he becomes responsible for the progress of pupils all the way up to the end of General Education. Whatever else he is, he is no longer foreman, for there are no longer instructional plants engaged in making parts. Every day his experience speaks to him of what is in principle, even if not in fact, Education. It is easy for him to think educationally, whereas it is difficult for the principal of an elementary school or high school or the president of one of our colleges so to think. In the Common School the Principal is at least Head of a school, a comprehensive unit in the performance of the common task of Public Instruction. Whether he actually is or is not Head depends upon himself and not upon the system in which he is caught.

II. THE MAJOR FUNCTIONS

We turn, then, for brief but comprehensive examination to the major functions of Headship in which the Principal operates.

GOVERNMENT

The government of the school and of the school community is like all government in that in the end it is coercive power applied to a group rather than persuasion. That is what it is at bottom and that is the quality to which we must always refer back. Nevertheless, school government is in the interest of the current welfare of the pupils and of their effective instruction rather than the exertion of power for the sake of enjoying authority. It may well be said that the Preamble to the Constitution contains the gist of our philosophy of school government as well as of civil government: "to establish Justice, insure domestic Tranquillity . . . . promote the general Welfare."

The first obligation of the school government is to see that all pupils are justly treated, by their teachers, by their fellow-pupils both individually and collectively, and by everybody else connected with the school.

The second obligation is the maintenance of good order, and that means not only orderliness among the pupils themselves but the order of the school community as a going concern.

The third major obligation is to see to it that the pupils receive that for which they are sent to school, namely, effective instruction —whether they desire it or not.

But the school government differs from our civil government in that it is not democratic; there is no sovereignty in the pupil body nor yet in the teaching body. In the eye of the law the school government is a parental absolutism. But it is not arbitrary personal government. Before the body politic of the community, the Principal is a responsible Head, sanctioned by the law and appointed by a representative of the people, namely, the School Board, and removable by it.

I will go farther, and I am sure that any successful and experienced and successful principal would agree with me, and say that the very conditions under which American pupils are in school make effective arbitrary government impossible. A temporary reign of terror on a small scale, perhaps, but not government. The school in the end is governed by its mores and customs, and the capable principal governs in the main through his influence upon these primary social factors. As we have seen before, the spirit of constructive government in school is the spirit of the Common Law in adult life: "You knew better than that, why did you do it? You will get exactly what you have been asking for." Turn up the biographies of the great schoolmasters wherever biographies have been written, and you will find that in one way or another this is the way in which they have governed. Contrast Arnold of Rugby and Dr. Busby.

All that is not to say that a refractory, disobedient, trouble-making pupil cannot or ought not to be dealt with summarily; he has to feel the weight of coercion, to learn that he *cannot* do as he pleases.

Learning how to hold authority.—The young principal is apt to think that he can govern his school by the sharp and ready methods which he supposes are the privilege of martial officers. So long as he does not inflict cruel punishment, he *may* do so; but he will find that not even his military prototype *can* govern that way. All people who are placed in authority have to *learn how to hold authority*. If they do not, they will soon find that their camps or factories or schools are in a state of anarchy.

How is it done? That is the question stubbornly proposed by stu-

dents in school-administration courses, the kind who are always looking for recipes. The answer is that nobody can give any rules for it;
the holding of authority cannot be taught. The young officer under a
wise and competent older man can sometimes be led to see in practice what the thing is. And one can analyze it in terms of some of the
qualities that enter into it.

In general, the pupils, even the little children in the Primary
School, and no less those older pupils who are near maturity, and the
teaching and administrative staffs as well, must feel personal respect
for the Principal. That is what at bottom makes him Head. And
they do estimate character surprisingly well. If they have affection
for the man or woman in addition to respect, that is a help. But affection never takes the place of respect and serves in its stead. It
has often been noted that pupils in a school and rough men at work
will follow and obey an head whom they respect but for whom they
feel no love.

Probably the main elements of that respect are:

First, a belief in the *fairness* of the Head. He has no meanness
about him. He deals with his subordinates with obvious justice. He
feeds no self-love with wanton insult to those who are for the time
in his power. He holds his place by reason of competency and not by
favor.

In the second place, he must be obviously competent. Pupils are
scarcely to be trusted to conduct an examination of candidates for a
principalship, but the man once in is somehow sized up as "knowing
his job" or not knowing it. And usually they are somehow not very
bad judges. Be the latter as it may, a reputation for competency
augments the respect in which any of us is held.

Finally, he must be strong. The weak principal wins no respect,
and there are several aspects of weakness which can seldom be con-
cealed from the influential pupils who are themselves leaders. There
is the traditional weakness of lack of firmness and resolution, the
sort of thing that "first shakes a fist and then shakes a finger." Then
there is the weakness which refuses to back up the classroom teacher in a case of discipline and its corollary of allowing the school to be
governed by a strong-minded teacher or group of teachers. And,
finally, the weakness of popularity-hunting. The principal who fol-

lows the advice to "win their love" will almost always end by being identified as spurious, a "stuffed shirt." Heading a school, or anything else for that matter, is not an episode in courtship. The popularity-hunter is likely to end by turning the school over to ambitious and intriguing individuals among the older pupils. He always has a formula for it. Sometimes the latter is "in the spirit of progress"; often it is "training the pupils in the art of self-government," which is usually allowing a few of them to get experience in the least admirable qualities of democracy—wire-pulling, demagoguery, individual self-seeking. The pupils may like a popularity-hunter on the ground that he is "easy boss," but they do not respect him.

Given wise, fair, firm, strong, school government, almost any school will become orderly and into its customs will come preference for orderly and law-abiding ways, in other words, self-government, the foundation of citizenship.

We are prone to confound self-government with democracy, and yet the two do not hang together as synonyms at all. Democracy is a body-politic in action; self-government pertains to individuals. Democratic processes can subsist in a population which is so devoid of self-government that the community is little better than organized crime and corruption. Given self-government in a democratic community, we have about the best guaranty of civilized community existence which the world has yet found.

Even if a school is in a state of infantile anarchy, and the only headship is in the hands of turbulent boys and self-willed girls, nevertheless a period of three or four years of strong school government will convert that school into a self-governing, self-respecting, community—provided only that the few really vicious pupils are segregated and placed where they belong.

SUPERVISION

When more than one person is engaged in a common task, there arises the function of *direction* in the interest of co-ordination. In school work we call it *supervision*, although there is more to supervision than direction alone. Supervision covers at least four activities on the part of the Head or his associates—inspection, direction, teacher-training, and recruitment.

1. *Inspection*, that is to say, visiting classes under instruction in quest of significant facts bearing upon the course of instruction—firsthand knowledge of what is going on. That is the first of all activities in Supervision if the latter is to be in any way objective and sincere.

2. *Direction*.—Direction covers classroom teaching and the relations between pupils and teachers. It reaches effectiveness in teaching pupils the subject-matter of the Curriculum and the conduct of those matters which enter into the common disciplinary purpose of the school and the maintenance of pupil morale. Teachers co-operate in improving instruction not as a generous attitude revocable at will but because it is their business to co-operate.

On the other hand, the processes of teaching cannot be directed by the same methods which can—somewhat doubtfully—be used in a regiment or in an industrial plant. The like of the latter can be used only where tasks are so simple that about all the direction needed is, "Do this and don't do that." Even if military and industrial direction can be carried out substantially in that way, instructional direction cannot be—not because there is anything ethically wrong in such methods but because instruction is not the kind of action that can be directed that way. In teaching, co-operation which is not intelligent is the same as if there were no co-operation at all. Only personal contact between the Head and the teachers individually and as a staff, in which the assumption is that the Head is as likely to learn from the teachers as the reverse, can achieve the ends which are the heart of effective teaching. It ought to be borne in mind that systematic teaching is in spirit scientific teaching, and in science there is no question of anything but truth and reality. Needless to say, a majority vote on right method is hardly in the picture. It follows, however, that the teacher who is so self-centered and self-willed that he or she cannot co-operate on any terms must go. The particular school concerned is part of a great social function which exists for the right and effective instruction of pupils and ultimately for the good of the community—and for nothing else whatever.

Closely related to the foregoing is the matter of *freedom of teaching* which, unless it be clearly understood, is capable of standing in the way of Supervision—and, indeed, often does—on the ground that the latter is an infringement of the teacher's liberty. In recent years the dogma has sometimes amounted to claims which would make both University and School little more than the tolerated soap-box area of a public park.

Lehrfreiheit und Lernfreiheit, as essential in the function of a true University, was laid down as doctrine at the University of Halle in 1711 and widely accepted. It meant that University students and teachers should as a matter of principle have freedom from outside interference in seeking for the Truth, wherever it might lead. But it was never contended that they might seek the Truth in any *manner* whatever, however repugnant the manner might be to the sense of decency common to civilized men everywhere. Nor was it contended that *Lehrfreiheit* extended to the teaching of the individual's views about the world, without regard to their truth or falsity. Neither State nor Church in those days had yet ceased to dictate what should be taught in the University and what must be left untouched. Professors were still in peril of being dismissed from their places for teaching the Copernican Astronomy and the new Experimental Physics. The phrase won its way as part of the definition of a true University throughout the Western World: the pursuit of Truth wherever it might lead. So it was understood for two hundred years.

And then came a remarkable recrudescence of the notion that liberty and freedom mean license and anarchy, a state in which each does what seems right in his own eyes; that teaching means not the inculcation of proven truth but the random expression of the teacher's own opinions about all things known and unknown.

So much for the University; now for the School.

One of the essential differences between the two institutions appears in the principle that the heart of the School resides in the Curriculum, whereas a curriculum is foreign to the purposes of the true University. The function of the School is not the search for Truth but the use of culture in the instruction of children and youth who are still in pupillary status. Freedom of teaching simply has no meaning in the School. Teachers are set to use the cultural material found in the Curriculum in the inculcation of the arts and sciences and moral attitudes of civilized existence. Pupils are in School to learn what they are taught. Neither pupils nor teachers are denied, nor can they be denied, *civil* liberty as it exists for all of us in the law.

3. *Training of teachers* appears as a third element in Supervision. That statement may easily be misunderstood, for is not the training of teachers emphatically the business of the Teachers' College? It is, indeed, but let us see.

Teachers' College training is invaluable certainly, especially in the subject-matter of teaching, in general pedagogy and its underlying sciences, in practice teaching. But when that is all done, there remains assimilation of the well-trained teacher into the teaching body of the particular school. That amounts in principle to continuous postgraduate instruction. Does all that ever end? The answer is obvious to the experienced principal and superintendent: as teachers grow older in successful teaching, like everybody else who is soundly educated, they become more and more adaptable and less and less in need of any kind of supervision. There only remains the task of keeping them from getting into ruts and becoming professionally obsolescent.

One of the most serious obstacles to efficiency in our school system centers in this training-in-service matter. The obstacle arises out of the preponderance of young women teachers and the consequent heavy turnover in employment. No sooner does the good Head get a young teacher well trained than he has to begin all over again with her successor.

Training-in-service is usually taken to mean apprentice training of persons who are not graduates of a teachers' college. That is passed over in the present discussion, for it simply ought not to exist. None but the well educated ought to be appointed to teaching positions. Nor can pupils justly be submitted to the ministrations of those who are professedly tyros.

4. *Recruitment of teachers and staff.*—The Principal as Head of the school is responsible for the fit performance of all the functions of the Headship and through them for the morale of the school and for the efficiency of the instruction. Responsibility is the key to efficiency and good conduct of every sort whatever everywhere, but it is only an empty word if the person has not the legal powers which go with responsibility. A school-board ordinance may assert that "he shall

be responsible for good conduct and efficiency of the school." Many a regulation does so assert, but it is all empty words. You cannot achieve an end merely by declaring that it is achieved. On the other hand, the words "responsible" and "responsibility" may appear nowhere in regulations, ordinances, or statutes; and, yet if the powers to achieve results be conferred, then the Head is made "responsible." The government of the school "shall be in his hands." "He shall direct the teaching." "He shall nominate the teachers and other employees." All these things *make him responsible.*

"Your school is a nuisance to the community. You have the power to govern. Why do you not govern?" If that be true, there is no rejoinder.

"Your instruction is miserably inefficient, and yet you have the undoubted power to direct the teaching. Why have you not seen to it that teaching is efficient?" There is a complete rejoinder if the Principal is able to say: "Because I have no voice in the kind of people who are placed in the classroom. They are sent to me by your Board. Besides being ignorant, they are contemptuous of my direction."

So it is that the recruitment of the entire personnel of the teaching body and staff ought in logic to be subject to the nomination of the Principal. In that case, he is in authority over them; otherwise he is not. Nomination, but not appointment, for the latter is an indubitable civil function. The Board is not constrained to accept his nomination, but in that case he must make another. The Board in principle should be forbidden by law to appoint other than according to nomination.

Right there is the point at which cheap city "politics" so called can get a foothold in the school system. If it is allowed to become the custom for anybody but the principals to place teachers in the several schools, then it is well-nigh impossible to bring the practice to an end. If it is made easy for strict nomination by the principals to become the custom, then the likelihood that cheap city politicians and greedy citizens will debauch the schools is reduced to the minimum. But a radical cure demands an electorate which will secure good school boards, either by direct election or else by keeping clean the channels of appointment, and the removal of the whole matter of Public Instruction from local control altogether.

The question may well be raised: "But are.you not opening the way for the principals themselves to become members of the city political ring?" Half the inefficiency and corruption in the United States is occasioned by just such questions and the attitude they disclose. In effect, the righteous prefer to refuse to endow with appropriate power an officer who on every count is most likely to use it rightly and leave the power to a board which is not qualified to use it rightly and is most likely to use it corruptly. If a principal so endowed is guilty of malfeasance in the use of his powers, he is subject to judicial notice. To get at the board, organized decency must wage a campaign in the next election.

In city systems the nomination, of course, runs through the Superintendent, who has a responsibility for the system kindred to that which the Principal has for his school. The presumption must be that the Superintendent will present the Principal's nominations for appointment to the Board. Inevitably, if the Superintendent refuses to present, some sort of an issue is raised with respect to the Principal, and thus another guaranty toward efficiency and honesty is set up.

But recruitment of a teaching force of high quality means hunting teachers. That in turn means that the Principal ought not to be tied to classroom teaching, nor to daily routine of any sort. He must be free to familiarize himself with the quality of available teachers in other local communities and to keep in contact with the teachers' colleges. Where the Superintendent takes that on his own shoulders, he not only overloads himself but interferes with the chain of responsibility at its very attachment.

THE PASTORAL FUNCTION OF THE PRINCIPAL

This function of Headship is noted in passing. With its substance we have already dealt in chapter viii, page 143.

MATERIÉL

No school in modern times can exist without more or less in the way of material equipment and supplies, ranging all the way from the building itself to fuel and to the paper used by the pupils.

Now, all this costs money, and money spent for goods and services connected with material equipment and material maintenance is money which cannot be spent on the essential instructional services.

The other day I read in a daily newspaper of a new high-school building erected at a cost of three and a half millions, of which the people
were apparently very proud. I venture to say that most of them
supposed that they were thereby giving their children an "high-
school education" of equivalent value. It is doubtful that any of
them realized that the building implied an annual cost of $140,000
forever, *in addition to* an annual debt-service charge of perhaps
$240,000 a year for thirty years. Many a school in the United States
today is but meagerly equipped for its proper work, and much that
is ancillary to good teaching is omitted, because the building is needlessly expensive, because a needlessly expensive building staff is employed, and because supplies of all sorts are heedlessly wasted. The
pupils, instead of learning habits of thrift, are learning habits of ex-
travagance—with the public money. Outside a romantic novel there
is no particular nobility in waste and nothing sordid about saving
money here in order that it may be used more advantageously there.

It has been our tradition that school people are in their nature
somehow incapable of economic intelligence of the practical sort.
They are in a way expressly told that they have no concern with the
economy of the school; that it is their business to attend to teaching
and leave money matters to those who are apparently supposed to
be inspired by election with that kind of intelligence—men and
women on school boards, mechanics and washerwomen about the
building, and those who feel called to bind up the bleeding tissues of
the body politic with honest graft. Naturally enough, the school
people come to take tradition for granted and not concern themselves
with waste of any kind. Instead, they consort with those who are
skilled in the art of prying more money out of the pockets of taxpayers and alumni bodies.

A generation of increasing generosity to all kinds of schools and
colleges seems to have led to public discontent with the meagerness
of the results. The public has only itself to thank.

Well, there is a good deal of human nature about it all. The trouble is that all concerned are under the delusions of a scholastic fallacy. This is an economic world as well as a physical world and a
world of the things of the spirit. We can none of us escape so long as
we have to eat, find the wherewithal to be clothed, and contrive a

shelter of some sort—unless we are willing to return to the days of subsistence farming. In that case school people would have to cultivate a sort of scholastic glebe in their spare time, set up home manufacture, and return from their palatial schoolhouse to the mythical pedagogical log of Mark Hopkins.

In truth, all the material goods and services which go into the process of making a school possible are quite as truly a part of instruction as are methods of teaching. It follows that the oversight and the conservation of the material economy of the school are as much a part of the responsibility of Headship as are school Government and the Supervision of teaching. The school is in logic a unity not only in the administration of the whole process of General Education but in the further administration of all that is ancillary thereto.

FINANCIAL

Things financial are economic, but not all the economics of the school is financial. Wealth is said to consist in economic goods and services, while money is but the medium in which these things are valued in exchange and exchange effected. Nevertheless, we live in a money economy and not in a manorial or subsistence-farming economy. So long as our school capital and operating expenses are expressed and managed in terms of money, we have to learn to think in important directions in terms of money.

A Common School of fifteen hundred pupils would presumably cost all told, in capital and operation, $150,000 a year or thereabout in normal times. Where shall all that in the first instance be administered and accounted for? Downtown in a central office, where there is no vivid awareness of the economy of the school? Or in the offices of the school itself, where every requisition, invoice, and delivery slip, every item of wear and tear, and every salary and wage check is naturally associated with some particular maintenance and in terms of the latter? As it seems to me, the answer is obvious.

Management of the school finances proper in the school itself would seem to be limited to accountancy, not only as bookkeeping but also in the application of the major concepts of accountancy as a science. Thereby hangs a tale.

Since the school people themselves have been read out of court as lacking in economic intelligence of any kind, school accountancy has usually been in the hands of men accustomed to commercial and industrial accountancy. Schoolmasters who are interested take courses in accountancy which are derived from the forms used in other and unlike institutions. The consequences appear in fallacies, particularly at two points.

First, and perhaps fundamentally, commercial and industrial accountancy takes on from the Profit-and-Loss account, to which there is nothing whatever corresponding in school and college accountancy. Hence a whole flock of concepts do not fit, and in devious ways they lead to fallacy in the vain attempt to make them fit.

Second, and perhaps the most conspicuous of these fallacies, found almost everywhere in the literature of monographs on school cost and in survey reports, is the concept of *unit costs*, so much so that almost any superintendent can show that his system is less expensive than most others in his class of city by the device of juggling unit costs. Nor does he know that he is guilty of juggling anything. He is dealing with a concept which fits the production and distribution of goods and services and does not fit the economic processes of the schools. Commerce and industry are concerned with the cost of material goods and simple services per unit turned out or distributed. There is nothing whatever like that in schools and colleges. There the corresponding substance is cost of services rendered in terms of the utility involved—and you cannot estimate services in terms of teaching-hours or anything like it. If there actually were anything exactly measurable in educational utilities so that it were possible to say, "It has cost $——— per unit of personality turned out," then the unit-cost concept would apply; and we could justly compare Chicago and Seattle schools in that respect. But to state the conditions is merely to show the obvious absurdity of any such estimates or comparisons.

Each school should be in a position to be constantly aware of its own financial behavior. It should further be concerned with economy as housekeeping, the prevention of waste in all the practices of the latter. If it seriously kept books on itself, the elimination of waste would probably drop into place as naturally as it does in the affairs of the private citizen who faithfully keeps his private books.

Beyond that it cannot go. The Headship cannot appropriate money or fix the pay of teachers and other employees. These are civil functions and can in the end be exercised only by the appropriating power.

Central office.—Aside from the economics of the individual school, in a local system which has several or many schools there are certain administrative functions which can properly be exercised only by a central office.

The most important of these is *purchasing.* That not only has to be systematized but it has to be done centrally for all schools, since advantage must be taken of buying in large quantities. The equivalent of a purchase is made by the individual school when a requisition is made upon the Central Office. Nevertheless, in central purchasing and school requisitioning is a fine opportunity for winding a spool of red tape. That tendency ought always to be nipped in the bud.

Beyond purchasing is the consolidation of school accounts for the system as a whole, analysis, check on the individual schools, making up the budget, and presentation to the Board.

I believe that it cannot too emphatically be urged that the Controller at the Central Office should always be a school man possessed of special training in the management of the school money and with a flair for that sort of thing. Not only are the principles urged above in respect to the differences between school and business finances in that way assured but the man in the Controllership is thus most likely to be intelligent about and sympathetic with the conduct of affairs in the schools.

III. THE PRINCIPAL'S ASSOCIATES

If the duties which in logic appertain to the Headship are accepted and made the responsibilities of the Principal, in a large school he must have associates, that is to say, men and women who have the qualifications of principals.

Let us take the rural-village consolidated school which has been further consolidated and extended into Common School and see what we can make of it in this respect. Let us assume an enrolment of three hundred. That would imply a general population of about fifteen hundred, typical of a great number of existing American communities and schools. The school is small, but it is still a workable school community.

The school government is no great matter, supposing that the Principal has in him the elementary qualities of Headship; no extended organization is required beyond that of a woman teacher on part time to act as personnel officer for girls.

Personnel work in general, especially that which has to do with problem cases, will meet with perhaps a dozen of the latter a year which call for extended investigation and treatment.

There are probably ten to fifteen teachers of all grades. Supervision is a matter of daily familiarity with what is going on in the schoolrooms and of intimate personal acquaintance with teachers.

Pastoral work is at a minimum, since the Principal presumably knows nearly everybody in the village, or at least knows about them, and all the parents of the pupils.

The supervision of the materiél and financial aspects of the school is a small matter.

The Principal stands in no need of assistants in his duties, save that mentioned above and perhaps of some clerical and secretarial assistance, but still he must be released from teaching. No administrative staff is needed, save that a local medical man on part time perhaps does the school medical work.[1] There is no Superintendent between the Principal and the School Board, since there is but one school in the district.

That is the kind of school in which the young principal can best get his early experience. After a term in such a school, he has himself done everything which any principal does and he presumably is prepared to direct associates and a staff.

Let us then turn to a city Common School of fifteen hundred. Conditions are at once complicated. Headship has to be distributed while the Principal remains Head. School government covers children of all pupillary ages, as, indeed, it does in the smaller school, and there are many of them. Building ideational background to something like adequacy and a parity among all children is likely to be a formidable matter, especially if the school is in a section in

[1] See below, p. 216.

which the homes are culturally meager or in another in which modern paganism has taken root and broken homes are numerous. Personnel work is likely to be at a maximum. There are probably fifty or more teachers, and that means a full-time job in supervision for one man. The materiél and financial sides have become those pertaining to a sizable business.

If the function of Headship is to be adequately carried out, the Principal requires associates and an administrative staff. Nevertheless, if the factory ideology is to be escaped, there is every reason why the whole Headship should still be a matter of intimate personal contacts and not an office-mimeograph job.

Let us see what the implications are, reasoning from our earlier study of functions and bearing in mind that schools will differ a good deal, depending chiefly on the character of the community.

Personnel.—In the first place, and most importantly, a Vice-Principal is needed for matters of personnel, and a woman assistant to deal with girls. The function covers: (1) general acquaintance-ship with the pupil body, on the basis of which school government is directed, not only acquaintanceship with the pupils individually, but awareness of what is going on among them; (2) the pastoral duties of the Headship, for which staff assistance in one or more visiting teachers is required; and (3) problem-case work, for which again one or more specially trained staff assistants are needed.

The school has probably an underlying general population of from 7,500 to 9,000. Densely populated areas with large families, of course, have a relatively small adult population, since the number of minors is relatively large. That is fortunate, since it is these areas in which the pastoral obligations and problem-case work bulk large, and charity organization and police contacts. The larger adult population, on the other hand, is what it is because the people are the sort in which personnel problems of all sorts tend to be at the minimum. "Tend" should be emphasized, for it is in these very areas that spoiled children and broken homes are often the most numerous.

Supervision.—There is certainly required a Vice-Principal for supervision, and he is busy with inspection, direction, teacher-training, and recruitment. He has, further, oversight of the important staff position of Records Secretary. In the nature of the matter, however, but one man is required if the school is limited to the size which seems to be the workable maximum. It will be observed that the number of teachers under his immediate oversight is about the same which experience seems to indicate is the number of families which a family physician can best look after, and again the number of cases, at any one time, commonly assigned under good management to charity case workers.

Money and materiél.—We have dealt with this issue at some length. It only remains to say that the function requires the time and energy of a school man who has had some training in school accountancy as well as in accountancy as a science and who has some taste and talent in that direction. He should have standing as a Vice-Principal, first, because that is what he is, since he has charge of one of the major functions in the Headship, and, second, because as a practical matter he needs the authority.

THE PRINCIPAL AND HIS ASSOCIATES

In thus describing the organization of Headship, there has also been described one of the obstacles to efficiency in any large school, even though the latter be not larger than fifteen hundred. Persons are rare who can act with and through associates or even learn to do so. Some Presidents of the United States have lacked this capacity—and it is not too common in commerce and industry. Men who lack it either find themselves with nothing to do, or else they ignore their associates and try to do it all themselves, or, finally, they are so egotistic and suspicious that they can work only through henchmen and favorites. A man who has all the other qualifications and does very well indeed as principal of a small school often fails to rise to the responsibility of promotion to a larger school because he has not this all-needful trait. Nor, so far as I can see, is it anything that can be taught didactically.

First of all, the government of the school community is still the chief obligation of the Principal. He probably does not need to know the pupils so intimately as does the principal of a small school with no personnel officer, but he still must know who they are and be able to get to know individuals well on occasion.

Second, the whole instructional policy and routine of the school are in the end in his hands, not as matter of command but because he sees what is right and is able to enlighten his associates and the teaching body. To that end, probably the best means among others is the frequent informal conference, not a "business-like" meeting with agenda, votes, and a secretary, but a talk over the school affairs in all their aspects. In that way the group may be knit together in common understandings.

All that means that a vital incidental qualification for the Principalship is a capacity for genuine friendship. Perhaps almost above everything else in the way of personal qualifications is that maturity in which egotism and vanity are so far sloughed off that there is little room left for jealousy, and room for one of the least common of human capacities, the ability to see that some things can be as well done by others in their own way as by one's self. So far from its being true that the presence of associates in the Headship leaves the Principal with little to do, the Principal is busier than ever. He is not released from any of his duties in the Headship but only has more time to study and reflect.

THE ADMINISTRATIVE STAFF

Historically, our schools were understaffed in the Headship. The Principal was a teacher with whipping powers. Perhaps that is where the name came from, as well as the English name of Headmaster. I recall that many years ago when I was a young principal in a town of four thousand population, I had occasion to appear before a local board for some purpose. One of the board asked another if he knew me. The answer was: "He is the teacher here." I suspect that a good deal of our school history was wrapped up in the answer.

But in the last generation all that has changed, and, in accordance with our American habit, we have flown to the opposite extreme. Where once four or five real deans were required in a large university to perform the decanal function, now on some campuses you can scarcely shy a stone without hitting a "dean." Where twenty years ago half-a-dozen clerks were thought to be needed, and in actual fact were amply sufficient, now that office swarms with young-girl clerks. All that not only makes needless expense but, what is worse, it shuts off the responsible officer from all personal contact with his task and duty; the red tape unwinds in long tangles, and bureaucracy begins to build up. In all such matters the primary question to be asked is, "What is the essential function?" and the second, "What do we have to provide in order to get the function performed?" Seemingly, the opposite course is often followed and staff assistance set up and inquiries about essential functions postponed.

The vice-principals are not part of the administrative staff. The staff which in principle is then needed in terms of essential function is that listed below. Bear in mind that the functions exist as truly in the small school as in the largest but that in the small school the principal can perform most of them himself, with some part-time help.

1. *The Medical Officer.*—Happily, one of the lines in which our schools have made marked progress in recent years is in the addition to all good schools of medical service of some kind. Sometimes the officer is a regular M.D., sometimes only a trained nurse. The function calls for a regular M.D. What is the function?

There would be no function at all if there were no relation between the current bodily condition of pupils and their progress at school and the health of future citizens. If a pupil has some malady, not manifest to a teacher but evident to a physician, which hinders him from normal learning—and there are many such—then the School Medical Officer is as truly a part of the forces of instruction as are the teachers.

The School Medical Service has regard chiefly to the following:

a) Check-up at least once a year on the growth and physical condition of all pupils for the purpose of (1) securing data for the guidance of the school Health and Physical Development Department; (2) detecting and watching over maladies and malformations in the individual pupil, with notification of parents and the family physician where that is called for in the circumstances; and (3) securing growth and other physical data for the master-card and perhaps for the pupil's case folder.

b) Receiving pupils from the classrooms who seem to their teachers to be ailing, and those who have met with accident, and administering first aid. This turns out to be one of the most valued services. The pupil has some trifling ailment or injury which can be set right then and there, and possible anxiety of teachers and parents laid at rest; or an incipient more serious malady which can be notified to the parent and, if the malady is transmissible, to the Board of Health.

In this phase of the service it is necessary to draw distinctions. The School Medical Officer does not assume to diagnose and treat disease or to perform surgical operations. The parents are notified and advised to consult their physician, the limit at the school being administration of first aid. That is all clear enough in the case of the well-to-do, but what about the necessitous parent? The answer is that modern, civilized, communities are organized to care for his child if need be, through public relief and organized charity. All that is in another field and it rests on another budget. The school cannot be responsible for any kind of medical or surgical treatment, for that is not its business.

c) Assisting in the diagnosis of problem cases, in which primary or contributory causation is not infrequently in some bodily condition.

The School Medical Service is not medical inspection which keeps watch and ward over the appearance of transmissible diseases in the community. That is part of the Public Health Service, and it has no more relation to the health of school children than to that of the rest of the public. The distinction is mentioned as a warning: local school boards not infrequently erroneously assume that they have school medical service through the City Board of Health. On the other hand, the School Medical Officer, like his colleagues in the local medical faculty, is under obligation to report transmissible diseases when he finds them.

Let it be repeated that the School Medical Service is as truly part of the process of systematic instruction as is maintenance of the Primary School or the provision of apparatus for use in the teaching of science. But it is not in itself instruction. For that reason, perhaps, it is not even a staff position but rather an independent part of the school enterprise.

2. *Problem-case teachers.*—These people do the work in systematic instruction which the classroom teacher cannot do, chiefly for lack of time as well as for lack of special training.[2]

---

[2] For description of problem-case investigation see chap. xxx of *The Practice of Teaching in the Secondary School* (rev. ed.).

The number required is very much a variable, for what they have
to do, especially in the early years of systematic teaching, varies
greatly according to different factors—character of the constituency,
previous schooling of pupils, effectiveness of teachers in noting learning difficulties, especially in prompt detection of learning that has
gone wrong and in applying corrective treatment.[3] When a problem-
case worker is first installed, there is a marked tendency for teachers
to "dump" all slow pupils on the new worker, as if they were all
remedial cases. Of course, the tendency must be resisted and teachers made intelligent about what problem-case work really is. Probably all cases assigned for investigation should be handled by the
Vice-Principal for personnel.

Judging from experience in the Laboratory Schools, one problem-
case teacher for every six hundred pupils in the enrolment should be
enough in schools which have a fairly well-cultivated constituency.
Generally speaking, the best way is probably to start with one and
then expand as the need becomes evident, bearing in mind always
the human tendency to "need assistance." As the discontinuous
school is broken up and systematic instruction more and more effectively applied, the number of such cases will steadily diminish toward the vanishing point at which the only cases left are those of
identified subnormals who do not belong in the Common School at
all.

The staff of psychological testers can be dispensed with for two
reasons: (1) systematic teaching properly done depends on a very
different notion of the nature of evidence touching learning than that
usually found in the psychological laboratory and (2) the problem-
case teacher should be equipped with the psychological methods
which he or she needs and equipped to be critical of psychological
proposals.

3. *Visiting teachers.*—The Visiting Teacher came into some prominence as a regular staff worker some twenty years ago. Doubtless
it was fashionable for a time and then, like all fashions, fell more or
less into desuetude. Nevertheless, it seems to me to have a thorough-

---

[3] "Corrective" treatment is done in the regular classroom under the regular teacher.
The correction of misunderstanding in the pupil is an instance. We speak of "remedial"
cases where the seat of the difficulty is not evident and prolonged study and investigation are required.

ly defensible place in the important pastoral functions of the school, and it ought to have a permanently recognized place.[4]

The position is not needed in the small school, since therein the whole pastoral function can be exercised by the Principal. In the large Common School neither the Principal nor the Vice-Principal in charge of personnel can give time to the details of pastoral work. The Visiting Teacher, besides her own direct influence on homes, is, in a manner of speaking, the eyes of the Headship in this field, but neither one of the executives should therefore suppose that the function itself has been subcontracted.

The number of such workers needed again depends upon the character of the school constituency. In this section the homes are all cultivated and well-to-do, and no visiting teacher at all is needed. That is not to say that the pastoral function itself is in abeyance, for to a surprising extent it is often most called for in such sections. But the work is not so extended and time-consuming as it is in some other types of neighborhood, and the assistance of police and charity organizations does not ordinarily have to be invoked. In areas in which the cultural level and economic status of the homes are low, two or three visiting teachers may be required.

4. *Records Secretary.*—In chapter viii it has been urged that a school is no school when it becomes so large that the individual pupil is little more than a card in the Principal's office. On the other hand, no school is so small that it can dispense with records altogether. Indeed, the Common School conducted on a thoroughly systematic basis will in principle require a fuller record than does the larger school which is still part of a discontinuous system and is conducted as a lesson-hearing enterprise.

There needs to be available as much information as possible about every pupil, from the time he enters school to maturity. Indeed, it is often desirable to know as much about graduates as may be and for as long as possible. All this is useful as matter of record when problem cases turn up, when disputes arise concerning the progress of particular pupils, and most of all for data in estimating school efficiency, in determining changes in the program of studies, and, in-

[4] For a description see J. J. Oppenheim, *The Visiting Teacher Movement*, and Mabel Ellis, *The Visiting Teacher in Rochester* (New York: Commonwealth Foundation [Joint Committee on Methods of Preventing Delinquency], 1925).

deed, for study of school policies in general. Beyond these administrative utilities is the fact that there is thus accumulated a great body of firsthand material for use in child study. But all that is not to say that such records can take the place of personal knowledge of pupils on the part of the Principal and his associates in personnel and in supervision. Again, let us give heed to functions.

The record starts with significant data concerning the pupil when he enters school—name, address, parental names, occupations, history of changes of residence, health history, disclosures of original physical examination. It is continued with amendments to and extension of these data as the pupil passes on through school.

It further continues with teachers' reports. Now these are properly concerned with the pupil's learning progress, but instead of being numeral or literal symbols—which rapidly become hypostatized into the reality of learning itself—they are brief reports *in language* with evidence similarly expressed. Reports to parents are stated in much the same form, but rather in terms of pupil conduct and attitude than in terms of the evidence presented to the Records Office.

The principle should be borne in mind that no records are collected or reports made save those which are clearly of use in forwarding pupil progress and those which throw light on school policies, notably arrangement of the program of study. Especially is the habit of collecting reports simply for the purpose of having them to be kept down, and similarly the furnishing of reports to external agencies resisted. Offices of various sorts all over the country are stacked with tons of reports, long since forgotten, originally asked for by individuals and offices which have nothing to do with schools and often motivated by nothing more important than the whims of people more or less in authority who had nothing better to do that day.

The record continues with the physical developmental history of the pupil derived from the Medical Officer.

All pertinent data concerning the pupil are collected in a large folder which bears his name and follows him through school. They are summarized on a master-card for ready reference at the hands of principals, vice-principals, and the teachers concerned. Nevertheless, the ideal thing about school records is that they contain little that the Headship does not already in substance know through personal contact.

Evidently, a very considerable person is required as Records Secretary. He or she must be well versed in the Theory of Education and that of Instruction, familiar with school work and the policies of the particular school, capable of sound judgment touching what reports are needed, critical in estimates of the validity of particular reports, and clever in devising economical forms and filing systems. At present, it is far better to select a person who has the educational and instructional qualifications required, and trust to his ingenuity, special study, and address for the rest, than to follow the reverse course and select a trained secretary without the other qualifications. In due season the teachers' colleges will be training the special kind of secretary needed.

Some clerical assistance will probably be needed, but probably not more than one reliable clerk.

BUREAUCRACY

All the foregoing is to write the formula for a school bureaucracy, unless what has been set down is followed in its substance rather than in form alone. I have tried to explain in such a manner as to minimize the likelihood that the hateful thing will arise.

Bureaucracy means "government by bureaus," that is to say, offices and office-holders, rather than by the duly constituted and responsible authority. In other words, what are properly administrative staffs of various kinds become the government itself. The typical bureaucrat is a past-master of intrigue and wire-pulling. He thus keeps himself in place and in power. The last thing he desires is interest in duties either in himself or his subordinates. In the place of these he devises "red tape." Indeed, a typical device of the bureaucrat is to "break the heart" of a subordinate who shows a disposition to become interested in his work and show efficiency.

It is wrong use to employ the term, as some writers do, to mean the administrative organization in government, school, university, and sometimes in commerce and industry, implying that there are good and bad bureaucracies. The word itself has a definite denotation which cannot be escaped: it means "government by bureaus" and nothing else. Government by bureaus is always bad. We use the term mostly to describe bad practice in the civil government, but it is prone to turn up in almost any large organization where there is no natural control as is likely to be the case in commerce and industry, through the profit motive. It is common enough in universities, especially in the registrars' offices, the buildings and grounds departments, and in the employment bureaus.

But probably the most miraculous example is to be found in our Federal Government, where it took root during the Civil War and has held on and expanded ever since. Mark Twain's humorous story of *The Great Corned Beef Contract* was when written, and still is, an authentic picture of the whole thing; but then it is all notorious. It is interesting to note that three recent Presidents, personally as unlike as possible, found themselves helpless in its presence and had to fall back on other agencies to do that which the administrative offices were supposed to be able to do. Wilson called in his "dollar-a-year" men; Hoover set up his numerous commissions; and Franklin Roosevelt resorted to his "brain trust."

IV. AMERICAN TREATMENT OF THE PRINCIPALSHIP

I suppose that the observations concerning the vital part played by the Principal in the Headship of the School made in the early part of the present chapter are sufficiently convincing. I suppose further that the lay reader will agree—and then go off and act as he always has acted. The truth is that the Principalship does not fit in anywhere in the existing mores of our people. He is "the teacher," and other teachers are his assistants; but he is not otherwise important, unless, to be sure, he has made a place for himself in the community outside the school. Here, as in so many other directions, we as a people have never grown up.

A good many years ago one of my associates had occasion to investigate the school affairs of a village community of perhaps two thousand people. The town maintained a small high school, and that was what led to the inspection. It appeared from the latter that the root of the worthlessness in the schools was a very weak sister of a man who was holding the principalship of the high school. He was the village schoolmaster. After inspection had been completed, inquiries were instituted among the citizens, especially those who were of some prominence and presumably well-informed. The conversations all followed about this line:

"What sort of a man is your principal, Mr. Blank?"

"Oh, he is fine—great church worker—no trouble with Mr. Blank."

"Well, that is most satisfactory—great thing that the school people should be religious."

"You bet it is."

"I suppose he is devoted to education too?"

"Can't tell you anything about that—don't know anything about education—out of my line—great help in the lodges."

"But you must know what he is doing for your children."

"Oh, yes, he is kind and they all love him—got up a sleigh ride for them only last week—good citizen too—foreman of our 'engyne' company."

"Did you know that your high school is not likely to be certified next year?"

"No—o, how's that?"

"Because it does not keep up to reputable standards." Pause.

"Tell you what—I'll see our representative and tell him to call in and see the superintendent."

Now, there is the tale. These people were all good folks as people go. Nobody was stealing the school money directly. And these citizens were no doubt unaware that they were stealing indirectly by using the services of a weak popularity-hunter for what they were reluctant to do for themselves. They probably paid most of the taxes, but they were weakening the schools to the detriment of the children and the future citizenship of the State. Moreover, they were planning to hold out a threat to a State officer to set up opposition to his measures in that session of the Legislature, unless he would ignore his sworn duty under the law and make other townships liable for tuition in their farcical high school. That probably seemed to them the smart and hence proper thing to do.

Moreover, that was more or less the regular thing all over the country at that time. Happily, many principals were made of strong stuff and did not allow their schools to degenerate; but these often had to waste time, energy, and interest in "keeping in."

That was far away and long ago. I suppose all the actors in the comedy are gone to a land where there are neither schools nor churches nor lodges—and hopefully no occasion for fire engines. But come down thirty years and travel in spirit over the national domain. I promise you that what you will find is that the churches have given place to country clubs where the local principal can demonstrate his qualities as a mixer. The lodges have been turned into downtown service clubs, and for the fire-engine company have been substituted parent-teachers' organizations, drives for this, that, or the other, and, above all, "athletics."

The other day I had a long talk with the principal of a high school of about the size of which we have heard so much, namely, fifteen hundred. He is a capable man, as well trained for his work as principals as yet ever get to be. Thinking to secure some data for this book, I asked him if he knew all his pupils. He replied that he knew most of the members of the graduating class "pretty well." This obviously compromising answer opened the flood gates, and I got my data after all, for he knew what he was about—or ought to be. Substantially the following apologia appeared:

I know that I ought to know my pupils better, for there are not too many of them; and I ought to do more supervising. I have an assistant, but I ought to know for myself. I simply haven't the time. Let me tell you.

In the first place, I have to fill out endless printed forms for the Federal Government, the State Government, and the local Superintendent. Then come still more from all sorts of organizations from all over the country. Of course, my clerks do the detail work, but I have to check over every one of them, and that means doing almost as much as if I had done it all myself from the beginning. [He might have added that a large part of this sort of thing comes from people who are too lazy or too ignorant to look up what they desire for themselves.]

I am expected to fill out endless questionnaires for students of education all over the country. That takes time. I suppose I could pass this up more easily than most things, but I am interested in many of them.

I am called upon to be an active member of various boards in town, to have a prominent part in service clubs, and of late to be chairman of emergency committees.

Worst of all, I am expected to steer the whole athletic program, and that takes more time and energy than anything else I do.

I tell you that I am not a high-school principal; I am just the manager of a three-ring circus.

Nor is that merely an isolated growl, and, moreover, he did not tell half the story. It is typical of what heads of most public schools get involved in all over the country. Just as in the former case of years ago, citizens utilize the services of perhaps the most important person in town to do work for them which they have taken upon themselves to do. He is not busy and besides he is a public servant. They are very busy—in making money—if they can. They take upon themselves a succession of causes, many of which are in themselves worthy, but none of them worthy enough to stand in the way of their school head and prevent him from carrying out effectively what is altogether the most vital of local functions. If they would leave him alone to do his work, and others like him, after a time there would not be nearly so many "causes."

The reader will perhaps remark: "Ah, but the man himself is weak; he ought not to allow himself to be exploited in that way." Well, he is not weak. He is a man who has found for himself a place in a world which has places for only a few. He has a family. He is getting toward the modern deadline of forty-five. Naturally, he is anxious to hold on to the place for which he has prepared himself and which he now holds. Let him devote himself to the work for which he is paid and presently the smear will get started: "Blank has become too much of a recluse; he has no interest in the city; we need a new man." The generation of new men are well prepared to cultivate a comfortable philosophy which bids them to leave the school to run itself in the interest of liberalism, while they devote themselves to pleasing the public—which is pleasing the influential people.

All the foregoing is part of a perverted conception of democracy which was already perverted when Horace Mann was conducting the Common School Revival in Massachusetts a century ago—the notion that there is something singularly democratic in leaving State functions to local control and support. Human nature being what it is, the civil function will be exploited by local and personal interests, as much in an age of labor unions as in an age of small local magnates in the employing and professional classes. If we, the people, really believed in the large pretensions we make in respect to universal education, then we should be as little inclined to tolerate local control of the United States Army or of a State Judiciary as of the civil function of Public Instruction.

V. QUALIFICATIONS OF THE PRINCIPAL

Perhaps it is the casual treatment of the Principalship which has operated to keep down and even to degrade the qualifications of Headship.

I do not profess to be able to estimate categorically the academic and professional and personal qualifications of the principals who now hold places in the United States or to compare them in these respects with their predecessors. I have never been able to make a census or to lay my hands on one already made. I have known a good many of them first and last, in schools large and small, in many of the States. Many of them I have seen at work in their schools. Of those I have known, very few, even of the best, have seemed to me to be fully qualified either academically or professionally. There is on the whole better personal qualification in other respects than that just named, for, after all, the office tends to select men who are roughly adequate to the job, so far as the common personal qualities of strength of character and good sense are concerned.

Nobody need hesitate to say that in one respect at least we have better principals today than were in their places forty or fifty years ago. In those days there were few principals indeed of good personal caliber who were career men. They were ambitious to become lawyers or physicians as soon as possible, and they were usually ready to give up school work in favor of a good business opening. As a consequence, they had little professional interest in what they were doing in school. They were the lineal descendants of the college student in *Snow Bound* who was "keeping the winter school." Moreover, the interested career schoolmaster was in those days looked down upon socially as being an individual who did not have force enough to become a lawyer, physician, or businessman.

Today, there is at least the presumption of preparation for a career calling. The preparation is, however, commonly a perfunctory Master's degree in some university department of education, with a thesis in school administration. Like most of our Masters' degrees, however, theirs is prevailingly a local ticket good as far as a job and not a through ticket good for the whole journey. The number who seek the Doctorate is certainly evidence of good faith as far as preparation is concerned, but the American doctorate is seldom, if, indeed, ever, anything more than a more arduous mastership.

But let us recall our analysis of the Common School and its Curriculum and ask ourselves what must be the qualifications of the men and women who are competent to govern and to supervise constructively the whole range.

ACADEMIC

In the first place, the prospective Principal should clearly be an *educated man*, or woman, in the nonspecialized sense. That seems obvious, for plainly nobody can direct that of which he is himself ignorant; nobody can supervise instruction leading to General Education who is not himself educated. Bear in mind that most—nearly all —principals today are products of the elective system, which means that they have been specialists from at least the day they entered high school. They are intelligent and well informed here, and densely ignorant there, in matters of common knowledge. They are estopped from supervision for the reason that they can have little idea of what it is that many of the teachers are talking about. But General Education imports much more than familiarity with subject-matter; there is included maturity in matters of Taste and Conscience as well.

UNIVERSITY TRAINING

But all that brings the ambitious young man up only to the level of maturity which the pupils are expected to attain. Beyond that is much more, for two good reasons.

First is the ancient expectation that he who teaches—or supervises teaching—shall know not only as much as his most advanced pupil but a great deal more. It has sometimes been held that the good principal should be able to teach any subject in his school. That is evidently part of the obsolete notion that the Principal is the head teacher and that the others are his assistants. The contention was true enough in the old academy days when society was simple and cultural products not numerous. It is not true today, for the Principal is not head teacher, and, furthermore, the teachers ought to be better qualified in their several fields than he. Nevertheless, since there must be inspection and supervision, the Head must be sufficiently catholic in his knowledge and taste to know when teaching is being competently done and when it is merely absurd from the standpoint of both knowledge and method—as a great deal of it is today. Moreover, every teacher in a school has a right to know that the Principal is capable of understanding what he or she is trying to do—in other words, a right to professional sympathy.

Second is the principle that heads of schools are, or ought to be, looked up to as the enlightened men of the community and the leaders of enlightenment. Since the clergy abdicated that eminence, or were deposed, our local communities have been sadly poverty-stricken in anything of the sort. The newspapers ought to perform the function, but they seldom do, nor are they likely to without capable public demand.

All of which implies that principals should have much the same academic qualifications which the best journalists ought to have.[5] In other words, the Principal should come to be a Doctor of Philosophy in the real and catholic meaning of scholarship and not that which is chiefly justified by researches in trivial and meaningless issues. But is not all this exaggerated? How can we expect our school men thus to prepare themselves? The answer is, in the first place, that we have got to expect it if we expect our schools ever to rise above a possible 10 per cent in institutional efficiency. In the second place, that they ought to desire it, and even now do desire it if they are of the personal caliber which justifies their ultimate induction into the Principalship. In the third place, that here and there a principal already has the qualifications, even if he has not the degree. There have always been such men. In the fourth place, that it is no more than we expect and get in the best of our medical men. Bear in mind that the Doctorate of Philosophy is hardly more, even when its full substance is present, than the Doctorate of Medicine. One is a philosophical profession and the other is a practicing profession, but they are on a parity otherwise. One is the culmination of studies in the Faculty of Philosophy and the other of studies in the co-ordinate Faculty of Medicine.

The real issue is: Are the folk as much concerned that their children shall be competently educated and the cultural future of their

[5] See above, p. 29.

country assured as that the practice of Medicine shall be in competent hands? Truth to tell, the folk care very little about either, but it is worth while to see what they ought to desire and ought to have. The forerunners of modern Medicine achieved their professional ends by leading the public to demand what they ought to have, and they did it largely through universities, chiefly Harvard and Johns Hopkins.

PROFESSIONAL

One of the best utilities which must arise out of adequate academic qualifications in the Principalship would be guaranties touching professional qualifications. Altogether the most serious lack in the professional qualifications of our school people today is their credulity in the presence of plausible but shallow philosophies of education and of life, their untutored proneness to be imposed upon and carried away by pseudo-science, and, in general, their susceptibility to fads and fashions, so that in the end they land in intellectual bewilderment in a world of wonders in which anything can be true.

The professional qualifications of the Principal certainly should include studies in Education as a science and in Instruction as a technology, which can be found only in an adequate Department of Education in a true University—which we as yet nowhere have. Beyond such university studies his academic and professional qualifications should enable him to master anything with which he may come to be concerned in his school.

PERSONAL

All the foregoing are in the end personal qualifications—certainly not physical—but there remains temperamental fitness, which is more or less native to the individual and which we often speak of, perhaps erroneously, as personality.

The adequate principal is, first of all, possessed of a scientific interest in Education and devoted to it as the chief agency in the diffusion of Civilization among the youth of a nation, who will presently become its adult citizens. He is strong in character, resolute, nervously and mentally well balanced, courageous in the face of opposition, strong in his own convictions, and willing to change in the face of clear evidence. He is neither subject to every fashionable change nor an intransigent. I was about to add, "not a popularity-hunter nor an intriguer." That is unnecessary, for if he has the other qualities he will not have these defects. The latter are probably always the defense behavior of individuals who have no confidence in their own strength and adequacy. He is not a "mixer," but he has great capacity for friendship. Finally, among his personal qualities ought to be ability to get along with and manage others. That I suppose is what Montaigne had in mind when he remarked that the competent schoolmaster ought to be a good politician. He must know how to hold authority.

All these things are matters of temperament and ripening wisdom and not of any sort of didactic teaching.

He is mature, not only in the educational sense with which we have been dealing all along, but in the further sense of wisdom which comes only with the years. Without it, he will make gross blunders, especially in school government, which will leave their scars behind. He may have proved himself a brilliant scholar and successful teacher, but the young fellow in the twenties who essays to supervise the work of teachers who are old enough to be his parents can scarcely inspire the confidence which is at the base of all constructive supervision.

Of course, it would be foolish to attempt to state the minimum age at which a young man should assume the Principalship, and certainly we cannot wait until the principal would be older than the oldest teacher. After all, there is usually an advantage in injecting new blood in most enterprises. However, it is worth remembering that the Great Teacher himself was thirty before he took up his ministry. By the time a young man has had adequate teaching experience and has completed his academic and professional training, he will be old enough—and probably not too old.

SCHOOL EXPERIENCE

It is probably more nearly true of competent executives, including school executives, than of most that they are born and not made. Nevertheless, an essential part of the process of turning natural gifts into professional competency in the Principalship is experience as a classroom teacher, at least enough to get the feeling of the school in its fundamental work, which is teaching. Beyond that is experience as principal in a small school and/or experience as vice-principal in a larger school.

It would undoubtedly be much easier to recruit highly competent men for the Principalship if the whole teaching, administrative, and executive personnel of each of the several States were appointed to State-organized teaching forces and sent where they are needed, rather than a matter of contract with one or more of a hundred and fifty thousand different school boards, which is now the absurdly obsolete practice. But that is another story to which we must presently turn.

CHAPTER XI

THE CITY SUPERINTENDENCY

THE City Superintendency of Schools, as we see it today, is ideally the Principalship extended into the professional Headship of a local system, although that extension has followed a course in its evolution different from simple growth out of one thing into another. The Superintendent who has not first been Principal, or at least been fully qualified to take upon himself the duties of the Principalship, may be the head of something else, but he is not the head of a school system. Indeed, in a local community in which there is but a single Common School, there is no occasion for the appointment of a superintendent, for he would have nothing to organize and superintend which the principal had not already organized and is superintending. In such cases, the latter has nobody between himself and the School Board and must himself learn to take on the political duties implied.

Especially must the warning be set up that neither in evolution nor in present aspect is there anything in common between the city superintendency and that of the county, save where a State is on the county system. The City Superintendent is ordinarily the executive of a school board having to do primarily with the organization and conduct of local schools. The County Superintendent is primarily a ministerial officer acting chiefly as the understudy of the Superintendent of Public Instruction, in a manner not unlike that in which the Sheriff was originally related to the Governor. He is ordinarily elected by the people and is not the executive of any board. Appointment of teachers and direction of their work are not functions which are in his hands, either directly or indirectly. His duties are typically the examination and certification of teachers, the apportionment of school money among the districts according to law, the hearing of appeals from the acts of district school boards, and the holding of teachers' institutes. The last is on the whole the most obsolete function, in an obsolete office, in an obsolete political unit, namely, the County of the Northern States.

I. EVOLUTION OF THE CITY SUPERINTENDENCY

The office as executive, or at least agent, of the School Board dates from the early part of the nineteenth century. The school historians make little of it, but piecing the story together, from fragments in the school laws, from old school reports, from the histories themselves, and from vestiges of old practices which were still in existence not long ago, the following account will be found to be not very far wrong.

As local communities grew into considerable size and increasing complexity, the school boards began to find that the details of school administration were taking more time than they could afford, and some of them at least felt that the oversight of teaching required more attention than their perfunctory visits could give. Bear in mind that in those days the "visitatorial power" over educational enterprises, now long forgotten, was taken seriously by those who knew enough. The solution was the appointment of a full-time or part-time paid man to do this part of a school board's work as its agent. That man was the precursor of the Superintendent of Schools. Sometimes, he was called "Superintendent," but mere agent and nothing more he long remained. In other sections he was definitely known as "Agent"—which, by the way, was in New England the term used to denote the head of a manufacturing plant. But there was also another kind of School Agent. Like this:

A variant of the foregoing organization was the establishment by law of "Superintending School Committees" for all the schools of a township, an equivalent in part of the County Superintendency in the Middle West, with a paid "School Agent," selected from the citizenry, on part time, in full control of the schools of each sub-township district. Now these were not legally agents at all, for an agent implies a principal, and these officers had no principals. They were statutory officers commonly chosen by the people in school-district meeting. The school committee visited schools, sometimes made comments on what the children were learning, and on occasion made addresses. They further certified the teachers. The functions of the superintending school committee seem at times to have been placed in the hands of a single professional man in town—an attorney, clergyman, or retired schoolmaster or professor—who examined and certified teachers; and this man was called "superintendent."

The district agent was the real power. He contracted with the certified teachers, built and repaired the schoolhouses, and bought fuel and other supplies. It is likely that he seldom meddled with methods of teaching or the curriculum or checked on the results.

A further variant was the "prudential committee" in each district in the place of the school agent, "prudential" being the old-fashioned word for looking after expenditures.

That type of organization lasted down until the end of the century, in many if not most places, especially in the Northern States. One-man power in the school agent appeared again in the superintendent who acted without school board in some of the cities, notably Buffalo.

So far, we see but little evidence of the emergence of the notion of Superintendent as having an accepted place as the legal Executive of the School Board, which is the board of directors of the quasi-corporation known as a School District. He is in all the foregoing but very much distributed. Still less do we hear of him as professional director of the school system and professional adviser of the School Board. For legal recognition we have to wait until the new century, and then we begin to find it in city charters. Nevertheless, an individual might be all the foregoing and more too, depending upon the intelligence and devotion of the school board and the address of the man himself.

The function of professional director of the school system emerged into clear light as a possibility when Charles Francis Adams II was made chairman of the school committee in Quincy, Massachusetts, and in 1875 was instrumental in calling Francis W. Parker to be Superintendent of Schools. The story may best be found in Mr. Adams' *The New Departure in the Schools of Quincy, and Other Papers on Educational Topics*, now preserved as a rare document. Adams' argument was straightforward common sense, which you would think would appeal to everybody who was not preoccupied with the use of the schools for selfish purposes.

Parker had been a teacher before the Civil War, volunteered, and rose to a colonelcy. After the War he found a place as principal in

Manchester, New Hampshire. Having fallen into a comfortable legacy, he went to Europe to study education. He worked in the University of Berlin for a time with professors who were pioneers in the field and traveled about Europe, visiting schools, much as Stowe and Mann had done a generation earlier. He was professionally qualified to direct schools if anybody was. And yet it is worth noting that what Adams had really done was to set up a Principalship over the Quincy schools. Colonel Parker was never in reality a City Superintendent. Nevertheless, the notion of a professional director of schools was established, for the "Quincy movement" became as famous as did the "Gary movement" a generation later. Adams himself remained the political head of the system—foreshadowing what was to become part of the structure of the local school system in the large cities fifty years later.

Out of the whole process of evolution has come into being the Superintendency as we know it, and the principle that the Superintendent is the Executive officer of the School Board qualified to direct Public Instruction in the community, that is, the school district; and that the School Board is in its nature representative of the local body politic and trustee of the school money. We find the principle but feebly recognized in law and even less in the current mores. But, law or no law, that is what the Superintendent tends to be if he is himself a man of force and competency and the Board is composed of honorable and intelligent citizens. It is no doubt unfortunate that the office has not as yet developed into an indubitably recognized place in the body of the public law.

So much for the evolution of the function and of the office. We can see well enough what has been happening through the years, and we can further see that it has happened because it had to. We can see the principles which have been emerging and escape the endless aprioristic speculation which has been the curse of Public Instruction—for ages, I suppose. We can make some progress in formulating principles and, applying them inductively, can see what the superintendent ought to be even when he is not, and entertain rational grounds for our convictions.

As we pause at this stage in our inquiry, it is interesting to note that the City Managership has come among us, a full-fledged equivalent of the Superintendency of Schools as applied to the executive management of the municipality as a whole. The schoolmaster may like to believe that the City Managership grew out of the ideology of the School Superintendency, and perhaps it did. We are on firmer ground if we say that both of them grew out of the necessities of corporate organization—executive, governing board, stockholders or some other commons.

The City Superintendency is peculiarly an American institution. It is probably a contribution to the rationale of school systems, save in so far as Canada has followed along with us. The European countries have nothing exactly corresponding to it, probably because such a thing as an incorporated school district is unknown there—or a corporate school board for that matter. The local executive in England and Scotland, for example, sometimes known as "Secretary of the Board of Education," even where there is no board in our sense, or "School Authority," is a civil officer somewhat like our county superintendent or like the superintendent in Buffalo in the days when there was no school board over the superintendent. On the other hand, our elective Superintendents of Public Instruction roughly correspond to Canadian and European Ministers of Education, in so far as differences in form of Government permit.

II. FUNCTIONS

If we attack the problem a priori, it seems obvious enough that the Superintendency is part of an hierarchy, leading from the classroom teacher upward to School Board: the individual teacher must have another teacher called head of department to watch him or her; there must be an associate principal to watch the heads of department; a principal to watch the associates; a superintendent to watch the principals; a school board to watch the superintendent; and the people to watch the school board. All of which is very lovely, hierarchical, military, feudal for all I know. The trouble is that it corresponds to no reality anywhere; that is not the way things are put together, in either fact or principle.

Lines of a supposed superiority come into the picture and create prestige—which is yielding to one of the baser traits in our original nature. Who of us who have ever been principals or superintendents have not been tormented by the ambitions of teachers to be heads of department—not that they ever did anything when they attained the place, or knew how to. Good principals spoil themselves by getting to be superintendents. Superintendents are unhappy and think they are not getting anywhere until they become presidents of third-rate colleges.

Of course, there is often the appeal of higher pay—and an ignorance of what is involved in that higher pay. Principals and superintendents command higher pay, not because it is "fitting" but because there are fewer individuals who are suited to such places. That is to say, that is the only justifiable reason. It is sometimes urged that preparation takes longer, costs a good deal, and must be recovered in pay. I have elsewhere shown that if the capital expenditure involved in even the most expensive preparation were to be recovered over a career period of forty years, the necessary increment to salary would be small compared with what such workers ordinarily receive.[1] Higher salaries ought to be established in terms of what experience has shown will make it possible for the best qualified to seek the places.

Moreover, risk is always an element in establishing economic price anywhere. Risk bulks highest in the highly paid places. Many a teacher is being paid as much as the principal if the latter consideration be taken into account, and many a principal as much as the superintendent.

The trouble is that what all these people desire has no place in a world of reality. There is no real superiority in the picture at all but only differences in function. If we have regard to the beginnings of the Superintendency, we can see that the office emerged not because they wanted more efficient schools but because the town was getting to be too large for the school board to manage in details. In other words, the Superintendency descended from the School Board, and developed greatly, not because something like a major general was required but because there was a function that had to get discharged.

As we have seen, where there is but one school, there is no occasion for a superintendent in the present setup of our system. We

[1] *The Management of the School Money* (Chicago: University of Chicago Press, 1932), p. 252.

may go farther and assert that in communities in which the general
level of culture is high and which show an high homogeneity of population, there is no real occasion for a superintendent, even though
there may be several Common Schools and a population of several
thousand, provided the principals are thoroughly effective in all the
functions of Headship discussed in the previous chapter.

It is the point at which *community complexity* begins to appear,
and what Herbert Spencer called the compound community, that a
well-integrated school system has to be set up, and a system requires an head. On the other hand, even in a very small community
in which a discontinuous system exists, there is need of a superintendent. A suburban community of fifteen thousand with two or
three Common Schools may be able to get along very well with its
two or three principals; whereas a mill town of a fifth that size, with
an heterogeneous population, with probably a juvenile-delinquent
problem, with need of classes for the handicapped, with bad political
conditions, may easily find the need of a qualified city superintendent imperative. In truth, the function of school superintendency is
far more one of *organization* and *executive management* than one of instruction alone, although the latter is, of course, the background of
all.

The notion of official superiority as the cure of all things seems to
me to be a widely-accepted fallacy which explains much of the failure
of our democracy to govern. It assumes that the superior must be
wise and good merely by virtue of official superiority. So we elect
any clown to some of our most important offices under the delusion
that the office itself will make him competent and good. The exact
opposite is manifestly the truth: an individual who is personally
qualified in all respects to perform the functions of the office will
ordinarily do well, not because he is Mayor, or Congressman, or Superintendent of Schools but because he is really qualified before-
hand. Outside of that, malfeasance comes within the purview of the
criminal law.

We turn, then, to what is more concretely involved in the Superintendent's functions, not because the law says so but because it is
historically and rationally true. Let us take them in order:

1. Direction of instruction, according to requirements determined scientifically and not politically, that is to say, as matter of principle and not as matter of policy. That touches especially the Curriculum and the organization of the kind of schools required. It touches pedagogy only in the sense that the superintendent must be familiar with what is going on in the classrooms. In the larger cities, of course, an inspectoral force and, it may be, associate superintendents are required for the purpose. Now right there is perhaps the most important issue in his own personality which the officer has to meet.

First of all, the superintendent must remember that he is not a principal. He must be able to know definitely whether each of the principals is doing his work competently or not, for he must be able to inform the board. Otherwise he leaves them alone in their own proper functions. Young superintendents—and sometimes older men, even up into the great cities—who have come up through the Principalship are prone to waste time and energy and disorganize the Headship in trying to do the work of the principals all over again. Especially, they seem obsessed to centralize the whole administration. They do not seem able to learn that they are Superintendents and not Principals.

Nevertheless, in respect to the Curriculum especially, to the place of each school in the local system, and to the development of the Common School, the superintendent must exercise much the same kind of direction over the principals which they exercise over the teachers. But it must be the kind of direction which we have noted in the last chapter. Direction is not command, nor yet persuasion, but enlightenment with a background of civil authority. And yet no School Board nor any law can make a Superintendent. They can only choose and constitute a man who is already a Superintendent in his person. Principals and others will follow, in the only way which makes following worth while, when they have confidence in the man as being better able to direct than themselves. Finally, the principals should feel that the superintendent is reaching the schools through them and is informed by them, not because of personal slights that might otherwise accrue but because none of the functions involved can otherwise act smoothly.

One of the utterly incongruous practices in the conduct of instruction is the preparation of examination papers and test questions in the superintendent's office and the correction of the papers there. It is bad from every point of view. Not only is the examination at its worst as a means of collecting evidence of the presence of learning[2] but it accentuates the process of hypostatization which has been so many times noted, and extends it to the point at which pupils get the notion that learning is a matter of jumping over hurdles.

2. Responsibility for financial and economic control as well as instructional. And here are two phases:

First, as we have seen in our discussion of Headship, so far as is possible that kind of control is properly decentralized and located where matters of use and of expenditure have their origins, namely, in the schools themselves.

Second, payment of bills, the making up of payrolls, purchases, consolidation of expenditure over against revenue for the school system as a whole, must be done at the central office under a competent and responsible officer who is bonded.

Once more the Superintendent's function is to know that it is all being done properly and yet not try to do it himself.

3. Ultimate responsibility for the nomination and renomination of teachers, principals, and all other appointees and employees, subject to final determination by the School Board. I say "ultimate responsibility." Here as elsewhere there should be decentralization. Nomination and renomination ought to originate where responsibility for competency and efficiency originates, namely, in the Headship of the particular school.

4. Recommendation to the Board in cases of discipline which are appealed to the ultimate political authority. Appeals of this sort ought to travel first to the Superintendent in order to minimize the number which must be heard by the Board.

5. Responsibility as educational adviser to the Board. This is one of the early recognitions of function, and it is still one of the most imperative.

In the first place, the duty is positive in that a good many instruc-

[2] See above, p. 183.

tional issues have in the end to be settled by the Board because they have civil implications. Among the chief issues likely to arise are:

a) Provision for new buildings, from convincing the Board of the need, to appropriate architectural and financial plans and the decision to ask for the needed appropriation.

b) Adoption of a curriculum. The latter looks like a purely professional matter, like a method of teaching, with which the Board ought to refuse to have anything to do. Certainly, a proposed curriculum ought to be wholly defensible on scientific grounds, but in the end the local curriculum more than anything else determines the kind of schools the community is to have and support. That means clearly that the representatives of the body politic should make the final decision. The programs of study, that is to say, the outlines adopted for attaining a curriculum, are, on the other hand, purely technical questions.

c) The establishment of new schools, all the way from a needed Common School in a particular section to the institution of classes or schools for the blind and the deaf and dumb. Such matters are permanent additions to the budget and, of course, must be settled by the trustees of the school money.

d) The preparation of the budget, supporting data, and presentation to the Board for adoption.

In the second place, in the present naïve state of our democracy, most school boards have to listen from time to time to the enthusiasms and importunities of minority pressure groups who are satisfied that they have found the true inwardness of Education and are anxious to have their views incorporated in the schools. Our local school systems are more or less cluttered up with the remains of the forgotten successes of such groups before weak boards. The Superintendent must know his profession well enough to be a clearheaded thinker on all such matters and able to head them off, or once in a while to accept and guide them. After all, nine-tenths of all such proposals are fads which in a few years will be forgotten, provided they do not become established in the schools.

All in all, this function of educational advisership tries the personal capacity of a superintendent as little else does. He must be utterly objective in his attitude, and that means never a partisan. If he knows his job thoroughly, he will be that. He must be ready to make haste slowly and patient in the matter of dealing with board members and the public. Even if he has reason to despise members individually, he must respect the lawful place which they hold in the community. Many a city superintendent, and some State superintendents or commissioners, possessed of very modest attainments as executives, have been highly prized because they were excellent counselors.

6. First, last, and all the time, the superintendent is an organizer. That is his most characteristic function. Nor are schools and school systems organized over night by writing up mimeographed directions. It is, on the contrary, a slow process which well may take a decade or more.

To that end, he must be able reliably to inform himself of the methods employed by the trained sociologist in social fact-finding and interpretation, in a whole series of problems which will inevitably arise in most communities in which the population is at all heterogeneous. Moreover, he ought to be a diligent lay student of the public law as it applies to Public Instruction. Needless to say, beyond any other person in the system, he must be a consistent student of his profession as long as he holds his place, if indeed not as long as he lives. Young lawyers have long been warned that the law is a jealous mistress. An analogous warning is even more applicable to the Superintendent of Schools. All that is certainly not to be taken to mean that he should become a studious recluse; but it does mean that he cannot afford to fritter away his time in doing unnecessary work or in any other kind of self-indulgence. All that was written in the last chapter concerning abuse of the Principal by loading upon him community services which are none of his business applies with even more force to the Superintendent.

III. THE SUPERINTENDENT AND THE BOARD

There are few principles under Anglo-American political institutions which are more inevitable in appearance and more truly a part of the fabric of democracy than that which holds that all governmental professional services shall be under the ultimate control of laymen who represent the body politic.

Thus our Army and Navy are controlled by civilian Secretaries
in the Cabinet of the President. The Commander-in-Chief since
Grant's time has never been a professional soldier. So it is in our
career diplomatic service. Ambassadors and Ministers and Consuls
in that service are professionals, but the control of foreign affairs
under the President is committed to the Secretary of State, a lay-
man. So it is in England, although there the device of permanent
undersecretaries in the various ministries makes for continuity in
policy.

All this is a clear response to that quality in human nature which
tends strongly to make the professional specialist a biased person,
and he is usually biased about in proportion to his devotion to his
profession. To many it seems patently absurd that government
heads of highly specialized services should be laymen. Well, we have
ample information touching what military and naval control of martial affairs will do to a nation and to the world.

So it is in the relations of School Board and Superintendent. It is
more difficult to draw the functional line there than it is in most similar situations, but let us see if we cannot make some progress in
clearing up matters.

Policy.—First of all, and fundamentally, the School Board is the
policy-determining authority, in other words, the political authority.
As such, it is directly or indirectly in fact the representative of the
local body politic.

We often hear it said, when vocal majorities of the righteous and
intelligent disbelieve in either the wisdom or the integrity of a given
board, that the latter does not "represent the people." The board
always does represent the people, even if it is the worst of boards. It
does so because the people have elected it by majority rule, either directly, or indirectly through election of the appointing power, or else
because they acquiesce in its misdeeds or make them possible
through neglect of civic duties.

But what is matter of policy? In general, what is desired rather
than what is compelled by logic or otherwise.

In the first place, the choice of a particular man to be Superintendent of Schools is a matter of policy.

It would be matter of policy whether there were to be any schools

at all, were it not for the fact that schools are now everywhere required by law. But if there are to be schools, there is still a wide
range in the possible character of the school system which is maintained.

It is a matter of policy how much school money shall be appropri-
ated each year or sought in appropriation.

In general, it is matter of policy whether consent be given to a
particular curriculum or to the appointment or reappointment of a
particular person as teacher or principal or employee. The initiative
in appointment is not a matter of policy but of competent professional knowledge of the candidate's qualifications. It must be assumed
that board and people desire efficient schools.

Municipal complications.—Most people forget that the policies
which govern schools under the local-control organization have to be
related to municipal policies in general, not only as matter of intelligent public policy but as a matter of consulting the interest of the
local machine. Otherwise, the schools will fare badly in the appropriations which they get, or else there will be a new and more amenable school board next year. Since woman suffrage came in, the connection has been closer than ever, for women teachers and their
friends make a very substantial voting bloc; and larger school appropriations make a very comfortable addition to the resources of the
local machine.

The *kind* of city machine which for about seventy years has been
common in the United States is inevitable in municipalities in which
city affairs proper are hopelessly entangled with State affairs, as is
nearly everywhere the case in the United States. The best citizens
complain and grieve over the situation, and at least one local paper
is always ready with denunciations of the school board for being
mixed up with the machine. But they ignore political facts and
processes and are hence futilely unintelligent about the political situation.

There have been machines always, only when they were the property of the clergy and of honorable citizens they were not called that.
The machine is but an efficient organization of citizens who have
common desires, be they patriotic and honorable or self-seeking and
corrupt. The machine is as inevitable in a democracy as are hordes of

henchmen and sycophants in an autocracy. It is an essential part of the actual democratic process. Time was, and still is in some places, when our people diligently "kept the schools out of politics," but that only meant that the intelligent and patriotic had an organization which kept things honest and the schools as untainted as the courts.

Leadership is always and everywhere determined by the mores. If the mores in a given community are bad or low or ignorant, there will be a city machine to match. No doubt the schools ought to have made the mores better. They have done so in some respects but not in the most important matter of all, namely, governmental intelligence and morality. To expect them to be efficient in this or in any other respect under the present system of control is like trying to lift one's self by the bootstraps. Control must be outside and divorced from the community which is also a municipality, as are the Post Office and, in the more progressive States, the Courts, the Constabulary, and Highways. So long as school policy must satisfy the requirements of an ignorant and corrupt city machine, Public Instruction is made futile from the beginning.

Technical conduct of the schools.—On the other hand, a given instructional policy being determined upon, it is fair presumption that it is to be carried out as efficiently as possible. If the policy keeps within the legitimate functions of the School as institution, the technique of carrying it out remains the same under one policy as under another. If our pipes spring a leak, we call in a plumber. He may advise us of several different ways of attacking the problem, of their respective advantages and costs. Choice in the light of advice is ours. But, having settled the matter, we do not stand by and tell the mechanic how to turn a thread or wipe a joint. Teachers, principals, staff, and the superintendent are presumably competent in the principles and practices which are required. They are not politicians but technologists.

It is further to be presumed that the executive will not be hampered by the self-interest of employees nor by the inefficiency of people who linger in the teaching body. Finally, it is to be presumed that school-board members, or the general public for that matter, will not meddle with purely technical details like the methods of teaching or with the government of pupils. I once knew a whole city of an unusually high level of general intelligence to be stirred up by a bossy woman who succeeded in making the method of teaching Latin in the high school a political issue.

Between professional and political functions, there is, of course, a middle ground in the Superintendent's function of adviser. Assuming that the desire is that the schools shall be as effective as possible, there is scarcely any matter of policy that ought not to be decided on the basis of pertinent facts and principles abundantly demonstrated and explained. It is the Superintendent's business to show the board the consequence of several different possible policies but not otherwise to influence the decision.

Intermeddling.—One of the principal reasons for disorder and inefficiency in our schools, and indeed in most of the other concerns of our Government, City, State, and Federal, is in the fact that professional and political officers are constantly intermeddling. The school board, or more likely individual members thereof, meddle with that which they do not understand. On one occasion, I found that a self-willed member of a school board made a practice of visiting schools and telling the teachers that they should "pay no attention" to the superintendent.

But the Superintendent, perhaps as often as members of the Board, meddles with that which does not concern him. For illustration:

He ardently desires the erection of a new building. Of the need it is emphatically his business to enlighten the Board and perhaps urge action. But he does not stop there; he begins to pull wires with individual members of the Board and in the end goes over their heads to interested groups of citizens. When he does that, he deserves to have the Board forthwith make a vacancy in his office.

Or he comes to worship what he calls his "policies," and upon them he makes speeches throughout the city, perhaps persuades one of the daily newspapers to support him, and ends by finding himself campaigning in a school-board election.

In all such instances, there is a fair presumption that he desires only the "best interests" of the schools; but they are not his schools. It is astonishing in the current state of the world to see how many people there are who are so thoroughly convinced that their views of the universe are the one thing necessary to salvation that they will cast off all restraints in order to realize their views. I suppose that most of us in this respect have never grown up. If the young man were gifted with the power of self-analysis, he would in most cases see in himself nothing more wonderful than an ambition to be known as a "great educational leader" among his brethren in other cities.

Such practices, I have no doubt, are responsible for the resentment at the Superintendency of Schools which one occasionally finds in works on Municipal Government and on Public Finance. "Here," they say in substance, "is an appointive officer who exerts powers unknown to the law, more indeed than the regularly constituted school authorities, and in so doing throws the whole municipality into confusion."

Outside all this is varied malfeasance and corruption, in the board more often than in the superintendent's office, some of it within the legal discretion of the school board and remediable only at the next election, much of it, however, capable of being permanently remedied by an alert and conscientious district attorney. All this is not germane to our study, otherwise than to point out that the chief underlying reason for it all is in the local control of Public Instruction, where the whole matter is left exposed to local gossip, malice, greed, small-town love of power.

IV. THE NOVELTY OF THE SUPERINTENDENCY

We have seen that the Superintendency of Schools is peculiarly an American institution. In its present common form we have been accustomed to it for scarcely half a century, very much less than that in some States; and over wide stretches of country, not at all. As a people, we have not had time enough to learn how to use the office.

The Principalship, on the other hand, is as old as schools. Varro apparently had something of the sort in mind in his famous formula: "Educit obstetrix, educat nutrix, *instituit pedagogus*, docet magister." It is likely a good deal older than Varro's time. Be that as it may, everywhere in the modern world is an officer who corresponds exactly to the American principal. Sometimes, he is called that and sometimes Headmaster or Rector, or by some non-English term. We know the Principalship, at least as it once was, and save for inexcusable faults in dealing with the man, on the whole we accept the

office as part of the established order of society. Not so with the
Superintendency; we have not yet assimilated the office. Sometimes the holder of it is looked upon as a troublesome lecturer on
"education." To some he resembles a county sheriff, and we all
know the shortcomings of that obsolete functionary. Sometimes, he
seems like an importation from a feudal world where men are called
dukes, earls, barons, and the like. I once knew a stalwart railway
conductor who, whenever he had occasion to call upon the local superintendent, would always inquire, "Is our lord and master at
home?" Well, sometime, perhaps in another generation or two, we
shall have learned what the Superintendent of Schools is and how to
use him. The present superintendents can do much to hasten that
day—and I know not who else can. At all events, as long as the
present organization of Public Instruction in local school districts
larger or smaller is adhered to, the powers and duties of the Superintendent should be defined in the public law.

V. THE QUALIFICATIONS OF THE SUPERINTENDENT

The academic and professional qualifications of the Superintendent are the same as those of the Principal.

In the first place, the competent superintendent must be able
readily and reliably to inform himself on a great variety of matters of
special knowledge. Of that we have seen instances. It is almost incredible to see how incompetent is the ordinary official and businessman, even if presumably well educated, to inform himself of what he
needs to know, even when little more is needed than to look up the
matter in an encyclopedia. He has been learning lesson assignments
all his days, and, unless a task is assigned and references given, he
is helpless. Reared in post-graduate days in the lip service of rever-
ence for "research," others cannot research at all outside the daily
walks; they cry loudly for the "expert." Well, the Superintendent—
and others similarly placed—will not get experts on everything that
turns up. Moreover, unless he is capable of informing himself, he
will not know when he needs an expert, or know a qualified expert
when he sees one, or be able to understand the real expert's report
when he gets it. Our governmental, instructional, and business enterprises are swarming with young "experts" whose main job reduces itself to preparing an analysis and drawing a salary.

In the second place, the Superintendent needs, even more than the Principal, the broad background of extensive and intensive advanced study in order to put himself in a position to resist the importunities of the quacks who flourish more vigorously and abundantly about our schools than anywhere else. The qualified superintendent is then a Doctor of Philosophy, but a doctor in the essential meaning of the degree and not merely a narrowly trained Master who has done a minor piece of research—a Doctor, indeed, even though he may never have been awarded the degree.

But, after all, the successful principal who is thoroughly qualified academically and professionally has not necessarily the critical qualifications which suit the Superintendency of Schools. The difference between the two comes in that aspect of temperament which we commonly call talent. We sometimes hear it said that "the good Lord never intended Mr. —————— to be a superintendent of schools." That is another way of saying that the good superintendent is an individual who is possessed of a rare balance in his temperamental qualities and of interests which are appropriate to the office. Intellectual and cultural interests in general are, of course, to be taken for granted, but the man is handicapped unless he has political interests and political talents as well—in the correct and worthy meaning of "political." I suppose the last can be made concrete by saying that he must have a genuine interest in people, in the processes of leading and managing men, and a keen sense of his place in a democratic order of society. Years ago I was in the habit of urging local superintendents to read John Fiske's *The Beginnings of New England*, which I thought a singularly illuminating portrayal of the social circumstances out of which our American phase of democracy has emerged. I believe I was right, but I do not suppose that many of them followed the advice. Probably it would not be good advice today, but in substance it would be good advice to urge reading and associations which would arouse an appreciation of the nature of our institutions and the place of officers like the Superintendent of Schools in their presence. I have known Governors, and we have all known a President or two, who were failures in their essential purposes because they did not understand their offices, and yet they were elective officers. How much easier is it for a Superintendent of Schools, who is of necessity an appointive officer, to fail for the same reason.

PART III

SCHOOL SYSTEM

INTRODUCTION

IN THE preceding divisions of our study we have been concerned in a critical purpose with, first, the School as institution and then with the University and various technical institutions and, second, with the structure of the American School. All the way along we have been demonstrating defects—most of them survivals of obsolete social conditions—which may go far to explain the ineffectiveness of our educational effort. In so doing, we have been proceeding from the proximate cause to the more nearly proximate. We now come to what to most people would seem the obvious center of things, namely, the organization of the school system as a whole and the character of the control which is applied to it through legal and democratic processes. It would seem to be clear enough that defects in structure, in curriculum, and in method must ultimately be traceable to those who have the system under control and to the limitations of that control. There is much truth in that view.

Nevertheless, here, as in most things social, you can never put your finger on cause, as cause is found in physics and to a less extent in biology. It is not possible to note university degeneration and say: "Here is the trouble; mend this and all will be well." Nor can we any better make the same remark of an obviously bad school structure or of an obsolete school system. There is no such thing as *vis medicatrix naturae* in the situation. Amendment must be personal and social rather than natural. The grave defects may be admitted, and we may say with truth that if they were corrected, efficiency would at least become possible. But, in the last analysis, who is to do the correcting?

At first blush the answer is: "Why of course the people in the form of popular demand." And yet that is completely to reason in a circle. Our fundamental assumption itself is that the whole educational setup exists for the enlightenment of the body politic. We can scarcely turn around and ask the public to correct the defects in our schools and school system. Is there any way out of the vicious circle?

If we turn back into recent history for the facts, we can see one clear instance in which a whole profession has been lifted to an higher plane of competency and effectiveness in less than a generation. The reader will recognize, I hope, that we are speaking of the Faculty of Medicine. It is plainly in the records that the medical renaissance of of the past thirty years did not originate in legislative enactment nor yet in public demand; it was brought to accomplishment from within the profession itself. The scientific bases upon which it was built had existed for many years, and the advance itself cannot inaccurately be described as the diffusion of rational, scientific methods of thought throughout the whole profession. Rational control of maladies was substituted for empiricism in the treatment of disease. Scientific diagnosis took the place of shrewd guesswork. In general, well-founded methods of thought were communicated to young medical men in the place of having them conning the rules for dealing with well-known symptoms.

So it must be with the whole field of Public Instruction and, indeed, with educational and cultural institutions in general. Reconstruction must issue, if at all, out of the intelligence and devotion of well-informed school people, teachers, school officers, and students, who have come to see that instruction is not a matter of varying popular fads which win space in the newspapers, nor yet of pedagogical eloquence, but is rather a matter of searching for significant facts, coming to well-founded conclusions as to what the facts mean, and then insisting that such conclusions shall govern in the place of mere tradition, the sentimentalities of speculative philosophy, or the vagaries of fashionable pseudo-science. Nor will they get any orders from the public, either directly or indirectly, for the people do not know any more about schools and education than, thirty or forty years ago, they knew what was wrong with Medicine or indeed that anything was wrong at all. The only pressure that is likely to be brought to bear on school people will probably come from increasing refusal of legislatures and other appropriating bodies to furnish school money. The ultimate attitude of the public is likely to be: "You are not delivering the goods according to your promises. Do not ask us what is the matter: you are supposed to know what is the matter or at least to be able to find out and correct your faults. We cannot do it for you. If you will not or cannot, then you must not ask us to support you."

CHAPTER XII

THE SCHOOL SYSTEM AS IT IS

WE COME to the School System, or the organization, support, and control of schools under which it is presumed that they will be able to achieve the institutional purpose of the School in Society. Note, however, that we are not concerned with the educational system as a whole, including universities and technological institutes. We are concerned with Public Instruction, with the common schools whether they be continuous in structure or discontinuous.

I. SOCIAL CHARACTER OF PUBLIC INSTRUCTION

If the School were not institutional but rather on the analogy of a farm or a business enterprise or the private practice of a profession, there need be no organized system or systems of schools at all. Each school would be an enterprise in itself, of interest and concern only to the parents who might furnish the children. Schools might be regulated in the statutes, as the trades and professions and commerce are regulated, but nothing further. In truth, that is at bottom the ideology behind our schools in the minds of most people. If you doubt it, attend a Parent Teachers meeting or read the communications signed "Anxious parent" or "Disgusted" or "Taxpayer" in the daily newspapers. The individual school, as they see it, is an enterprise in a free economy like other enterprises. Of course, the notion is quite inconsistent with the institution of free schools, for if the schools actually were what people suppose them to be, parents would pay tuition just as they pay the grocer, the landlord, the physician, or the lawyer.

And yet we undoubtedly do have free schools in State school systems in each of the forty-eight States.

The dilemma can be escaped only by realizing the truth about the social nature of our schools—the truth which those who understand them and who have in large measure been responsible for them have perceived these three hundred years—the principle, namely, that the School is institutional in its nature, that schools are maintained not primarily in the interest of the parents and their children but rather in the interest of the defense of commonwealths from the menace of an ignorant citizenry. Instead of being private enterprises either severally or communally maintained, they are part of the machinery of Government under popular sovereignty. So our courts have reasoned whenever the legal and constitutional bases of public tax-supported schools have been the issue.[1]

Nevertheless, through negligence and public ignorance of public affairs, most of the State systems which we have belong to a state of society which came to an end in the Eastern States well over a century ago and everywhere on the disappearance of frontier conditions sixty years ago or more. I propose to devote the present chapter to a description and analysis of our State school systems as they exist today.

II. THE SCHOOL DISTRICT

The cell of the political, instructional, and fiscal organism which is the American type of State school system is what is called the "School District," larger or smaller. Nobody can understand the school system or comprehend its obsolete character without some clear notions of this peculiar legal and political institution. Few there be who have any inkling of the nature of the thing save here and there a schoolmaster, or a rural politician and office-holder, or a very rare lawyer who happens to have been concerned in some school litigation.

In brief, the school-district system means that the great function of Public Instruction is conducted and in the main supported by more than a hundred and fifty thousand independent political units scattered through the nation, each of them conducted by a school board of one sort or another. By them teachers and school officers are employed, curriculums sanctioned or prescribed, money raised, supplies and equipment purchased, and pupils governed and graded.

[1] See E. P. Cubberley and E. C. Elliot, *State and County School Administration* (New York: Macmillan Co., 1915); Henry C. Morrison, *School Revenue* (Chicago: University of Chicago Press, 1930), chap. iv; and Newton Edwards, *The Courts and the Public Schools* (Chicago: University of Chicago Press, 1933).

In some of the States, Illinois, for example, there are more school-board members than there are teachers; and in the United States as a whole there must be nearly or quite as many.

These districts are set up for all sorts of purposes. The fundamental unit, however, is one set up to support and administer a local school system. As you drive through the country, you will now and then come upon a schoolhouse bearing over the door the sign "School District No. ——." That means that the building is the capitol of one of ten to thirty or forty little republics in that township or county. New York, Chicago, Philadelphia, and the rest of our cities differ from these in essential school organization principally in the fact they have scores or hundreds of school buildings instead of but one. But there are other kinds of school districts, all of them independent and each of them with a governing board of its own—high-school districts, supervisory districts, districts for vocational schooling, for the employment of school nurses—and many others.

Here, as in most things social and biological, we find it hard to come at any meaning at all, save by the road of history: how did it all get this way?

ORIGINS

I have pointed out earlier that our system is in most respects an evolution out of New England, and chiefly Massachusetts, origins. There is undoubtedly where the school-district idea came from, not only the general concept itself, but that rather hateful variation in the subtownship district. We have the great authority of Horace Mann to the effect that the latter never worked, not even in the beginning. The history of the school-district system of support and government shows what often happens in social evolution. A form corresponding to valid and useful substance appears in the customs because the substance responds to the requirements of social circumstance in a given age. The form persists and itself becomes institutionalized, in this case by taking on political and legal concepts. In the course of years the substantial meaning disappears in a new set of circumstances, but the form remains, and it is the form in which we do our thinking. Thought inevitably goes wrong when it rests on no valid substance. It is perhaps not too much to say that even our great cities in some ways organize their schools in the way they do because that was the right way in Colonial Massachusetts. Indeed, we might say that the style of our system is "late New England Colonial."

If we recall the development of schools in the Northeastern States in the seventeenth and eighteenth centuries, we are left in no doubt as to the principles upon which they acted when they acted on principle at all. Schools were social in their meaning and were indeed presumed to be at the heart of the free commonwealths which were growing up. The Colonial legislatures required that schools be maintained, and Massachusetts sanctioned the use of general taxation for the support of what the Colonial Government required. But there was no sign that the latter would itself assume the burden and responsibility. Maintenance of schools was a burden laid upon the towns: that was the kind of Government that was developing. It fitted the circumstances of the times. Why?

Suppose the Colony had set up the machinery of a system to be directly supported and administered by the Colonial Government, how could it have been operated? Bear in mind that any executive officer charged with the necessary duties could have reached most of the schools, and indeed of the towns in which the schools were located, only after a journey of several days, largely on horseback. He could have had no prompt communication with his subordinates scattered over the Colonial domain as it then was. Postal facilities, as we now know them, were nonexistent, and of course telegraph, telephone, railroads, rural free delivery, the automobile, and hard roads were all several generations in the future. A form of system came to be set up which was well suited to the circumstances; and we still have most of the essentials of that system in a day when we could visit schools by airplane if need be.

There was good geographical reason for the policy of local control and support throughout the Colonial and well over into the National period, while the State sanctified the form in the building-up of a sort of school jurisprudence covering the legal nature of the school district, pupillary status, teachers' contracts, and civil rights and obligations with respect to schools and attendance thereon.

So the form persists, long years—say five generations—after the circumstances which produced it disappeared.

THE SUBTOWNSHIP DISTRICT

But what has, on the whole, proved to be the most serious obstacle to progress in our Public Instruction—the subtownship district—owed its origin to social conditions which did not appear until the last quarter of the eighteenth century. These conditions have already been described in chapter viii in exhibiting the patternless character of our national and local communities. Farmers moved out and settled on cleared land, remote from the old village community. If they were to have schooling at all, a school must be established within walking distance for the children, and the formal political pattern already established meant that the school must be supported and controlled by this knot of farmers. Thus there came to be constituted organized school districts about each of the schoolhouses. The latter would ordinarily be one-room buildings, housing what in conception was a continuous school such as has been described in chapter iv. We call them "subtownship" districts because there were typically many of them in each township. They constituted what was known as the "district system" par excellence, but they were no more truly that than were systems founded on the township, city, or county. Indeed, the cities for many years were subdivided into these little districts. There are a few such cities still left.

Perhaps there was no other device which could have carried the elements of Civilization, as Civilization in the country then was, into the backwoods and beyond the frontiers, not only in New England but Westward, so long as the task of conquering a continent for Civilization remained. The task was long ago completed, but the subtownship district and the special districts for high schools and the like still remain in many of the States, including the largest, like a vermiform appendix in the body politic. Once more, substance had disappeared and form remained. It was toward the end of the nineteenth century before the subtownship began to be abolished in the States which had it, in favor of the town system and, later, county system; that is to say, the townships or in some cases the counties were made single districts. That eliminated the most troublesome symptom of disease but did not cure the disease itself, which is in the school-district concept.

You are not likely to find qualified people enough to make up from several hundred to twelve thousand good school boards in a single State. Nature does not produce ability and devotion in that degree of profusion, at least not in ordinary times. Even if you could do it, the good school boards would be well-nigh helpless in this day of the world's development.

III. LOCAL GOVERNMENT

It has been suggested that the political concept behind the local control of schools is perhaps more important than the visible school district itself. It is part and parcel of our devotion to Local Government. It is well to be clear about that concept itself, to see what it is and what it is not.

In practice we are likely to confuse Local Government with two other concepts which in reality have nothing to do with it. These are Municipal Self-government and State Sovereignty. All three are commonly lumped together as being the same thing by journalists and candiates for office. Let us take the last first and work backward.

STATE SOVEREIGNTY

State Sovereignty is a fundamental fact and principle in our Federal Republic. It means that certain sovereign powers are specifically committed to the Federal Government and others reserved to the several States. We thus have Federal Government and Government in forty-eight States in a dual sovereignty, but some of our lives and activities are regulated by one of the sovereigns and the rest by the other. That is all the Government we have. Town, city, and county governments are creatures of the States. State Government is not a form of local government; it is Commonwealth Government.

LOCAL SELF-GOVERNMENT

Local self-government, on the other hand, refers to the principle that matters which concern a given local community, and in their nature do not concern any other community, are left to the incorporated municipality to provide for and administer. That is Municipal Government proper, and it is the same thing when it is carried out by a township, an incorporated village, or a county, as it is when it is operated by a chartered city. Illustrations of Municipal Government are found in the maintenance of fire departments, streets and sewers, public parks, and enactment of ordinances to govern existence within the municipality as such. Traffic regulations and sanitary ordinances are good illustrations.

Local Government, however, as we are accustomed to the term, means the commitment of affairs which are admittedly Civil in their nature and not Municipal, that is to say, which are of the State and affect everybody in the State and often in other States as well, to the several counties and municipalities. We say that they are State affairs locally administered by *locally-chosen* officers. Instances in most States are the prevention and punishment of crime as distinguished from misdemeanors, the care of the public health, the maintenance of courts for the trial of both civil and criminal cases, the registering of deeds, the probating of wills, and especially the maintenance of Public Instruction. The tendency, no doubt, is to transfer these Civil functions to the State Government where they belong, but the process lingers unduly.

All the foregoing Local Government, not local self-government but Government locally conducted, has been part of our theory of Government itself. In point of fact, it is tradition handed down from other days, other conditions, and another kind of society. Some of it comes down to us from Medieval England and indeed from Anglo-Saxon England. In our country the tradition goes back to frontier days, isolated communities, and poor transportation, and then there was reason for it. There could be no central State administration of Civil affairs, when communication was so slow that even in the smaller States not even a message could be got through to the seat of Government and an answer received under several days at the best. Constabulary had to be local if criminals were to be apprehended at all. Courts had to be locally provided for, since it would be intolerable for litigants to be obliged to travel to a remote city in quest of justice.

These were all reasonable grounds for Local Government; but it is more than likely that other grounds were the main motive, or at least would have been motive if there had been no good geographical reasons. Here, again, is particularism in all public affairs as well as in those of the schools, and out of particularist interests and attitudes came intense suspicion of any kind of central Government. But keeping Government "in the hands of the people" meant not Commonwealth democracy but rather keeping it in their own hands and those of their neighbors. There may be something admirable in that, for it at least meant a willingness to assume the responsibilities of Government. That is the generous way to look at it all. More cynically, one may suspect that it arose out of an overweening love of having one's fingers in every pie. So long as conditions persisted in which tradition originated, and so long as the population was mainly British in origin, it worked fairly well, or at least not ill, and more than one chapter might be written showing how it did contribute to the secure foundations of the Republic.

But, once more, content changed and substance was lost. The form has lasted over to a day in which it is easier to get to the State Capital than it used to be to get to the county seat, and in which, so far from desiring to have a finger in every pie, most of us are unwilling to have a finger in any pie other than our own business. We desire honest and competent Government, but we cannot devote a large part of our lives to doing the governing ourselves. Moreover, the population has ceased to be mainly English with racial talent for self-government, and our body politic has come to be made up in large part of peoples who in their former homelands hardly conceived of such a thing as their own participation in Government. The obsolete form becomes a gift of grace to the machine politician, because it provides him with an abundance of offices with which to gratify his henchmen.

The school district is simply an extreme and special case of Local Government, and the subtownship district an ultra-extreme case.

QUASI-CORPORATION

Dillon in *Municipal Corporations* has this to say about school districts large and small:

An incorporated city or town sometimes embraces by legislative provision two *distinct corporations*, as, for example, the municipal and the school corporations existing within the same territory. It is in such cases a distinct corporation for school purposes. . . . . More generally, however, *school districts* are organized under the general law of the State, and fall within the class of corporations known as *quasi*-corporations. . . . . It [the school district] is but an instrumentality of the State, and the State incorporates it that it may the more effectively discharge its appointed duties.

This corporate character has important consequences in the whole popular conception of the School and in the manner in which schools are carried on.

In the first place, let the legal theory be what it may, the corporate character of the school district makes the School as enterprise conform to the ideology of a communally-supported undertaking maintained for the benefit of citizens who have children of pupillary age, and the School as an instrumentality of the Commonwealth falls into the background and is forgotten. It becomes hard for people to understand the School as an institution or to see it as anything else than a public enterprise set up for their special benefit, conducted according to their ideas and desires in curriculum, methods of teaching, and extra-curriculum activities. Hence it is notoriously easy for ill-considered and even nonsensical instruction to invade the schools and divert them entirely not only from their general social function but from their civil purpose as well, under the eloquent leadership of an army of quacks who no doubt make the most enthusiastic gland doctor green with envy.

Second, while the indubitable civil function of the schools is analogous to those of the courts, the civil service, and the Army and Navy, that is to say, the function of an instrument of democratic Government, the corporate character puts teachers and school officers in the status of labor under contract. We do not contract with the servants of the State and Federal Governments: we elect them or appoint them or enlist them. A formidable body of law has grown up around the contractual relations of teachers.

One of the most unfortunate consequences is the universal tendency of the best teachers to drift into the wealthier districts and into those in which the teaching is easiest. The effect is that the districts which have but slender fiscal resources, and those in which teaching is most difficult—and which by consequence need good teaching most—have to put up with relatively inferior and frequently incom-

petent teaching. We do not allow the wealthier and more comfortable sections to monopolize the best judges, nor do we reserve the
most desirable Army and Navy service to the best soldiers and sea-
men.

While few people in the cities or larger towns have any notion that
they are citizens of school districts, supposing that the term is reserved to something in the rural sections, nevertheless the school-district ideology appears as truly in the large cities as in the crossroads
country schoolhouse. The possible exception is in those chartered
cities in which by the terms of the charter the school system is part
of the city government. But Chicago, for instance, is a school district in Cook County, having its own budget and not on all fours
with Fire, Police, Streets, and other municipal enterprises.

STATE CONTROL

Has, then, the State Government no control over its instrumentalities? It has more control than was formerly the case in all the
States, and in a few of them it has substantially full control, but in
all that counts toward actual efficiency in Public Instruction the answer is still, in the main, "No."

State control is almost entirely in the domain of legislation governing the civil rights and obligations of citizens in respect to taxation
and the schooling of their children; governing the institution of
school districts and the conduct of their affairs; and to some extent
prescribing what shall and shall not be taught. From that point on,
State regulation appears chiefly in court decisions which arise out of
litigation instituted by citizens who conceive themselves to be
wronged by some action arising out of the conduct of schools. Thus,
there is legislative and judicial regulation aplenty, but the all-important executive and administrative control appears almost entirely in
the local school boards.

True enough, either the office of Superintendent of Public Instruction or that of the State Board of Education is now to be found in
every State, but its duties are chiefly:

1. Executive control of State enterprises like teachers' colleges.

2. Ministerial functions, such as computing the apportionment of
State school money.

3. Semijudicial functions, such as hearing complaints concerning the conduct of local schools and issuing approval to schools, usually high schools.

4. Hortatory missions over the State, in which it is hoped to arouse the people to better efforts and more intelligence through sheer eloquence.

INEQUALITY IN RESOURCES

The absurdity of the school-district form of managing and supporting schools has chiefly appeared in works which exhibit and analyze gross inequalities in the money resources of the several districts in all the States which still have the system. That attack runs back fifty years and longer. It is perhaps the most critical problem of all, or at least the most immediate.

Most of the States have essayed the task of correcting the evils by the apportionment of State school aid according to some mathematical formula. I have shown that any such policy involves a mathematical absurdity.[2] The only way in which inequalities in support, and other inequalities as well, can be eliminated is through consolidation of management and support in the State Government itself, even as the cities have similarly abolished their own internal inequalities.

But even if we could find a formula which would accomplish all our mathematical aspirations, so that the resources per child to be schooled would be on a parity throughout the State, and so that money could be thrown into each district according to the varying *instructional* requirements of children, and so that the tax burdens in all of several thousand school districts would also be on a parity, it does not follow that *educational* opportunities would be made equal. That depends upon the quality of the supervisory and teaching personnel that can be secured, and the latter in turn upon the qualities of the school-board members who are available in the several districts. Moreover, mere equalization of educational opportunity gets us nowhere. The education may be meager, misdirected, quite without validity. What is imperative in the modern world, in the interests of both justice to individuals and of sound society and good Gov-

---

[2] See *School Revenue*, chap. viii and esp. Sec. V.

ernment, is General Education for all future citizens, not "an education" that is as good here as it is there and adequate nowhere.

The sum of the whole matter seems plainly to be that the school-district system itself is so obsolete, so far removed from the society in which it was once valid, that it has become an incurable malady in our commonwealths.

IV. EVOLUTION OF THE LOCAL UNIT

To leave the last statement wholly unqualified would be to be guilty of gross overemphasis. For more than half a century past many of the States have been taking steps designed to correct the evil, and it is worth while to review such steps for the purpose especially of seeing what they have all been tending toward.

1. The absurdity of the division of cities into fiscally and politically independent school districts long ago become manifest and, save in a negligible number of instances, that practice has long been forgotten. The city school district is made coterminous with the municipality. Commonly the district conception remains, but the term has disappeared in ordinary usage, as, for instance, in Indiana, where we hear the expression "school city." Often the only thing left of the old corporate district idea is seen in the fact that "Board of Education" is the same thing under another name. Be that as it may, there comes to exist full equalization throughout the city, save inequalities which are traceable to the human limitations of the governing board and its officers.

2. Similarly, the subtownship districts have long ago been abolished in several of the States which formerly had them, and the township district substituted for the State as a whole. The effect is of course the same as in the preceding paragraph.

3. Continuing, the county unit appears—or rather county district, for the county in such cases is the same kind of corporation as the subtownship or town district—but it appears in incomplete form. All schools in the county, outside chartered cities ordinarily, are brought under a county board of education, with a county superintendent as the executive of the board and appointed by it, and not merely an elective ministerial officer.

4. Finally, all distinctions in political and fiscal local units are abolished, save perhaps for a single overpowering city, and we have the State unit, with a State Board of Education, and a Commissioner as its executive officer, in direct control of all schools, and teachers and school officers a State body of professional people. Three States —Delaware, Maryland, and New Hampshire—have in substance, by one route or another, reached that stage, but I can find no other of which the statement could truly be made.

Amelioration of inequality.—In this process of evolution inequality has been mitigated in the only way in which that evil can be mitigated and finally abolished.

In a State which still retains the subtownship system, there may easily be a range of fiscal inequality within the State, amounting to 250 or more to 1. That is to say, there will be one district somewhere in the State which has 250 times the taxable wealth behind each child to be schooled which some other district has, and the others string along between.

When a State goes on the town-district basis, the range will fall to about 10–15 to 1—a great improvement over the preceding but still entirely unacceptable.

Similarly, the true county unit brings the range down to 5 or less to 1, and, of course, the State unit abolishes the range altogether, even as was the case when the cities abolished their internal districts.

OPPOSITION

In all this transition from very small units to larger and larger units, pretty much the same opposition has been found everywhere and always. The school district as a political and legal conception has been defended largely on the following grounds, whether the issue be passing from the subtownship district to the town district or from that to the county unit.

1. *It keeps the schools close to the people and is thus a corner-stone of democracy.*

That is a sort of *ex post facto* reasoning. The local control of schools was not set up on any kind of political theory but because that was the only way in which it seemed feasible to get any schools at all. If the admitted purpose of public schools, ever since the Massachusetts Act of 1642, reaffirmed by the Northwest Ordinance of 1787, and justified in practically every court decision which has had to pass on the constitutionality of any kind of a public school, has been to carry out a State function in the schooling of young citizens, then it is of small moment whether the schools are kept close to the people and of great moment whether it is made likely that representatives of the people will carry on effective schools.

Local control of schools is not a corner-stone of democracy; effective schools are such a corner-stone.

2. *It performs the cardinal function of throwing responsibility on the people in their local assemblies.*

If good schools redounded to the exclusive benefit of the local communities which support them, and the local community alone suffered from the consequences of poor schools; and if, further, there were no such things as Federal and State elective officers—then the contention might be sound. But that is not the case.

The schooling or lack of it which children receive in a particular local community has its effect on the whole State and on the Nation. That would be true even if every child were destined to spend his life where he was born and went to school, for he would still be a voter in Federal and State affairs, but it is notorious that only a small proportion of us are now living and carrying on our adult activities in our native towns or even in our native States. Local responsibility for good schools is too remote to be felt.

3. *It gives local people an education in the conduct of schools through service on school boards.*

I think the plea can sufficiently be answered by putting the simple question, "Do the schools exist for the education of school boards or for that of the children?"

4. *We must avoid centralization, and a multitude of school districts is the best way to do it.*

That is, of course, mere verbal tradition lingering on since the election of 1800.

Centralization in *administrative* affairs is almost always bad, but what is centralization? Well, to confine ourselves to school experience, if examination papers are made up in the superintendent's office and the returns corrected there, that is a good illustration of centralization. It is worse when the same thing is done from the State capital. But *consolidation* is not centralization. When all the schools of a city are brought together in a single organization, there is no centralization about it. What has been done is in the interest of justice to the school children and of efficiency in Public Instruction. The schools are governed and administered, no doubt, as one system, but no more centralized than when they are governed by a board of three in a small rural district.

5. *A multitude of school districts gives room for experiment.*

That may be called the academic plea for localism.

Experimenting is an highly technical process, and so far as schools are concerned it belongs in the psychological laboratory and other laboratories in the search for light on educational and pedagogical processes. Even so, most of the experimenting has been done by the race and is recorded in history. This whole volume essays a critical study of the experience of our people with schools and universities and technical schools.

6. *Too many eggs in one basket.*

An objection to giving up local control rather than a defense of the district system may perhaps be conveniently summarized in the phraseology of this section title. Of the six, it is altogether the most respectable and is ordinarily quite sincere—which none of the others usually is.

There are a good many school, city, and village school districts which secured special charters years ago in order to make it possible for them to have good schools of their own, for which they were willing to pay and which they were entirely capable of managing. People in such districts are naturally reluctant to commit themselves to the control of a Board of Education in a larger unit about whose capacity they are at best uncertain. But granted that the objection has merit, it has that quality only as the principle is defensible that schools exist primarily for the good of the community which supports them. We know well enough that the principle is not defensible. Excellent schools for the children of an enlightened community will not solve the problem of an enlightened citizenry in the State at large.

But all the foregoing objections, or most of them, are now and long have been merely academic scruples furnished ready-made to the gullible and temperamentally intransigent by intriguing and often corrupt politicians.

When the proposal was first made to abolish the subtownship district in New Hampshire, as the story came to me from one who had been a member of the reforming group, they went to the legislative boss of the day, the original of Jethro Bass in Churchill's *Coniston*, for permission and support. His response was: "D-don't w-want to d-do that—t-take c-care of lot of them that w-way." That has been the real reason for objections to enlarging the local unit. It was the reason why Massachusetts had to abolish the subtownship district five times before it would stay abolished, why New York not so very long ago got it abolished and then had to restore it in the next administration, and why Indiana a few years ago rejected the county unit.

The way our democracy as a form of government actually works is sometimes through bribery and corruption on a larger or smaller scale but far more often by appeal to the vanity of men—and women. "Take care of a lot of them that way." Uncle Reuel as a machine politician knew perfectly well that one of his chief problems was to provide his henchmen with enough offices to distribute, and places on school boards appealed greatly to the vanity of people—and later on to the lovers of graft in sundry forms. Two or three thousand such places in a small State were a gold mine of influence for his lieutenants. That was more than half a century gone by. The political observer in other times and another part of the country must be aware of another gold mine for the machine politician in places on election boards for women whose vanity is thus tickled to the point of worship of the dispenser of such blessings. Curiously enough, in the old days—I know not how it may be now—secret societies wondrously helped in the great task of democratic government—in this way. Energetic aspirants to official dignity could usually be satisfied, and more than satisfied, when there were not enough offices to go round, if they were helped into an office in which they would be addressed as Worshipful, or Noble, or Illustrious.

Learning from experience, our people have been adjusting their school systems from the beginning, hastening the process somewhat for the last fifty years; but the process has been purely empirical and pragmatic, without widely recognized principles upon which deliberate action could be founded. The effect is that adjustment has been altogether too slow to keep pace with advancing material culture and the rapid social changes which are the consequence. Some States are still in the main on a basis which suited frontier days, even the Colonial frontier. Three perhaps have completed or nearly completed, at least for the time being, the adjustment which reasoning based on facts suggests as the complete adjustment. Other States are at various stages between. All of them in varying degrees are still under the curse of ignorant or corrupt politics. We ought to realize by this time that muddling through in any kind of public matters is no longer safe.

In the next chapter we shall seek for some of the principles which ought to be employed in the rational setting-up of a modern public school system.

CHAPTER XIII

A MODERN SCHOOL SYSTEM

THE preceding chapter has shown on almost every page, or at least suggested, how obsolete is our national system of Public Instruction, how illy adapted to the requirements of Society, to an order of living which in its very nature is always changing and expanding in the relationships among humans in which all societies consist. To place our State systems on the best and surest foundations is to discover the rationale of an adaptable system good in any society and capable of prompt adjustment without sacrifice of principle. That is an ambitious task, altogether beyond the capacity of any one student and certainly beyond the space available in a single chapter. While that is doubtless true, if we have in mind the problem in its entirety, it is perhaps not too much to expect that we may be able to throw some light on what are the sound lines of development.

To state all the foregoing is to state nothing new. The present author is not the first to point out the absurd incongruities which are inherent in the whole school-district conception in all its implications. Some writers have set themselves down to the task of proposing amendments by merely "standing to reason." Things cannot be done that way; at least the present writer has no ambitions to try it. Rather, we shall follow the method used in our study of school structure. We shall adhere to the belief that wisdom was not born with any of the generations now living and that our predecessors for the most part acted according to reasonable judgments in their time. We shall remind ourselves of the experience of our people in seeking to make over their systems, and we shall seek to substitute for their empirics some principles which will be useful in guiding us to a more deliberate and rational course of action.

A. THE ENLARGING UNIT

I. THE LARGER POLITICAL AND FISCAL UNIT

If we turn back for the moment to the outline of development found on page 266, we can see plainly enough the gross picture of what has been taking place and from it derive what is perhaps the simplest and most enlightening of our principles. The picture may be summed up as one of an enlarging political and fiscal unit of school support and management.

Development, however, has not been merely *enlargement* but also *comprehension*, that is to say, enlargement has tended toward the inclusion of all local schools out to the boundaries of some political unit other than the subtownship district—first in township and city, then county, and finally State.

If we recall the history of popular movements which eventuated in legislation, we shall see that the reasons urged for change have been, in the main, three.

First, the patent absurdity of the old-time school-district system which became manifest when one such district after another came to have legal organization but no schools. A recent bulletin of the United States Office of Education shows that at the time of publication there were thirty-four districts which had no schools in Pennsylvania alone.[1] That sort of thing has been common enough in the subtownship States, ever since the drift of population to the cities began. Inflexibility in town-district systems, as well as in subtownship systems, is illustrated by an experience of my own.

I was once besought to come to the aid of a town school district to the extent of drafting an act to relieve them of surplus school money, no less. The district had for several years been in receipt of greatly increased revenue derived from taxation of the estate of a rich man who had recently become a resident. They had raised only the minimum required by law, but that amounted to more than they could possibly spend, and funds accumulated in a frozen condition. And yet there were two hundred and more towns and cities in the State which could very gratefully make use of that money in carrying out their obligations as "instrumentalities of the State."

Second, neglect, arising out of the fact that nowhere can you find school boards enough, composed of persons of intelligence and character, to equip several thousand, or several hundred for that matter, of these small districts in the same State.

Third, fiscal inequality and injustice, always a powerful motive

[1] Alves, Anderson, and Fowlkes, *Local School Unit in Ten States* (U.S. Office of Education Bull. 10 [Washington, D.C., 1938]).

for abolishing the subtownship system, in spite of the principle that gross inequality applies to the town and county systems as well as to the other.

Enlargement in principle.—Now enlargement brings about improvement not merely because it "seems to work well" but because there is an ameliorating principle in its very nature.

In the first place, it reduces the number of necessary school boards from thousands to hundreds and thus makes it a good deal easier to find qualified people to serve.

Second, superannuated districts automatically disappear.

Third, the range of fiscal inequality is necessarily greatly shortened by reason of the fact that there is far less room for variation in economic circumstances.

Clearly, every argument that has ever justified enlargement of the local unit has the more forcibly justified the ultimate unit, namely, the State itself.

THE COUNTY UNIT

For several years past there has tended to be a good deal of faith among school people in the county as the ultimate political and fiscal unit. Perhaps confidence is fading out; perhaps the enthusiasm was only fashion after all. Be that as it may, the faith is so very much misplaced that I think it desirable to interrupt our main argument briefly to clear up that issue.

In the first place, especially in the States which still adhere to the subtownship district, there is undoubtedly a county organization, but it is perfunctory and long obsolete. The county superintendent elected on a party ticket is a wholly superfluous ministerial officer. He has no executive and administrative powers and duties; there is no county board of education. Typically, the local school districts, through their school boards, make up their local budgets within legal limits, and the aggregate of them all is then consolidated in a county levy. But the revenue thus derived is distributed back to the districts in proportion to the budgets which the school boards have adopted. The county itself is neither a political nor a fiscal unit; and the districts are such.

The county would become both political and fiscal unit, if:

1. There were constituted a County Board of Education, with a professional County Superintendent of Schools as its appointee and

executive, having full executive and administrative control of all the schools in the county, in the same sense as that in which the ordinary city school board through its city superintendent has such control within the city school district; in such wise that there were no districts smaller than the county and no school boards other than the county board.

2. School support were on the basis of a county budget, administered by the Board according to the several needs of all schools and pupils in the county; and the budget were supported by a county tax levy.

In that case, there would be a real political and fiscal County Unit.

Now there are several States which purport to have that kind of organization, but a close scrutiny of the statutory setup shows that the real test of the political and fiscal unit does not exist. There are usually still a good many more or less autonomous school districts, and the county control is only in part real. Moreover, at the best, the cities in the county are commonly excluded from the county unit, which is to surrender the whole principle. However, some gain is made, and the local district bulks much smaller in these than it does in most of the States. Kentucky, for instance, reports 300 districts— 120 counties and 180 independent—as contrasted with 4,879 of all sorts in the comparable State of Iowa. In North Carolina there are 167 districts, of which 100 are counties and 67 are cities. In Tennessee there are 95 counties and 79 cities and special districts.[2]

The County an obsolete political unit.—The chief ground, however, for lack of confidence in the County as the ultimate unit of school support and government is in the principle that the County itself is nearly everywhere an obsolete political unit.

In the South and West the County was commonly the original local unit. In sparsely-settled regions civil government had to be organized long before urbanization even began. In the Northeast the reverse was true. But in either section the unit was a convenience where certain civil functions had to get performed in which there

---

[2] All the data for States reported in this chapter are from the latest available documents. There is no guaranty that the findings are up to date. Nobody knows what a session of a State legislature may bring forth. But, after all, these chapters are accounts of the evolution of ideas and not an history of legislation.

would not be business enough in each of the several local communities, while the State Capital was too remote. Today, most of the original reasons for the County have disappeared, some of them with great improvement in communications, the rest with the growth of State constabularies and organized militia.

It is perhaps not too much to say that, just as the subtownship school district was a response to the settlement of isolated farms, so the County as a political unit ceased to have any substantial meaning after the automobile and the modern highway net became common.

II. THE END OF THE ROAD

The logic of the enlarging political and fiscal unit evidently tends toward the State itself becoming the unit, comprehensive of all schools in respect to both control and financial support. At that point the local "instrumentalities of the State" disappear, and the Government of the State or Commonwealth assumes the burden of maintaining and governing and administering its school system, in an executive as well as in a legislative and judicial sense. The school district of Colonial and frontier times, having long since served its purpose, lapses, and with it goes corporate as well as local political implications.

The argument is greatly reinforced by the fact that it is possible to cite the three States mentioned in the last chapter as having in substance reached that end. From their experience we can learn much. For the convenience of students of school administration I present in an appendix sketches of the organization in each. Suffice it at this point to say that the cardinal tests are met by each according to the following list:

1. An appointive State Board of Education is made supreme in executive and administrative control of the school system of the State save that Baltimore in Maryland and Wilmington in Delaware are left wholly or in part outside the State unit.

2. The support of schools is made, directly in Delaware and indirectly in Maryland and New Hampshire, a responsibility of the State.

3. The teaching force of the State is already in essentials a State force and, without much doubt, will presently become fully that.

III. COMPARABLE EVOLUTION IN OTHER STATE FUNCTIONS

We have in the preceding chapter devoted some attention to Local Government as contrasted with Municipal self-government and have seen how necessary Local Government was in an earlier state of community development. It will perhaps be useful to trace the evolution of some other State functions from control by a multitude of small governing and supporting units to support and control by the State Government itself. We shall see that the enlargement of the local school unit to the point where it disappears in the State unit is but part of a process which is not peculiar to educational enterprises—a process which is part of the evolution of our political conceptions as we have grown from universal frontier conditions to what is perhaps one of the most complex communities in the world.

ROADS, STREETS, AND HIGHWAYS

Over the larger part of the country the maintenance and support of schools has long been the largest single item in the gross local budget. Easily next has been the maintenance of roads. We might well anticipate that we should find a story in the development of a road system comparable to what we have found in the development of a school system. And so we do.

As we all know, in 1607 and 1620, in what afterward became Virginia and Massachusetts, there was no such thing as ways of land communication with which civilized men had long been familiar.

So our people started from scratch.

Especially in the Bay Colony after 1630, population increased rapidly and pushed inland, establishing new villages as they went. In the country at large that process continued over into the present century, although the Census of 1880 disclosed the fact that there was "no more frontier." It is easy enough to see that for nearly three hundred years the building of roads has been one of our chief problems—roads to connect farms with the trading centers, city streets, roads to make Provincial and State capitals and the county towns accessible, roads to connect one village with another. It was a long, long time before any township, not to say any county, any State, or the Nation, had such a thing as a road net. Distance travel was chiefly by water and, in the South, a large part of local travel as well.

There was scarcely such a thing as a true highway in the United States until after the completion of the National Road over the Alleghenies in the early part of the nineteenth century. The function of highway was for the most part discharged only by the accident that the roads of one town happened to make physical contact with those of the next.

How was a road system to be developed, as population increased and spread inland from ocean and waterway? The answer is that it could not be *developed*, for nobody knew what to plan for. It had to grow.

The whole problem of road communication had to be met locally by a people which in those days had a genius for managing their own affairs and postponing the crossing of bridges—metaphorically as well as literally—until they got to them. The outcome was that they provided country roads much as they provided country schools. The subtownship road district suggested itself, as did the subtownship school district, as being a feasible way to achieve a public end.

In time there came to be distance travel, as farmers, perhaps twice a year, hauled their surplus product to the nearest seaport or large trading center, where Sunday dresses and fine furniture, among other contributions to the standard of living, could be had in exchange. There thus came to be customary "routes" through many townships and several counties. Legislative sanction and requirements of road maintenance came to be required, as they had been required in the evolving school system. Turnpikes were sometimes chartered, as the old academies were chartered. For a long time these went far to solve the problem, since the turnpike company could be depended on to keep up an highway as an highway rather than as a succession of town roads. Bear in mind that the only way in which either town or turnpike company could be forced to keep roads in safe condition was by suit at law against the company or the town. In short, you see, the method of *administering* the road system was by litigation, just as the only method of *administering* State school systems in most of the States today is litigation plus politics plus pressure groups.

But the fateful thing with roads, as with schools, was that having found a way to keep up roads through the road district, they kept on

doing it long after they knew how to build good roads if the legal
highway system had let them. John McAdam *died* in 1836.

Very much as in the case of the school district, the town or county
system for roads generated unbearable neglect and incompetency;
and, as soon as through routes developed, grievous fiscal injustice.
The neglect is understandable: that is what always happens when
what is everybody's business naturally becomes nobody's business.
The fiscal injustice arose from the fact that along the routes this
township would have good road foundations and few watercourses to
be bridged, whereas the next might easily have many bridges to
build and keep up, and long stretches over boggy ground which had
to be corduroyed or filled. And yet it was the wider community
which profited from the through route rather than the towns which
kept it up.

Here, then, is an accurate picture of school support and control,
and the need of equalization laws, done in a medium of dirt roads.

That state of things persisted at least half a century beyond the
time when the conditions which brought it about had disappeared.
We can still see traces of it when, traveling over a great United
States highway, we are reminded by a sudden change in the character of the surface that we have passed into another county.

Nevertheless, when automobiles, which transmit the badness of
roads most effectively to the consciousness of drivers, had come to
exist in the proportion of something like one to every family, the
highway system on a national scale came into existence and made
rapid strides toward efficient maintenance. In the fall of 1919, there
were scarcely a hundred miles of surfaced highway between Buffalo
and Chicago. Today, if a Roman of Hadrian's time could come back
to visit us, I fancy that the thing he would most appreciate in our
national economy would be our highways. U.S. 20 would seem like
his Appian or Flaminian Way, only a lot longer. After all, it takes a
long time to recover Civilization when it has once been lost out of
the mores. Our present-day roads and highways, however, were
made possible only through the organization of nonpolitical State
Highway Commissions, equipped with a trained personnel of engineers and modern machinery and given authority over highways as
distinguished from streets and byways. The end of the story comes

in those States in which the layout, construction, support, and maintenance of all accepted highways are in the hands of State Highway Commissions, and the revenue is derived from gasoline taxes earmarked for that purpose and that alone.

The evolution of the highway net is almost a complete parallel to the evolution of the school system, starting later and reaching an advanced stage earlier.

CONSTABULARY

The salient defect in the local support and management of both schools and highways has been neglect and incompetency. The function of the constabulary, or the prevention of crime, shows much the same defects, and the course of correction and improvement follows much the same lines.

Our record in the exercise of the police function is one of the black spots in our national history, the one most often cited by those who are skeptical about the ability of the folk to govern. There is not in mind the exercise of the police power in legislation, in itself a sorry chapter, but rather the executive function, which is the Constabulary, a police matter, but not all of the latter. Failure in dealing with criminals, and often silly injustice and arrogant tyranny in the persecution of the inoffensive, have given us altogether the worst criminal record among the civilized nations.

But our police organization is in the main local and always has been, all the way back to "watch-and-ward" days. Much of it, like much else in our devotion to localism, comes down to us from old days in England. Periodically, an honest and effective district attorney turns up who overhauls the incompetent, undisciplined, and corrupt local police, and for a time things are better. But the district attorney is an elective officer, and that means that he usually has political ambitions. He presently hears the invitation, "Come up higher, friend," and that is the end of reform—until the next time. His action is, I suppose, a reflection of our passion for administration by litigation.

And yet it is noteworthy that exactly the same force which drives about in squad cars, lounging in disarray, the very picture of undiscipline, when put on traffic duty will show admirable competency and in personal tenue decidedly "look the part." Traffic duty on city streets is very much a local interest. The apprehension of a murderer at the best makes news.

Our fire departments are variants of police, that is to say, they exercise a police function in the community. And yet we seldom hear of an incompetent city fire department; most of them are wonderfully skilful, intelligent, and accomplished in dealing with fire. But what they have to do is acutely a local interest. No reforming district attorney is necessary to keep them up to the mark; public sentiment does that.

On the other hand, some of the States have organized efficient State constabularies, not motor police who are also ordinarily a State body. The well-organized State Constabulary is usually an efficient, intelligent, well-disciplined, semimilitary body of men trained for its work.

The story is much the same with schools, highways, and constabulary. From the neighborhood road district to the Highway Commission; from the village constable to the New York, Pennsylvania, or Texas State Constabulary, or the Royal Mounted in Canada—the development follows much the same lines as might be followed in our school systems—from the subtownship school district to the Maryland State Board of Education.

Apparently, when a given function is in its nature municipal, as are fire protection, traffic control, city parks, streets and sewers, and a host of others, it tends to get well done locally. When the function is civil rather than municipal, as is the case with schools, highways, and constabulary, it tends to be poorly done locally.

Much more might be written, but we are interested only in seeing that the correct organization of Public Instruction is only a particular case in the working-out of a general principle. The latter will in the end have its way, but to leave it at that is to wait a long time, perhaps to the beginning of another period of Dark Ages. If we can see principles at work, and in their light set our houses in order, we may yet escape the penalties of ignorance meted out to those who believe that we can always muddle through and that in the end the cult of democracy will save us.

B. The State Unit

In all the foregoing there has been unfolding a picture of what social forces seem to have been trying to teach us to do. In this part of the chapter it is sought to demonstrate more at length what is involved in the State Unit of control and support and particularly in what respects anything of that sort departs from the concepts attached to local control and support to which most of us are habituated.

I. THE HEART OF THE MATTER

The national problem in Public Instruction in the second quarter of the twentieth century, or any other century, is in fundamentals no different from what it was in the second quarter of the seventeenth in Colonial Massachusetts. It is the transmission of Civilization to the whole generation of children and young people who are presently to be part of our body politic.

The problem does not countenance a solution which merely provides for schools which may follow any courses which the vagaries, or the fads, or the ignorance, or the poverty of each of a hundred and fifty thousand different school boards and teaching bodies may dictate. The solution is positive and definitive, not opinionative and wilful and indeterminate. The task is not one of making it legally and fiscally possible for each of a multitude of local communities "to give *an* education suited to their needs"—or what they think are their needs and what is suited—but rather to guarantee that, so far as is humanly possible and in so far as circumstances do not prohibit, all children shall be put in possession of full General Education.

We have seen more than once that any factual and rational analysis of what we call "education" discloses that it is a natural process giving rise to natural products; that it is no more subject to the arbitrary whims of humans than are their own bodily processes; and that normal and valid Education is objective and determinate, to be apprehended by rational and positive methods of thinking which are the same as those employed in all scientific and philosophical inquiry rather than a matter of varying popular opinion. That the *methods of instruction*, on the other hand, which are intended to bring about Education must vary according to the present learning capacity of pupils is scarcely to be doubted but that, too, is a matter of objective apprehension and not a matter of the fashions of the day or of the uninformed opinion prevailing in different communities. The varying of methods of instruction, however, is altogether a different matter from varying education in order to suit individual needs. What is suited to the individual needs of all mankind is Education.

II. STATE BOARD OF EDUCATION

If there were no body of accumulated experience, as there is, it would still be inferable from the premises themselves that the task of guaranteeing General Education to all implies a unit for the government, administration, and support of schools which is coextensive with the sovereignty which undertakes the guaranty—a unit which is headed by an executive and administrative authority which is supreme in its functions throughout the area and in control of a fiscal system which is capable of directly reaching every school. In our Federal Republic the smallest unit which is capable of being used for the purpose is each one of our sovereign States.

Such an authority is, in our present use of terms, a State Board of Education.

BOARD AND LEGISLATURE

All State Boards of Education are of necessity constituted by the lawmaking bodies, and there the normal relation ends, save for the legislative function of appropriating money.

There is, however, a function connected with the administration of public schools which a legislature cannot delegate. It is the enactment of laws governing the civil rights and obligations of citizens, parents, and pupils, in so far as these are related to schooling. Herein come such matters as required school attendance, the kind of punitive discipline which the law will tolerate, and many other similar issues which from time to time arise. This is what is properly meant by the clause, "except as limited by law" in the New Hampshire act. The Board of Education is set up to govern and administer a school system but not to define civil rights and duties.

But in the very act of constituting such a board as has been described, a legislature provides that its regulations which are not repugnant to law shall have the force of law. It thus sets up a body, one of many in the modern world, which is empowered to make what is called administrative law. Others, State and Federal, are railways and utilities commissions, banking commissions, boards of health, highway commissions, police commissions, the Federal Reserve Board —and many others. The State Board of Education differs from all these, save highway and police commissions, in that it is the directorate of a great public enterprise, while the others supervise private enterprises.

The crucial thing is that, having created an executive and administrative board, the Legislature should henceforth refuse to meddle in the executive and administrative field.

One of the cardinal defects in our school system has been, and in most States still is, the fact that our legislatures, and by consequence our courts, act as State Boards of Education, even where there is nominally such a body in existence. The consequence is that they interfere with the Curriculum, with the grading of schools, with examinations, with school building design, with school government, with school budgets—and many other similar things. All that is executive and belongs in the field of administration. It is hard to think of anything more absurd to be made part of the law of the land than such things as eight grades, or the passing grade on a teachers' examination, or the use of a particular textbook. Such practices operate to create inflexibility, for laws cannot be changed at every session of a legislature and certainly not oftener. Moreover, they make it possible for minority pressure groups to get their way with respect to things which they desire to have "taught in the schools" and other things which they want the schools "to take up." In the end, the Curriculum and the School itself tend to become an hodgepodge of unrelated fragments—and those fragments badly conceived. One of the important ends to be served in erecting fully empowered State Boards of Education is to relieve legislatures of purely administrative measures and the courts of litigation which has little or nothing to do with either law and order or substantial justice.

All this is part and parcel of an abuse in our current political notions which has long persisted and still is very much to the fore, both at the State capitals and at Washington. Multitudes of our people, and apparently many of our legislators, seem never to have learned that our theory of Government, and all valid theory, differentiates sharply between legislative, executive, and judicial functions. They act as if Legislatures and Congress were boards of directors of which the Governors and the President were executive secretaries. Far from being "democratic process," it is one of the most effective ways of preventing democracy working at all. We elect our President and the Governors and indirectly all the officers and boards whom they appoint. They are on the whole far more representative of the people as a whole than are members of the legislative bodies.

MEMBERSHIP OF THE STATE BOARD OF EDUCATION

The State Board of Education is only indirectly representative, and even so it represents only the presumptive desire of the people to have good and efficient schools. Its measures are not political, for they would be the same whatever political party is dominant in the State or country. It is not representative of the many groups in our population: good and efficient schools are the same whether boys or girls are the pupils; whether the pupils are descendants of the original immigrants or of the many waves which have followed 1607 and 1620; whether they are the children of wage-earners, or farmers, or capitalists; of Catholic, or Jewish, or Protestant families; whether the schools are in the North, West, or South.

A Governor, in constituting the membership of the State Board, ought to have in mind solely the ablest men he can persuade to serve, and he ought resolutely decline to appoint members because of sex, color, racial antecedents, or because "representation" of constituent blocs in the population is demanded. The members certainly ought to be of the personal caliber of the men whom a good Governor would be likely to appoint on the State Tax Commission or the Board of Public Utilities.

III. THE ADMINISTRATIVE DISTRICT

A large part of the present chapter and the preceding have been devoted to criticism of the school district, both as a political unit and as a legal conception. That does not imply the proscription of the word "district" entirely—although if there were an equally convenient term, even that would be well, in order to escape the unsavory connotations it has collected.

Every elementary school in a city, and every high school if there be more than one, is necessarily given a *district* from which it draws its pupils, by act of the city Board of Education, and pupils who live outside the district boundaries are expected to attend school in another district. But such districts are administrative in their nature, and their boundaries are subject to change as equity and convenience dictate. They have no district boards of control; the schools are not supported by taxation within the administrative area. Such a district, in short, is not a political and fiscal unit.

Very much the same principle applies to the State at large. It may be convenient for administrative purposes that there should exist districts of suitable area, or larger cities, in order to make the State Board a real State Board, governing largely by administrative law rather than as a directorate, which is easily possible in the smaller States where the problems are not so formidable. But administrative law is not merely a set of rules and regulations; it is rather a well-thought-out set of principles which can be used for *guidance* rather than for express direction. Moreover, in order to avoid the vice of administrative centralization, to minimize the growth of bureaucracy, and to make it possible to vest school property in a legal and orderly manner, it may often be well to establish boards over some of the cities and wider areas and to constitute the boards themselves corporations. Such administrative units, however, should never be made political and fiscal units. Public Instruction in the State should be the same throughout the State. The regional boards should be appointed by the State Board and be made by law representative of the latter. The regional boards would bear much the same relation to the State Board which the city principal bears to his superintendent. That relation we have discussed at length in chapters x and xi.

IV. KEEPING THE SCHOOLS OUT OF POLITICS

The title of the section names an end ardently desired by enlightened people from the beginning. To many, the expression merely means that political partisanship should have no place in the appointment of teachers and school officers. But that is a small matter today compared with personal intrigue, favoritism, nepotism, and an hundred other abuses which make for avoidance of the sole test which ought to prevail, namely, the test of merit. I was once besought to interfere with a village school board which appointed an high-school principal because they thought him a Baptist and afterward dismissed him when they found that he was a Congregationalist. Our schools have in truth been kept out of politics in many enlightened districts in which it has long been possible to secure men and women to serve on school boards who have themselves been educated people with no axes to grind, no disposition to make money out of the schools, either directly or indirectly, and no talent for intrigue.

But these abuses are only symptoms of the political fallacy of local control of a civil function. It is pretty hard for the best of us to resist the importunities of neighbors who desire places for their relatives or friends, regardless of the competency of the latter. "After all, they are our schools," whereas as matter of principle they belong to the Community at large in its Civil capacity and not to individuals or whole townfuls of individuals.

What does the phrase: "Keep the schools out of politics" mean as the words stand, without regard to the intent of people who may have coined the expression and without regard to the wide fringe of connotations which may have grown up about it?

I take it that Politics is the theory and practice of Government. If the form of Government is a democracy, it means popular participation in the election of certain officers and often participation in the determination of public policy. Therein is the inescapable focus of what we call "politics" in the ignoble sense—corruption, underhand seeking of private advantage, favoritism, and all the kingdom of evils. These things grow up just because people participate in election through their votes. We recognize it when we say of a particularly contemptible scoundrel that "he will do anything for votes." Well, we have to struggle along and fight that sort of politics or else surrender the elective principle altogether. That would be tantamount to giving up democracy and even popular sovereignty itself.

But the word "politics" is a cognate of "policy." Political action in its direct form applies only where there is, directly or indirectly, public policy involved and the officers who make and execute policy. There is chiefly involved the party system. There and there alone is where elective processes belong. To keep any kind of public function out of politics is to keep it out of election.

Hence, we do not elect Federal judges and ought not to elect any judges, since the courts have nothing to do with policy or with matters of public opinion or desire, and we certainly do not wish them to. The elective judge is under sore temptation to make his rulings with an eye to the next election—and particularly to the desires of those who he knows will manage the next election—and not with an eye single to law and justice.

And yet the Federal judges do not inherit office; they come into it by democratic process in that they are appointed by a President who has been elected, and sanctioned by a Senate the members of which have also been elected.

In the more enlightened States the new highway commissions are appointed for their presumable ability to choose competent executives and engineers. The construction and maintenance of highways are not matters of public policy but rather of engineering principles.

Once more, so it is with tax commissions. Whether a tax shall be laid at all or not is emphatically a matter of policy, to be settled by some policy-forming body, usually a State Legislature. But the economic laws which govern salutary taxation, the equitable imposition of taxes on individuals, and the collection and accounting of taxes— these things are matters of principle and not of policy. In some notable instances competent and courageous tax commissioners have resisted plausible politicians and have given States just, scientific, and productive tax systems and tax administration. But such men have rarely been elective officers.

Humans are on the whole much better judges of persons than of policies. From earliest infancy we have had much practice in estimating the character and quality of our fellow-beings. But we seldom are good judges of public policy, for we do not know enough about most such matters. That is why we have Congress and State Legislatures.

We are the best judges as to what we *desire* and do not desire in the way of *public action*, but not more than once or twice in a generation are such matters placed squarely before us. Usually, what we desire are such matters as good schools and good highways, good courts, safe banks, and just taxes. And yet we know nothing about the operation of effective schools, or the laying-out and construction of highways, or the principles of jurisprudence, or the solvency of banks—and most of us do not pretend to. The sensible thing to do is what we always do in the conduct of our private affairs. We do not summon a lawyer or physician, an electrician or a plumber, or a watchmaker and put him through a technical examination as to his competency. We trust ourselves to him on our estimate of his personal character and our knowledge of his reputation. Similarly, we trust our Governors and the President whom we have elected to appoint for us boards in fields in which special knowledge is required. Sometimes we get badly betrayed, but in the long run these boards are much more likely to give us the service we desire than are those which we elect by majority vote.

And so, if we desire to keep the schools out of politics, the starting-point at least is to keep all who have to do with schools as far away from election as possible.

V. THE SCHOOL MONEY

The heart of the fiscal aspect of the State School Unit is that the school money in its entirety be State money and not, as now, primarily school district money eked out by gifts from the State Treasury. To state the matter in another way, the taxable resources of the State as a whole must be made immediately available to meet equitably the instructional needs of all school children in the State taken collectively.

Justice to the taxpayer can be achieved only through direct State taxation of the individual rather than through the use of local units as leviers and collectors of State taxes. Moreover, it can be achieved only through the use of a scientifically drawn State income tax, universally agreed upon by taxationists as being the most just form of taxation and one which least easily destroys its base. The property tax, especially the realty tax, ought to be left in the main to the use of municipalities.

Justice to the child, and to the commonwealth in which he will presently be a voter, worker, and citizen, can be secured only through the consolidation of all instructional authority, supported by a con-

solidated budget, in a single board legally and fiscally and professionally capable of supplying instructional instrumentalities throughout
the State, and special instruction wherever it is needed. That is what
our cities have long been doing for all children within their boundaries, for so long that few people are old enough to remember the old
ward districts and ward schools.

The prima facie objection is that most States are too large to make
such consolidation a practical matter.

Size may be a matter of area or a matter of population.

"Area" is a very relative term. In practical actuality it is measured not in square miles but in available means of communication,
both physical and in the transmission of messages—in other words,
in time. Two places are five hundred miles apart. In the days of
saddle horses, the distance between them might be expressed in terms
of perhaps a week or ten days. The railroad comes to connect them,
and the distance becomes an easy overnight journey, or twelve hours
by mail. The automobile and paved highways arrive, and what was
before inaccessible by rail becomes equivalently accessible by road.
For many matters the telephone reduces distance to a few minutes.

The size of population introduces no peculiar impossibilities in
school administration as such. It is worth noting that there are
only three States which are larger in population than New York
City, one of the three barely larger; twelve larger than Chicago.
More than half the States are smaller than Philadelphia. Boston is
larger than thirteen of the States, Milwaukee larger than ten, Rochester, New York, larger than three. There are thirteen States which
have populations of less than a million each, and five cities of over
a million each. Six States have populations of less than 500,000,
while twelve cities are of that size and larger. And yet we take it for
granted, and have long done so, that every one of the cities counted
should have a fully consolidated school system.

VI. SPECIAL INSTRUMENTALITIES IN INSTRUCTION
HIGH SCHOOLS

It has repeatedly been shown that not only is the High School
obsolete as institution but that it operates as an unavoidable ground
of inequality in the district system. We have long endeavored to correct the evils by making every school district which maintains no

high school liable for the tuition of its children in a district which does maintain such a school. The charge is often met by some form of grant-in-aid out of the State Treasury. Of course, that is but a make-shift way of doing things and it operates only as a mitigation of in-equality. Moreover, it is ordinarily thought of as a benefit extended to children, a portion decreed by the laws of a benevolent State rath-er than as needful instruction for future citizens.

Forty years ago or more, when high-school tuition was beginning to be paid this way, the High School was still an institution main-tained for the few as part of the higher schooling of the talented and the fortunate. Even then that condition in our society was begin-ning to come to an end, as we have seen, or else there would have been no demand for the tuition laws. Today, the four years which have traditionally been assigned to the High School are imperatively required in the Common School in the process of making an intelli-gent citizenship.

Under a consolidated State System with a State Board of Educa-tion at the head, it would be possible to locate high schools—if such enterprises were retained at all—where they would best subserve the interests of the schooling of future citizens, without reference to local fiscal ability to maintain such schools or to local address in es-tablishing and managing them. Moreover, it would be much more likely to happen that the Common School as discussed in Part II would become the typical school everywhere. In the end there would be few children anywhere in the United States who would not have access to full General Education within their own townships.

SPECIAL SCHOOLS

We have already discussed the problem of instruction for special classes of handicapped children, having due regard to those who are in principle Common School pupils.[3]

We have this problem well underway to solution—in some of the cities. Like most such things, it has been slowly and sparsely de-veloped in the intense localism of our existing system, usually under pressure from local minority groups actuated by the crusading spirit. Ordinarily, the course of events has been: (1) a period of agitation; (2) legislative sanction of the use of money for the purpose; (3) some-

[3] See above, p. 127.

times a suit in the State Supreme Court to test constitutionality; (4) the establishment of schools or classes; and (5) a period, more or less prolonged, during which the schools were establishing themselves in local public esteem.

In a consolidated State system the Board of Education could, and presumably would, establish schools for all the Common School handicapped of the State. Having control of the teacher's colleges, the Board would be able to provide systematically for the special training of teachers.

MAINTENANCE IN PECULIAR SECTIONS

Many of the States, perhaps most of them, have within their boundaries areas or local sections in which it is difficult or impossible to maintain regular organized schools. We have met the problem in one phase in our study of the Community. In general, such sections include: (1) sparsely settled territory; (2) remote coves in the mountains; (3) small islands off the seacoast or in the Great Lakes; (4) slum sections in cities; (5) communities of the abnormal consisting of the wreckage of humanity cast out of the cities; and (6) temporary communities founded chiefly on the exploitation of forest and mineral wealth.

In some of the States in recent years the existing State Boards of Education and Departments of Public Instruction have been empowered to deal with some such areas and sections by such means as seem to be indicated. Now and then an individual turns up in a State Education office who seems to be imbued with the true missionary spirit, and endowed with a sort of special talent, who devotes himself heroically to the task and sometimes saves a whole State. Ordinarily, however, development is along much the same lines as those described in the case of the special schools. Somebody, often a clergyman, has noted such a section and devoted himself to amelioration until that particular problem has been solved; but it takes a very long time to clean up a whole State in that way. Meantime, thousands of children suffer deprivation, and the human scrap-heap accumulates.

Under a consolidated State system, the Board and its officers are in position not only to take the initiative but to study the problems objectively and put them in the way of solution.

VII. THE BUDGET

There can be no Consolidated State School System, and neither Public Instruction in the large nor the special ends can be accomplished, without a common budget for the system flexible enough to be usable, and there is one of the chief difficulties in administration at our present level of political intelligence. It must be borne in mind that budgets are still rather new, especially in the United States. We have made progress, but the same difficulty appears which in other forms we have already noted: there is apt to be no clear distinction between executive and legislative functions, either in city councils, or State Legislatures, or in Congress. The policy-forming and lawmaking body has still a strong predilection for not only appropriating money but for defining in specific terms how it shall be spent. The appropriation is distinctly legislative; the expenditure thereof is with equal distinction executive and administrative. Let us see.

The annual or biennial budget of a city, or of a State, or of the United States is one thing; that of one of the Branches of Government or of one of the administrative boards or departments is quite another. The State budget proper, for example, appears before the appropriating body, namely, the Legislature. It covers appropriations recommended by the Executive for *various State activities*—support of the Legislative, Executive, and Judicial Branches, State Constabulary, National Guard, Highways, Public Instruction, and usually many others. All this has presumably already been co-ordinated and matched with the revenue by the Director of the Budget in consultation with the Governor, and the Legislature ought to give full faith and credit to the other Branch of Government. That is to say, it ought to be prima facie assumption that the budget as recommended will be adopted by the Legislature.

Nevertheless, the budget appears before the lawmaking body as a proposal in policy, and in matters of policy the Legislature is the ultimate authority. It would be remiss if it did not inform itself about the proposals. Hence, the Appropriations Committee of the House will want to know what the money is to be used for. That calls for the budget in detail of each branch, or board, or commission, or department which will make the expenditures. Each particular agency, having worked out its budget and defended it before the Director of the Budget, and indirectly before the Governor, must expect that it may still be called before the legislative committee.

So far, so good. Nevertheless, most executives in State affairs have, I suppose, had experience with appropriations committees which, instead of confining themselves to the fiscal merits and limitations of particular budgets as wholes, devote themselves to two vicious practices.

First, the merits of particular expenditures in themselves considered, a matter already passed upon by some other committee organized for the purpose, are scrutinized. In the orderly conduct of public business the other committee passes on the desirability of particular undertakings as such—if there be money enough. The latter issue and that alone is within the functions of the Appropriations Committee.

Second, influential members devote themselves to the paring of items which they do not like, or the elimination of which will "get back" at an officer whom they detest. Quite as bad as this is the fact that members will sometimes insist on adding expenditures which appeal to their fancy or which form a basis for the later appointment of friends to useless offices or other jobs.

These two abuses taken together are responsible for a large amount of log-rolling, lobbying, and bloc organizing which to some extent take the place of responsible legislation in many, if not most, of our States, as well as in Congress. The practices are not only wanton abuse of power but they contribute to the inefficiency of democratic government itself, the worst count against it.

If now, the Appropriation Committee, and after them the legislative body, is so far convinced that it accepts the estimates of a particular board or department, it ought to accept them as a whole. If there is insistence on reduction of expenditures all along the line, the responsible department should do the paring rather than the committee. Instead of dealing with the department as a whole, however, the detailed departmental budget is sometimes itself enacted into law, perhaps in many pages of the session laws. The effect is always more or less disastrous, for all flexibility is taken out of the budget. While every board ought to know very closely what it will spend during the year or other fiscal period, no board or department can foresee in detail what ups and downs in particular enterprises it will experience. The practice referred to is undoubtedly one of the roots of our abominable growth of bureaucracy and red tape.

VIII. THE CITY PROBLEM

Of the three States studied, Baltimore seems to be outside the State Unit without question; Wilmington is politically outside but not fiscally, and the city may come fully into the State Unit by action of its own board of education; Manchester is as truly a part of the State Unit as is any other local community. These are the largest cities. Now the population of Baltimore as found by the Census of 1940 is 859,100; that of Wilmington, 112,504; that of Manchester, 77,685. Baltimore classes as in truth one of the great cities; the other two do not. It seems plausible to infer that, in the minds of those responsible for the legislation, Baltimore appeared in the nature of things to be outside the classification in which the smaller cities of Maryland appear. Is there any truth in that view of things, even supposing it to be held? Is there anything about even New York, Chicago, and Philadelphia which places their schools on an essentially different basis from those of smaller places?

In the States which are organized on the county-unit system, the cities are left outside as special districts. Is there any inherent justification in the practice? Is there anything, on the other hand, essentially peculiar in country schools?

One of the commonplaces of Public Finance is that the cost of Government, as population grows larger, increases not in arithmetical but in some geometrical ratio. There are doubtless reasons, the chief of which are centered around increasing complexity, especially in city life, and in the fact that, as cities grow, true self-government becomes weaker. The inevitable consequence is that sooner or later the point is reached at which the ordinary functions of municipal government, to say nothing of the civil functions left to the cities, cannot be supported as they are in smaller places. When we recall that the bulk of city revenue comes from the taxation of real estate and that the tax base begins to be destroyed at a low tax rate, it is

easy to see that under American standards of living the size of sol-
vent cities is strictly self-limited.

In recent years, as is well-known, industry has been deserting the
large cities, and sundry devices have been adopted to protect property from the consequences of destructive taxation.

Notable is the retreat of population from the inner city to the less-
heavily taxed suburbs. That has been going on for the last forty or
fifty years until it has become the accepted thing. But excessive
taxation is not the only cause. The automobile with its reckless driving and tendency to make night hideous with needless horn-blowing,
apparently quite beyond the power of city police to prevent, is an
illustration of many causes which tend to drive away everybody who
can get away. The movement tends to remove a class of citizens
which is on the whole composed of the most capable individuals, and
these are drawn off from participation in sundry community interests including politics.

Tall business structures are demolished, to the enormous waste of
capital, and their places taken by two-story buildings aptly called
"taxpayers." Retail trade moves into the outskirts and suburbs in
order to cut high tax and rental costs out of its overhead.

Probably all this would continue to be true on a smaller scale even
if the burden of costs which are essentially civil rather than municipal were removed. Removal would, however, at least distribute the
cost of schooling the State's future citizens, and of enforcing the
State's laws, over suburbs, other residential and lightly-taxed communities, and over "tax colonies" which have grown up merely in
order to escape heavy taxation. It would somewhat raise the critical
point above which the city becomes self-destructive. But turn
whichever way you will, the great city is and always has been, since
the days of Babylon, a sort of cancerous growth on the body politic;
and neither this work nor any other need pretend to solve the problem. We are in the presence of *Acceleration toward the Center* which
never in itself has had any other outcome than progressive destruction of national culture and of Civilization among the people of a
nation.[4] You can go out any day and see the process at work in any

[4] See Brooks Adams, *Law of Civilization and Decay* (New York: Macmillan Co.,
1896).

of our great cities and see the malady transmitting itself to the smaller places. Thomas Jefferson was right about it.

If an observant schoolmaster of long experience who has traveled a good deal within our country were asked to tell us the size of the local communities in which the best schools are most often to be found, I am confident that he would reply: "From about 5,000 to perhaps 250,000." In smaller places it tends to be hard to find people of requisite caliber who are willing to serve on school boards; in places above the upper limit, the city is drawing near its critical population point, the selective movement out of the city runs stronger and stronger, and school boards are more and more becoming parts of ignorant and corrupt city political machines.

It is the common belief that cities are opulent in the fiscal sense, mere size of population being confounded with taxable resources. No doubt, in absolute amount of wealth, a city of 500,000 has many times the wealth of a village of 5,000, not to say of a small rural township of 500. But the city is in very much the situation of a businessman who is over extended but still has access at any given time to a good deal of money. He can live luxuriously and even pay his bills—until the inevitable crash comes. Bear in mind that even New York City is only a corporation, is not sovereign, and has none of the attributes of sovereignty. It can lay taxes and borrow money within legal limits, but it cannot coin money nor establish a banking system.

When we place over against aggregate taxable wealth the burden of local costs which are inherent in city conditions, the picture looks far otherwise than one of opulency. Instead of being rich in relation to necessary school support, cities are commonly poor.

THE CITY IN THE STATE UNIT

How, then, can we picture the City as fitting into the State Unit?

In those States which are under the county system so called, both the counties and the independent cities are in legal concept still corporate school districts. The problem has partly been solved by the enlargement of the political and fiscal unit, but the obsolete corporate school district still remains. No way out along that line.

On the other hand, where the County Board is itself a corporation and not the county, in law is the representative of the State Board, and the State itself is the fiscal unit—the school district defect has been eliminated. We may reasonably infer that the cities, large and small, should be organized along the same lines, with city boards appointed by the Governor or by the State Board, made corporations, empowered to make regulations not repugnant to law or to the superior regulations of the State Board, and the city schools along with those of other local communities supported by State taxes.

One is reminded that such a proposal must seem strange to those who are in the habit of supposing that the chartered city is coordinate with the State if the city is big enough. Such people often speak of "State law" as if city ordinances were simply another kind of law. Of course, the latter are not law at all.

Well, we are as used to the Post Office as to any function which is carried on by any city unless it may possibly be streets, water, and sewers. The Post Office is an example of a civil function which is consolidated not on a State-wide but on a national basis. It would not be of much account if it were not. Nobody ever supposes that the local post office should be made part of local Government and supported locally or that cities in this respect should be made independent of Federal control. The function of the Post Office is to deliver the mail, and it would be hard to find any office—city, State, or Federal—which does its essential job better. It does its job because it is Federal and not State or local, since it is a national function. It is not otherwise with Public Instruction, which is a State-wide job. State schools in the City would ere long seem as natural as a Federal Post Office in the City.

IX. TECHNICAL SCHOOLS

Should the State Board of Education have control of the technical schools, treated in chapter iii? Let us see if it should.

The State's function in Public Instruction has been accepted throughout our history, even from Colonial times. Practically every reasoned analysis found in court decisions and elsewhere has justified the statutes enacted and the taxes imposed for the purpose, solely on the ground that the public schools exist for the general education of prospective citizens. That is the function which the State Board takes over when it becomes the executive and administrative authority over the school system.

The Technical School, with the exception of the Teachers' College, serves another kind of function. Such schools are as different from the common schools in institutional purpose as is the University.

How they should be organized and supported is foreign to the subject matter of the present work. Suffice it to say that they are either private, Federal, State, or it may be municipal concerns, but no part of Public Instruction proper. An Art Museum or Institute, for instance, may easily be a matter for municipal support, as truly as are public parks. Naval and military technical schools are plainly the obligation of the Federal Government and very possibly schools of forestry.

X. THE BOARD AND ITS EXECUTIVE

The two combined, as we find them in most of the States which have the board-and-commissioner organization, have taken over functions which belonged to the older office of Superintendent of Public Instruction. As one scrutinizes the statute books, it is not difficult to see that this newer organization of the State Education office has not yet settled down into a coherent and logical structure in conformity with our political institutions. Notably, the Commissioner or State Superintendent, or Superintendent of Public Instruction as appointee and executive of the State Board, seems to retain certain powers and exercise certain duties independently of the Board.

It is easy to theorize about what ought to be, but it is a good deal better to take a look at the evolutior of the State school office, see what has been happening, and what we can make out of a development that has been going on for a century or more.

EVOLUTION OF THE DEPARTMENT OF PUBLIC INSTRUCTION

In the early stages of the Superintendency of Public Instruction there was naturally enough only a vague notion of what the officer was for. The public mind had been assimilating the ideology of district control of schools for two hundred years, and while this new officer seemed to the progressives obvious enough, in actuality he did not fit into any official pattern then in existence. It is not surprising to learn that the office was for some time bandied back and forth between a regular and an ex officio incumbent, the latter being usually the Secretary of State, that catch-all of all the odds and ends of Government.

In the educational renaissance of the thirties and forties of the last century, there emerged the notion of a Superintendent of Public Instruction as a permanency, usually defined as having "general supervision and control of the school system of the State." This statutory phraseology would have made a State School Unit three generations ago had it meant what it said. But its meaning was to be taken in a strictly Pickwickian sense, for having endowed the officer with full powers in the introductory clause defining the office, all the rest of the statute book took the powers away. And yet I will venture to say that most people have always supposed that the statute meant what it said and that the Superintendent of Public Instruction is indeed the responsible head of the school system. As late as the second decade of the twentieth century, while holding the office, I recall that I was frequently in receipt of letters from citizens taking me to task for not "doing something about it," referring to poor local schools. And yet I had no such powers as the statute ostensibly conferred on me, nor had my brethren, from Maine to California.

Probably because most of our people, including their organs of public opinion, believed that the law meant what it said, all but a few of the States elected their Superintendents of Public Instruction on a party ticket. Of course, since the officer's salary was also his living, most of them conducted their offices and issued their public statements with a view to re-election.

Now all this confusion was apparently due to the fact that the State school office, so long as the district system remained in existence, was long years ahead of its time. In reality it belonged to the era of administrative law which came in with the State Railway Commissions and the Interstate Commerce Commission.

Expansion in the office.—There has often been noted the expansion of enrolment and in the curriculum which came in about 1900. Whereas prior to that time most of the duties of the State officer were clerical and quasi-judicial and hortatory in character, now there came to be reposed in the Superintendent considerable actual administrative authority.

THE STATE BOARDS OF EDUCATION

As part of the expansion after 1900 came what may be called the "era of surveys." Most of the State surveys condemned the method of choosing the Superintendent of Public Instruction by popular vote on a party ticket and at the same time recognized the repugnance of our people to one-man power in appointed officials. Hence the period of appointive State Boards of Education with executive officers called Commissioners. The pattern was, of course, the City Board of Education and its Superintendent. But the pattern was form without substance, for the City Board of Education has control of a city consolidated school system, and these State boards had no such control. The corporate school district as political and fiscal unit was left the method of control and support.

Just as we have seen the development which gradually eliminated the subtownship district in the more progressive States and substituted larger units; so we can see that a sort of vague public consciousness of the need of some sort of integration in school systems led from the stage of no State officer at all to that of an ex officio functionary; to the Superintendent of Public Instruction as a ministerial and quasi-judicial officer; to the same officer endowed with some real administrative authority; to the Board of Education and its Commissioner, with the school-district support and control left intact; and, finally, to States in which the State assumes responsibility for adequate support of the entire school system and is placed in a legal position in which it can define adequacy.

Observe that the whole development has been a matter of force of circumstances under a democratic regime, in which in the more enlightened States the school system has been moving in the direction of adjustment to a mature society and away from adjustment to an earlier and now obsolete society—but the process has already taken a full century and more.

THE BOARD AND COMMISSIONER IN THE STATE UNIT

We might hastily dismiss this subsection with the statement, "See chapter xi." It is indeed easy to think of Board and Commissioner in the State Unit as being fully parallel to the City Board and its Superintendent. That, however, is not true, largely because the State office has always more or less extensive legislative responsibilities which city boards seldom have.

Generally speaking, in all matters which in their nature pertain to the administration of instruction, the executive officer ought to be supreme and the law ought not to tolerate interference of the Board. save when there is appeal from the acts of the Commissioner and his subordinates—and appeal ought to be allowed only when there is something vital involved.

Especially does the issue of executive responsibility arise in the case of appointments of school officers and teachers. That should be recognized as peculiarly a part of the professional authority of the Commissioner and his subordinate county, regional, or city superintendents. The power should not be subject to being overridden by either the State Board or by any local board. Nevertheless, the power is subject to limitation.

Where the local district board, under present conditions, has the ultimate power of appointment, there inevitably arises the use of the schools as a source of political patronage. That is especially true when there are several thousand boards in a State. The only remedy is to remove power of appointment from the boards. After all, the power is the crux of the whole administrative set-up. Nevertheless, to endow the executive with unlimited power is to invite public dissatisfaction and perhaps justifiable accusation of autocracy. The middle ground is to place nomination in the hands of the executive and confirmation in those of the board. Any board should be able to refuse to accept any really undesirable nominee no matter how well qualified; but in the event of such refusal it should be obliged to wait on the executive's further nomination, so that in the end any appointment whatever would be on the initiative of the responsible executive, and the latter in that way be made responsible.

Further, the Commissioner ought to have power to vacate any school office or teacher's chair in the State for immorality, malfeasance, incompetency, or unfitness; and the several superintendents ought to have similar powers within their own jurisdictions. But action should be taken only on charges duly filed and proven, and appeal on the facts and findings to the appropriate board should be allowed. Failure of the Commissioner or of a superintendent to act when he ought to act should be good cause for his removal by the State Board. Long experience and much observation have convinced the present writer that a potent cause of poor discipline in the teaching force of a State arises out of the reluctance of the school authorities to face delinquencies among teachers and school officers so long as they can escape action by simply refusing to renew a teacher's contract. I do not suppose that is a denial of the teacher's or officer's constitutional rights, but it is tantamount to that, since the person may well be dismissed without being informed of the charges against him.

The whole question of appointment and dismissal strikes closer to the efficiency of Public Instruction than most things. Nevertheless, most of the issues which might arise, and do arise under the present system, would never be heard of after the teaching force of State had been made a State force, such as is discussed in the next section.

On the other hand, the State Board ought to have the last word in matters which are in the nature of administrative law. The chief example is perhaps to be found in the Curriculum. Any good board will as a matter of course, in such an issue, consult with and be guided by its professional officer—and perhaps consult with other qualified persons. But in the end the decision should be that of the Board. That is principle. It is doubtful that much is gained by legislating to that intent, for an enlightened and strong Board, working with a strong Commissioner whom it has appointed, will arrive at that end anyway; while no law will lead to the right result with an ignorant Board and a weak Commissioner.

In general, the relations which ought to subsist in administrative matters between Board and Commissioner in the State unit are pretty much those which ought logically to obtain between the City Board and its Superintendent, where the city is a political unit. All that has been argued in chapter xi. In the relations between the Commissioner and the local superintendents the same principles apply which are found in the relations between the superintendent and his principals.

POLITICAL MATTERS

In matters which are essentially political as well as educational, the board ought to be competent to take the leadership, especially in matters where legislation is required and other forms of public contact. But leadership is unitary and not divided. That means, just as it does with the City Board under the present system, that the Chairman of the State Board tends to become the real political head of the school system of the State. The Board is in consultation with the Commissioner, and it leaves instructional detail and administration to him without consultation; but when matters of policy emerge, then decision is with the Board, and where political action is implied that also ought to be with the Board through its chairman. Nor is this mere theorizing.

In the first place, in any group of citizens such as a board or committee, some one will tend to go ahead and become the leader. In cases such as that which we are studying, it is better that such a one have the responsibility of recognized place.

In the second place, experience seems to show that where state railway or utilities boards, tax commissions, boards of health, police boards, and bank commissions have rendered distinguished service, as many of them have, it has usually been the chairman of the board who has made scientific or professional policies effective by assuring them of needful public understanding and support.

In the third place, it is always a bad business when what in reality is political in its nature, although it may also be educational, has to become the obligation of the Commissioner or State Superintendent. It has often happened that a devoted and even brilliant State officer has impaired his usefulness because he has been obliged to dabble in political matters, either because he had no Board or because his Board was a do-nothing body, with nobody on it capable of leading others. Mann himself fell into that kind of situation, and at times made himself the best-hated person in the Commonwealth. In due season no doubt his statue was placed before the State House—but that was post-mortem appreciation.

XI. A STATE TEACHING FORCE

It has hitherto several times been noted that one of the troublesome anomalies which the obsolete district system has carried with it is the contractual status of teachers, principals, and other school officers. Contract for personal services in the schools goes back to a time when the maintenance of schools was felt to be parallel to the conduct of any private enterprise. Teachers were "hired to teach" the coming term very much as hands were hired on the farm or a ship's company signed on for a voyage. The churches under which the regime grew up similarly hired their clergy, although a parish might in time go through the process of "settling the minister." Even so the minister seldom had any protection against a domineering deacon or bossy woman in the congregation.

All that has long been forgotten, especially in the cities; nevertheless, status remains. Once more the form abides, although substance has for the most part been lost.

It is pretty hard to get that wholly desirable *esprit de corps* called "devotion to the service" unless the service be on a State or Federal basis. In a local contract for teaching there is simply a job to the fore, and if a job, then a better job soon. Where the teaching position is subject to annual contract, or annual appointment, and all the neighborhood is engaged in expressing opinion about the teacher's methods and personal character, there will not likely ever be good methods or really self-respecting teachers.

Assuming, on the other hand, that the State School Unit were in operation, administered by a State Board of Education having also control of the instrumentalities for training teachers, the whole picture changes.

The State Unit implies a State Teaching Force, the pay of which is not a matter of contract but rather depends upon a regular salary schedule for all teachers in a class wherever they teach, with such local adjustments, also part of the schedule, as the Board may find expedient. It implies that school people shall receive their checks directly from the treasurer of the Board, who may also be the State Treasurer, and not be subject to the financial naïveté of city officials who periodically set up the institution of payless paydays, sometimes to the unconcern of a State court which has to be engaged in the administration of a school system by litigation.

We may learn something from the long experience of the Federal Government with the appointment, training, pay, and dismissal of Army and Navy officers, and similar career persons.

A young man is selected for appointment to West Point or Annapolis. After due examination, he is admitted and at once goes under pay as a cadet. He then goes under severe training as an officer of the Army or Navy as the case may be. If he survives a continuous process of testing and is graduated, he is appointed to the branch of the service for which he seems best fitted and enters the grade of second lieutenant or ensign at the salary fixed for those grades. He will be ordered to the station where he is needed. He cannot thereafter be dismissed from the service save on the verdict of a court-martial or in consequence of an Act of Congress—no question of not renewing the contract for no reasons given.

That is in general the conception of recruiting and training and status of professional personnel in sundry forms of the public service the world over, and in similar private service as well, notably in the episcopal and synodical churches.

There is still further implied that the only person in the whole working staff who is elected by a board is the Commissioner; that the others are all appointed, or at least nominated, by members of their own profession. But the appointment of an Army or Navy officer is a very different thing from the appointment of a teacher, school officer, or parish clergyman. The former has no goings-in and comings-out before the people; the latter has. The appointment of a teacher or school officer who is not acceptable to the people among whom he or she must work is a serious matter, provided the unacceptability is real and is not the fabrication of some domineering individual in the local community or of some group of chronic malcontents. The appointing or nominating officer who knows his job will ordinarily avoid such misfortunes. Nevertheless, what is a great deal more important is the fact that a teacher, principal, or superintendent who is already a member of a State force does not suffer miserable injustice from the whims of a local constituency which finds him or her *persona non grata;* the person may be located elsewhere in more grateful surroundings.

TEACHER-TRAINING AND TEACHER RECRUITMENT

Let us take the training of Army and Navy officers as a point of departure and ask ourselves what the corresponding method of training and recruiting the teaching force would be. I take it that it would follow very much these lines:

1. Promising teacher material would tentatively be selected in the Junior College, as schools now are, and encouraged to look forward to a school career. The possible candidates would thus be put through a preliminary selective process. Then would follow examination or some other method of surveying relative qualifications. The successful would be admitted to a teachers' college for study and training. Thereby hangs a tale.

One of the serious defects of our present method of training is that altogether too many are admitted, more than the actual recruitment of the force will ever require, and that only a perfunctory selection of likely teacher material is ever made. Not only are State teachers' colleges duplicated beyond all likely needs of annual recruitment, but the State university and many endowed science-arts colleges enter the field. The natural result is, of course, a lowering of standards for the sake of keeping up enrolment.

The history of the legislative establishment of many of our teachers' colleges, running back over the years, yields an interesting body of evidence bearing on the way a State Legislature works when it functions as a State Board of Education. Rarely has such an enterprise been established after a thorough study of the need for it in terms of prospective enrolment and the annual needs in recruitment of the section of the State that the college is intended to serve. Establishment has often, if not usually, been the result of a wire-pulling contest between different communities, each of them anxious to have some "State institution." This one would, like the reform school; this, the hospital for the insane; this, the State University; this, the penitentiary; and this, bursting with ambition, the State Capitol and the Capital buildings. When teachers' colleges are to be established, the plum tree is shaken indeed. All this is democracy in its childhood. No wonder that American teachers' colleges do not bear a good reputation for scholarship and standards.

Evidently the reform indicated under a State School Unit is broadly:

a) Retirement of institutions not under the control of the State Board of Education from the function of training teachers.

b) Limitation of the total admissions to all teachers' colleges to the number actually required for recruitment of the teaching force plus an allowance for wastage.

c) Confining the teachers' colleges to preparation of teachers for service in the common schools of the State, up through the Junior College, as schools now are.

2. When once admitted to training, it would be assumed that students are already cadets of the teaching force of the State, and they might well be paid a subsistence salary as such.

3. They would then be submitted to a full course of training, intended:

a) To complete their full General Education. If a full Common School establishment were in existence, graduation therefrom would carry the presumption that General Education was already complete.

b) To give them full academic qualifications in the fields in which they propose to teach, but qualification in the catholic or comprehensive sense and not in that of the specialist.

c) To give them a sound basis in educational and instructional principles.

4. Along with the foregoing, they would be put through adequate observation and practice as practice teachers.

5. Like all other suitable forms of post-school training, the whole course would be selective, indeed severely selective, and by no means all would survive to graduation.

Nevertheless, when people are admitted to higher technical training of any sort, the faculty which admits them assumes an obligation, and good faith enters the picture. Admission carries with it the obligation of systematic teaching, that is to say, if a student seems to be failing, of finding out why and correcting the learning process where that is possible. And yet *graduation* entails an obligation to the State and not to the individual.

6. Finally, upon graduation each of them would be given an appointment under pay to the regular teaching force of the State and would be subject to assignment to the position in which his or her services might be needed.

Training of special teachers and school officers.—We have dealt with the legitimate implications of post-graduate training in service in chapter x. There is, however, a further matter which we need to consider, namely, the training of special workers and school officers.

As we have already seen, the special training which is required in the routine of instruction anywhere in the common school, whether continuous or discontinuous, ought to be covered in the State teachers' colleges in specialized departments. That applies chiefly to work with problem cases, visiting-teacher work, and teaching the deaf, dumb, and blind. When young teachers in service show that they have interest and talent in these fields, as many as are likely to be needed should receive appointments for a period of post-graduate special training. On the completion of their training, they would receive assignments wherever they are needed.

But nobody can foresee where or when new needs in systematic teaching will appear. When such needs do arise, it would be competent for officers of the Board to select promising teachers and send them for special study wherever the facilities exist.

There remains the special training of school officers in the line and staff. I repeat that these people should normally be recruited from among those who have had considerable experience in the schoolroom and have given promise of executive and administrative ability. That implies that they will already have received the general training which has been described. They in their turn should be appointed to experience as cadet personnel, supervisory, and financial officers in the regular schools and afterward sent for special study to institutions where it can best be given. Presumably the latter would be done in University Departments of Education, or very possibly Science-Arts Colleges. The mere formal matter of University training ought not, however, to be the determining factor, but rather the place where constructive courses can best be found. If there are none such available, the young man who seems to have in him the qualities and interests, needed in the principalship, for instance, ought not to be encouraged to waste time in a university which in truth has little or nothing to give him. Rather he should keep on as a cadet until he is as a matter of practicality fit for appointment.

Nevertheless, before a man should be considered for the Principalship in any considerable community, he ought to have acquired the qualifications presumed in the true Doctorate of Philosophy, whether he has ever been awarded the degree or not. The same qualifications are of course implied for the Superintendent and the Commissioner.[5]

5 See also chap. x, p. 228.

SUGGESTED READING REFERENCES

SUGGESTED READING REFERENCES
FOR STUDENTS

BROWN, E. E. *The Making of Our Middle Schools.* New York: Longmans, Green & Co., 1910.

CUBBERLEY, E. P. *Public Education in the United States.* Boston: Houghton Mifflin Co., 1919.

CUBBERLEY, E. P., and ELLIOTT, E. C. *State and County School Administration.* New York: Macmillan Co., 1915.

EELLS, W. C. *The Junior College.* Boston: Houghton Mifflin Co., 1931.

———. *Present Status of Junior College Terminal Education.* American Association of Junior Colleges, 1941.

FLEXNER, ABRAHAM. *Universities: American, English, German.* New York: Oxford University Press, 1930.

GILMAN, D. C. *The Launching of a University.* New York: Dodd, Mead & Co., 1906.

HASKINS, C. H. *The Rise of the Universities.* New York: Henry Holt & Co., 1923.

JUDD, C. H. *Evolution of a Democratic School System.* Boston: Houghton Mifflin Co., 1918.

KNIGHT, E. W. *Reports on European Education.* New York: McGraw-Hill Book Co., 1930.

KOOS, L. V. *The Junior High School.* Boston: Ginn & Co., 1927.

PERRY, C. A. *Housing in the Machine Age.* New York: Russell Sage Foundation, 1936.

RUSSELL, J. D., and JUDD, C. H. *The American Educational System.* Boston: Houghton Mifflin Co., 1940.

APPENDIX

APPENDIX

THE STATE UNIT IN DELAWARE, MARY-
LAND, AND NEW HAMPSHIRE

DELAWARE

In Delaware the county is ignored—there are but three counties—and the State is consolidated into a single unit outside the City of Wilmington. The latter is a political unit, but in essentials it is no more truly fiscal unit than are the other districts. The *State Board of Education* is appointed by the Governor in individual appointments for the term of three years.

It is the executive and administrative head of the school system of the State, the actual directorate under the law.

The Superintendent of Public Instruction is chosen by the Board and is its executive officer.

THE SCHOOL DISTRICTS

The local school district is retained, presumably because it is territorially constitutional, but it is neither politically nor fiscally a fundamental unit in the system.

Each district is headed by a board of trustees appointed by the resident judge of the county, and the boards are by law made representatives of the State Board of Education.

The annual local budget is adopted jointly by the boards of trustees and the State Board of Education, and the local budgets taken collectively are then met by direct State appropriation. The State bears the cost of Public Instruction instead of leaving the matter to instrumentalities of the State. The State accepts in full the principle that what is everywhere a State obligation shall be met by the State.

The district trustees contract with teachers qualified by the State Board of Education, the contracts are filed with the State Board, and salaries are paid by the State Treasurer on the certificates of the trustees.

MARYLAND

Outside Baltimore the State Board of Education has the same kind of control over Public Instruction in the State that a City board of education has over the city schools.[1] Nevertheless, the Board is a State and not a city board.

---

[1] An excellent account of the school system may be found in a Maryland school bulletin of 1935, entitled *Summary of Important Sections of the Maryland School Laws* (Baltimore: State Department of Education, 1935).

STATE BOARD OF EDUCATION

The State Board of Education is appointed by the Governor, and members thereof may be removed by the Governor for specified reasons. The Governor is admonished in the statute touching the kind of citizens he shall apppoint. Ultimate responsibility for the decent conduct of schools is thus lodged definitively in the Governor.

The State Board has definite jurisdiction over the whole course of Public Instruction in the State, including enterprises which may be set up to deal with the handicapped and other ancillary matters. It is not only empowered to enact administrative law but it may intervene in the administration of the schools anywhere in the State, outside Baltimore. It appoints a qualified executive in the State Superintendent of Schools, who is also the secretary and treasurer of the Board.

COUNTY BOARDS

There are twenty-three counties. Over each of them presides a County Board of Education, the members of which are appointed by the Governor as are members of the State Board.

The County Board is itself corporation with power to hold title to property, to sue and be sued, and all school property in the county vests in the Board. Note that the latter is corporation and not the county, as is in substance the case in States which have the county unit—or think they do. The Board is corporation in the same sense in which a university board of trustees is corporation.

The Board appoints its executive officer in the County Superintendent of Schools who is qualified by the State Board. It is charged with the administration of Public Instruction within the county, subject to the law and the rules and regulations of the State Board of Education. The county superintendent nominates teachers and directs instruction.

The County Board as thus set up must make for flexibility in the school system of the State, and in principle be a deterrent of the growth of bureaucracy in the State office. The County is not, however, a political school unit and only in part a fiscal unit.

LOCAL DISTRICTS

There are local districts, but they are unlike those which we have thus far met. They are set up as needed by the county boards, the trustees thereof are appointed by the same authority and are removable as in the case of the other boards. But these local districts are not corporations and neither political nor fiscal units. They exist purely for the conduct of prudential matters connected with the maintenance and operation of schools, and the trustees to some extent are the spokesmen of the local public.

FISCAL

The school money is at bottom county money. Each county must levy a minimum school tax rate. Beyond that it may levy a somewhat higher rate and thus become entitled to aid from the State. If the revenue thus derived is insufficient to maintain schools at the standard prescribed by the State Board of Education, the latter may make up the difference with State money.

NEW HAMPSHIRE

The third of the States which seem to have gone farthest in the process of developing a State Unit is New Hampshire.

The local town school districts are retained, but they have become what are in substance for the most part administrative districts, although they are in form still quasi-corporations. In erecting the State Unit, they are utilized rather than abolished. For the enlightenment of those who are puzzled by the New England term "town" it ought perhaps to be explained that the expression is roughly equivalent to "township" in the States which were built on the Land Survey.

THE STATE BOARD OF EDUCATION

"The State Board shall have the same powers of management, supervision and direction over all public schools in this State as the directors of a business corporation have over its affairs, except as otherwise limited by law."

That seems conclusive and comprehensive. Note that the Board is in terms made a directorate and not merely an authority for the enactment of administrative law. Note further that it is given authority over all public schools and not over district boards. In other words, it is given the same control over all the schools in the State which the typical city board has over the city schools.

The members of the Board are appointed by the Governor.

It sets up standards with respect to the qualifications of teachers and school officers, with respect to subjects required to be taught, and with respect to instructional procedures for all grades.

High schools are specifically subject to approval and certification by the State Board, but whether there shall be an high school at all or not is left to the discretion of the local board. The *Commissioner of Education* is appointed by the Board and is their executive.

SUPERVISION

With the establishment of the State Board of Education, all the schools of the State were placed under professional supervision, in the cities and in supervisory unions of local districts set up under authority of the State Board. All such superintendents are appointed by the State Board and are paid by the State. The persons appointed must, however, be acceptable to the local authorities. Nomination of teachers and school officers is with the superintendent.

SCHOOL MONEY

Bear in mind that standards for both elementary and high schools are determined by the State Board. Hence the local budgets are in large measure so determined.

Each district is required by law to levy school taxes on property, largely real estate, at the rate of three and one-half mills regardless of its budget.

If the budget for the elementary schools of the district requires less than the revenue so derived, the surplus is paid into the State Treasury as a contribution to State school funds.

If the local revenue barely matches the budget for elementary schools, then the books are closed without reference to the State Treasury.

If the levy required by law is insufficient to support the budget for elementary schools at the standards required by the State Board, the balance is made up by the State Treasurer on the certificate of the Board of Education.[2]

COMMENT

Despite three different ways of arriving at the result, the policy established by law in the three States is in principle essentially the same. Delaware is evidently the most unequivocally a State Unit. Policy as established in the other two is, however, such that they might easily advance to the position held by Delaware, and both Delaware and Maryland might take the final step of including their largest cities in the State Unit.

Policy in all three amounts to this:

Public Instruction is an affair of the State. The State Government therefore undertakes to guarantee efficient instruction and pay for it regardless of the assumed interests of local communities and their resources. Public Instruction, like the establishment of Justice, ought to be excluded from the reign of politics of any kind, even of good politics; it ought to be impartial, objective, scientifically guided, rather than a matter of bloc prejudices, local fads, and local neglects. Therefore, the appointive principle is adhered to.

All in all, it is perhaps sufficiently evident why the author believes that these States, so far as he knows, have gone farthest along the road on which the more enlightened States have slowly been traveling these many years. Maryland can be rated as a middle-sized State; the other two are, of course, among the smallest. But size has nothing to do with the principles which these States are following. The principles are equally applicable to New York, Pennsylvania, Ohio, and Illinois.

Let us bear in mind, however, that Delaware puts the resources of the State directly behind the support of the school system, while the others do it only indirectly.

The counties in Maryland are required by law to levy school taxes to support their school budgets, within major and minor limits. That leaves the problem of equalization, although greatly simplified, on the old basis. It is certainly true in principle, and I doubt not in practice, that a given *tax rate* will produce more in some counties than in others and bear harder on the taxpayer in some than in

[2] The foregoing sketch of the organization of the three States is taken from the published school laws as of 1939.

others of a different economic type.[3] Moreover, Maryland apparently foregoes the use of surplus revenue in rich counties.

New Hampshire uses much the same method as Maryland, but uses the township rather than the county as the primary levier of taxes. She does not, however, ignore the surplus of the rich town; it is paid into the State Treasury. On the other hand, this use of the township would be prohibitively complicated in a larger State.

Maryland may well be leading the way into a feasible organization of the larger States through her administrative use of counties. Not only, as it seems to me, is the Maryland use of counties, divorced as it is from political considerations and the variability of local autonomy, an eminently useful method of reaching a balance between centralized government and decentralized administration, but it suggests an entirely feasible use of other administrative units, notably the larger cities, and territorial units larger than counties.

THE REGIONAL UNIT

In the larger States, that is, territorially larger, in the more recently settled sections of the country, the counties are usually the vestigial remainders of an earlier and more thinly settled community. There are necessarily more of them. Maryland has twenty-three counties; Michigan, eighty-three; Indiana, ninety-two; Illinois, one hundred and two; Iowa, ninety-nine; Ohio, eighty-eight; New York, sixty-two; North Carolina, one hundred. On the other hand, Massachusetts, which rates as one of the larger States in point of population, has but fourteen. In time, the existing counties nearly everywhere will be consolidated into a few convenient regional subdivisions.

It is noteworthy that consolidated highway administrations, which came in much later than schools, have tended in that direction from the beginning. For example, Iowa administers its highways in six regional districts, whereas the traditional county affairs require ninety-nine counties, and the school system is made up of 4,879 school districts. If it were desirable to retain as much of the local administrative district as does Maryland in her counties, the large regional district would furnish the appropriate unit.

[3] See the author's *School Revenue*, pp. 180 ff.

INDEX

INDEX

Academy, 57; nature and social placing, 58; structure and curriculum, 60; parallel with college, 61

Accomplishments of our school system, 108

Adams, Brooks, cited, 296

Adams, Charles F., 234

Adams, Henry, *History of the United States in the Administration of Thomas Jefferson*, 45

Administrative staff in Common School, 215 ff.; Medical Officer, 216; problem-case teachers, 217; visiting teachers, 218; Records Secretary, 219

Adolescence as primitive majority, 118; no ground for divisions in school structure, 120

Advancement of pupils in systematic teaching, 180 ff.

Anatomical and physiological grounds for school structure nonexistent, 118

Apprenticeship, 33

Art Institute, 39

Bass, Jethro, in Churchill's *Coniston*, 270

Bassett, E. M., cited, 152

Beauchamp, Wilbur L., cited, 189

Bismarck, Otto von, 82

Brown, E. E., on Academy, 60

Budget: appropriation legislative, expenditure executive, 293; attitude of legislative committee, 293 f.

Bunker, F. F., cited, 78

Bureaucracy, 221

Carnegie units, 69

Caste obsessions, 174

Central office in business management, 211

Certification boards, 70

Chicago, University of, 21; and junior college, 25

City managership, 235

City problem: cities become impossible as they grow larger, 295 ff.; city in State unit, 297

Classified schools, 74

Colburn, Warren, 84

College: as term, 19; in Paris and England, 20; incorrect American use, 20; in State universities, 20

Comment on three States, 320; regional unit, 321

Committee of Ten, Report of, 97, 113

Common School, 1, 9; complete in itself, 15; contrasted with university and technological institute, 16; attributes of, 44; possibility of, 45; origins, 45; concerns common man, 45; derived meaning, 46; early village and rural, 47; dates from Reformation, 49; instances in New England and Illinois, 49; structure of old, 52; terminal, 53; end of old common school, 70; modern common school, 110 ff.; in fact, 123 ff.; evidence for modern, 170; structure in large places, 191 ff.; in small cities, 196

Common School Revival: characteristics of, 75; period of, 76

Community: American local, 147; lack of pattern, 148; frontier, 148; isolated farm and subtownship district, 149; urban, 150; zoning, 151; rural, 164

Conservatory of Music, 38

Contracts with teachers: obsolete and vicious, 263; due to corporate school district, 263

County unit, 274; criticized, 275

Cousin, Victor, 77

Cubberley, E. P., cited, 74, 256

Curriculum: point of departure in systematic teaching, 172; feasibility of Curriculum of Common School, 186

Dame School, 55

Degree: Master's, 28; Doctor's, 29

Delaware, 276; State unit described, 317

Delinquent pupils, custodial treatment of, 128

Dexter, E. G., on academies, 61

Dillon, *Municipal Corporations*, cited, 262

Discipline: defined, 13; appropriate to School, 14; curricular disciplines, 14

Discontinuity, 73 ff.; to about 1900, 86; since 1900, 97

Double-track system, 88

McGuffey, William, 84
Mann, Horace, 53, 77, 78 f., 149
Maryland, 216; State unit described, 317
Mastery: in systematic instruction, 175
Matériel, control in individual schools, 207
Maturity: personal, 10; social or ethical, 10; volitional, 10; intellectual, 10; not completeness nor perfection, 12
Meaningless terms, 120
Mental defectives, 132
Mentality: higher attainable only by breeding, 174; mental ability grouping uncritical, 188
Municipal government, 260

Negative evidence worthless, 51, 170
Neighborhood unit, 160; school in, 161; applicable to villages as well as to large cities, 164
New Hampshire, 276; State unit described, 319
Nursery schools not of the Common School, 124

Off the track, 111; efforts to get back, 112
Overhead: explained, 156; critical term in school management, 156 ff.; effect of Common School on, 158

Parker, Francis W., 234
Pastoral relations of the school head, 143
Performance estimated, 91
Perry, C. A., cited, 161
Phillips Andover Academy, Fuess' History of, 59
Physiological and anatomical grounds for school structure fallacious, 118
Politics, keeping schools out of, 286 ff.
Polkinghorne, Ada R., cited, 126
Post Office in cities, 298
Primary School: as term, 116; as educational status, 116; beginnings of, 125; untaught learnings, 126; change of primary status, 176; as separate school community, 177
Principalship: most critical place in the system, 198; in the Common School, 198; not an head in a discontinuous school, 198; government, 199; learning to hold authority, 201; qualities, 201; supervision, 202 ff.; training teachers, 205; recruitment of teachers and staff,

205; basis of responsibility, 205; pastoral function, 143; materiél, 207; financial, 209; associates, 211; as vice-principals, 211; administrative staff, 215; abuse of principalship, 222; qualifications of principal, 226
Problem pupil in systematic instruction, 173
Product of the system as is, critical estimate, 100 ff.
Program of studies, 187
Pupilage: common school, 9; pupils under discipline, 13

Quincy movement, 234

Rational evidence, 170
Reason, age of, in children, 120, 127
Recruitment of teachers and staff, 205
Regression, cultural, 7
Research, 22
Reverse movement in junior high school, junior college, and consolidated school, 70
Rostovtzeff, M., cited, 35

School as Community, 134 ff.; social foundations of instruction, 134–35; government of, 136; effective size, 138; pupil acquaintanceship, 139; principal's knowledge of pupils, 140; teachers' knowledge, 141; involved in wider community, 142; government, 142; pastoral relations, 143; sanitation, 145; recreation, 146
School district: the cell of the system, 256; origins, 257; essential in pioneer and frontier times, 258; subtownship form, 259; original justification, 259; quasi-corporation, 262; inequality among districts, 265; evolution of local unit, 266; administrative district, 285
School in the Glen, 49
School money under State unit, 289; in principle, entirely State money, 276
School structure, terms in, 115
School system, 255 ff.; schools not private enterprises, 255
School as universal institution, 6; common school, 7, 9; common school complete in itself, 15; contrasted with university and technical school, 16; attributes, 44; possibility of common school, 44; as community, 134